AFTER THATCHER

Paul Hirst is Professor of Social Theory at Birkbeck College, University of London and a frequent contributor to *New Statesman & Society*, the *Political Quarterly* and other publications.

AFTER THATCHER

Paul Hirst

COLLINS
8 Grafton Street London W1
1989

William Collins Sons and Co. Ltd
London · Glasgow · Sydney · Auckland
Toronto · Johannesburg

BRITISH LIBRARY CATALOGUING IN PUBLICATION DATA

Hirst, Paul Q. (Paul Quentin), *1946*–
After Thatcher.
1. Great Britain. Politics
I. Title
320.941

ISBN 0-00-215169-3

First published 1989
© Paul Hirst

Photoset in Linotron Janson by
Rowland Phototypesetting Ltd,
Bury St Edmunds, Suffolk

Printed and Bound in Great Britain by
Hartnolls Limited, Bodmin, Cornwall.

For Penny and Jamie

Contents

Preface

This is something very unusual in English terms, a sustained argument about politics aimed at the general reader. Books about modern British politics break down into three species: politicians' statements of their world-view, more or less systematic, more or less ghost-written, varying in quality from the instantly forgettable to the moderately thoughtful; journalists' offerings, which are often readable contemporary history, but seldom amount to sustained political argument; academic tomes, many of which are more honest and approachable than their scholarly apparatus might suggest. This book takes something from each species, but aims above all to be readable. I have taken the risk with my academic colleagues of arguing in as plain and simple a way as I can, cutting the mass of defensive scholarly references to well below the bare minimum in order to avoid boring the reader.

I have been encouraged to try writing an extended political essay and letting academic niceties go hang by two facts. First, the publication of David Marquand's *The Unprincipled Society*, which persuaded me that accessible political argument need sacrifice nothing of substance and seriousness and still reach the non-academic reader. Secondly, the existence of a body of more detailed academic work on the future of British manufacturing. This book could not have been written without several years' collaborative work with my colleague at Birkbeck College, Jonathan Zeitlin. It draws heavily on our edited collection *Reversing Industrial Decline?* Whatever strengths this book has in economic analysis are due largely to him and needless to say the faults are my own. My friends Professor John Williams and Dr Karel Williams have likewise encouraged and inspired my efforts, more by criticism and debate since they are severe opponents of the thesis of 'flexible specialization' which is central to this book. But inspiration takes many forms and cosy collusion is only one. I owe a considerable debt to JoAnne Robertson, my editor at

Collins, for her encouragement and unfailing help. Lastly, the book could not have been written had not the *New Statesman* and its successor *New Statesman and Society* allowed me to try out my ideas in a series of articles written over the last few years. I am particularly grateful to John Lloyd, the previous editor, and Stuart Weir, the current editor, for giving me the room to air my opinions.

This book involves a deliberate gamble. It has been written in the middle of the Labour Party's policy review process. I have made the rather presumptuous choice of arguing *ex cathedra* what the Labour Party should do, rather than trying to guess what it will propose or waiting until all its policies are safely on public view. Parts of the argument here will doubtless correspond to the thinking in the policy review, parts will contradict it. My reason for writing now is to try to add something that I see missing in the process of policy modernization; that missing element consists less in the detail of policy than in the overall political approach to governing the economy and dealing with the other opposition parties. Labour's policy is still too exclusively the policy of a single party and too geared to traditional forms of government. Neither such inwardness nor such traditionalism will do for the difficult economic conditions Britain will face in the 1990s. The strategy for dealing with such conditions is the argument of this book.

CHAPTER 1

The Mirage of Thatcherism

THIS IS NOT a crystal ball. The reader seeking a precise answer to when and how the present Conservative government will be defeated is asking an impossible question. No sensible person who has carefully considered the scale of the electoral task facing the opposition can exclude the possibility that the Conservatives can win the next general election in 1991 and perhaps the one thereafter. It is the combination of a divided opposition and the British electoral system that has given the Conservatives two massive election victories in 1983 and 1987. The opposition remains divided. Ten years of Conservative rule stem from this fact, rather than from any special political wisdom on the part of Mrs Thatcher or from any conversion of the country to the ideology of economic liberalism. 'Thatcherism' is a myth that tries to justify Conservative victory by ascribing it to fundamental social and attitudinal changes, rather than to the default of any credible alternative political force. It is a myth propagated by the left, notably the Communist Party's magazine *Marxism Today*. It is a myth enthusiastically taken up by sections of the mainstream quality media and given wide coverage in the early and mid-1980s.

The myth is less credible today. Mrs Thatcher and the Conservatives lack that sureness of political touch, that efficiency and competence in government, and that broad cultural and ideological appeal necessary to explain their success by their own efforts and their own strength. Conservative rule has been marked by political disasters and scandals as much as by political success. It is easy to forget that when Mrs Thatcher became Conservative leader in 1975 many political commentators saw her as unelectable, impossibly partisan and unacceptably right wing. Even in 1978 many commentators saw Labour as the natural party of government and the Conservatives as faced with a long spell in the political wilderness. Many Conservatives, not merely Heathites, feared this would be the case. Politics is an activity prey to contingency and chance. Striking reversals of personal and party fortune are frequent and yet unpredictable. The Conservative government could be wrecked by a political crisis before 1991 or suffer from one of those unaccountable reversals of fortune that all politicians fear. That is unlikely, but not impossible. Political prediction is the riskiest business of all. The Conservatives may rule until the year 2000, or they may be swept from office by a scandal tomorrow.[1]

My purpose is not to predict the exact circumstances of the Conservatives' demise but to look at what the opposition needs to do to make that demise possible and the tasks facing an alternative government in the 1990s. In order to make itself electable, the opposition needs to address those tasks carefully and objectively and devise a strategy to meet them. Political success will come by seeking a credible alternative form of government appropriate to tackling the political and economic problems I shall analyse in this book.

If Mrs Thatcher has ruled largely by default, the opposition cannot bank on the same luck. It cannot hope merely to inherit power because people are tired of Tory rule and seek a change. It is the default of the opposition that needs to be overcome. That default is not merely that the opposition is split but that it lacks a credible alternative way of governing the economy to that of the Tories. The centre parties are confused about policy and at each other's throats. Labour has lacked a successor doctrine to the marriage of Keynes and Beveridge celebrated in practice by the 1945 Labour government, confirmed in theory by Tony Crosland in the 1950s, and which unravelled in the 1970s. Labour's swing to the left in the early 1980s did not provide that alternative. It made Labour appear more partisan and unacceptably doctrinaire than Mrs Thatcher. It gave the Conservatives the 'socialist' enemy they so badly needed to make their own views tolerable. There is very little evidence that the electorate wanted a partisan right-wing government in the 1980s, but there is a lot of evidence that they did not want a partisan left-wing government. Nationalization, the growth of state collectivism, over-powerful trade unions and high taxes were all bitterly unpopular, especially with successful manual workers in private industry. If this was what 'socialism' meant, and that is how it was perceived by voters, then it was, indeed, a loser.

It will be a central theme of this book that, while the Labour Party has emphatically rejected the left fundamentalism of the early 1980s, while it has sought to modernize its policies and drop those very features of 'socialism' that made it unelectable, it has also failed to appreciate the full political logic of these new policies. Labour is struggling to become a consensus party once again, but it is changing its policies on the assumption that it will form a single majority government. My case is that the new policies require a new political style, and that if Labour does not change its very traditional conception of how to govern it will be unable to carry these policies out. It will be unable to do so, first, because it is unlikely to win the next election by its own unaided efforts. Too many voters do not want a purely Labour government; they may be anti-Thatcher or wavering in their support for Conservatism, but they are not pro-Labour. It will be unable to do so, secondly, because its policy goals – economic modernization and the revitalization of British manufacturing industry – require a very strong and very stable government. Labour alone cannot form a government strong enough or stable enough. The tasks it has made the core of its new policies require a revolution in its own political thinking, and that (despite the policy review) has not occurred.

When this book appears Labour will have unveiled its new policies. Many of these policies will correspond closely to the strategy for a new reforming government outlined here. One element that will almost certainly be missing is a full appreciation of the political concomitants of implementing these policies. Labour needs to recognize that the logic of its own policies requires cooperation with the other opposition parties and the building of a strong coalition government. Only a 'national government' with broad support can overcome Britain's growing economic problems. Such a government is not a concession to the other opposition parties, a reflection of Labour's weakness, but a condition of its strength.

This political logic is still being refused by the Labour leadership. Labour is willing to modernize its policies, but not to modernize the Party's political role and outlook. It seeks to return to power in Westminster as a single majority party government, ruling in the traditional way. That conception of government causes least upset to the Labour Party's own internal workings and its political traditions – policy can be changed more easily than the Party. The Party Conference will swallow the new policies, but all three major sections of the Party – the parliamentary leadership, the union bosses and the constituency party rank and file – will find it difficult to swallow the political changes necessary to realize these policies. This is why *After Thatcher* has been written: it is an essay in political persuasion directed toward driving this lesson home. The argument here is that the failings of the British political system and the economy are such that they require a major change both in political institutions and in political culture if they are to be overcome. Labour is central to that change, and must change itself to meet it.

The core of this book is an analysis of the workings of British political institutions, of defence policy, and of the economy. The three chapters on the economy form the bulk of the book. The reason for this is that economic failure and how to remedy it has been at the heart of British politics since the early 1960s. Chapter 4, 'The Fading Economic Miracle?', argues that Conservative rule has not solved the problems of the British economy and reversed a century of economic decline. On the contrary, Britain has failed as a manufacturing and trading nation most seriously and acutely under the Conservatives. Chapter 5, 'Economic Recovery: the Failed Contenders', dismisses a number of alternative programmes for dealing with Britain's economic problems. Chapter 6, 'A Strategy for Industrial Renewal', outlines a programme for the revitalization of manufacturing industry. It argues that a change in the form of governing the economy is more important than any narrowly economic strategy or purely technical methods of economic management. Central in this respect is a lasting coalition government backed by a strong social consensus, the objective of which is to switch the balance of national income decisively from short-term consumption to long-term investment.

Although the centre of this book is an argument about the economy it is not a technical and forbidding treatise in economics.

It is written for the general reader and avoids as far as possible economists' jargon. This is not simply a concession to the non-technical reader; rather it arises from my contention that the main sources of economic failure and hence its solutions are social and political rather than 'economic' in the strict sense.

After Thatcher concentrates on the three major policy areas where the opposition in general, and the Labour Party in particular, has faced a problem of a lack of a convincing alternative to Mrs Thatcher's government. The opposition has been consistently vocal in criticizing Conservative policy, but criticism is no substitute for an effective alternative. *After Thatcher* analyses the problems that will face Britain in the 1990s and how to deal with them; it does not waste its time criticizing Conservative policy. A majority of the public do not need convincing that Mrs Thatcher's rule has been partisan, often incompetent, authoritarian and socially divisive. They do need to be shown how an alternative government could do better and how it could avoid being equally partisan and divisive from an opposing stance. The reader will find no long litany of criticism of Tory policy in health, education, welfare, the public services and local government. Too many books about the Thatcher years have concentrated on doing just that, without notable effect. It is increasingly obvious that a majority of electors do not share Mrs Thatcher's goals and values in the matter of welfare and the public services. Even many Tories and many of the affluent wanted higher public spending rather than tax cuts at the time of the 1988 Budget. Mrs Thatcher has not converted the British into a nation of hard-nosed individualists and enthusiastic economic liberals.

If electors could choose a government for each policy area, and if there were no spending constraints on government, Labour would be elected as the health, education and welfare government every time. Labour is far closer to the core attitudes of the British public on many social issues than are the Tories. But the voters can only elect one government, and Labour has been perceived as weak on the key issue of overall economic management. Progressive health, education and welfare policies can only be strengths for a party that has a real alternative economic policy. Voters want to spend more of the nation's wealth on welfare than the Conservatives have done, but they also want that wealth to be created and to grow. Voters have feared that a Labour government would mean economic chaos and instability, high taxes and industrial strife. The Conservatives have promised to create wealth, and for six years from 1983 to 1988 have offered its semblance. The myth of 'recovery' is now fading and public perceptions of current 'prosperity' are tinged with uncertainty and the threat of growing economic failure: balance of payments difficulties, high inflation and high interest rates. The Conservatives today can less credibly claim to have ensured sustainable growth and genuine industrial recovery than they could in 1987. But Labour has to show that it can do better, not only that it will spend more of the national income on desirable social programmes but that it will make national income grow. Voters want personal prosperity *and* public spending. They will not sacrifice the former to the latter. To have both requires strong and sustainable economic growth. Labour must convince them that it can achieve such growth and until it tackles the hard issues of governing the economy it will fail in that task.

The reader who wants a denunciation of Mrs Thatcher and all her works should look for another book. Mrs Thatcher is the object of a great deal of unfocused whingeing and hostility. How often one hears the phrase 'I hate Mrs Thatcher'; it usually comes from the lips of someone who is too ineffectual to hate properly and it is little more than a confession of political impotence. Mrs Thatcher is a tough and uncompromising politician, but she is by no means as inflexible or consistent as her opponents make out. She has made the most of the advantages the 1980s have given her. She has played the electoral and governmental game ruthlessly and to win. Those who have played the game less well should blame themselves and not her. She lacks depth of analysis and genuine political imagination, and is the victim of certain fundamental prejudices. Her faults are, however, uninteresting and beside the point. Converting Mrs Thatcher into a monster, and elevating her into the master politician that the myth implies, are the parallel errors of her critics. The one seeks to displace the impotence of the opposition onto the flaws of her character: we failed because she is wicked and unfair. Whoever expected leaders in the rough and tumble of electoral politics to be nice or fair? The other opposition mythology, in good old Marxist style, turns the defeat of the left into the necessity of history: we have failed because Mrs Thatcher is in tune with fundamental changes in society and ideology. These changes are actually very hard to find, but so is the evidence for the view of her as an evil genius, a political Svengali mesmerizing the voters. Mrs Thatcher has survived because she has given enough of the voters enough of what they want. She is far too much of a political opportunist and far too much of an orthodox party politician for either of those myths of her critics to be true. She has consistently abandoned 'conviction' when necessary for political advantage and she has repeatedly changed policy when that would win her support.[2]

Labour lost the election in 1979 for reasons that were everything to do with its own failures in government, and little to do with the opposition. It lost the election in 1983 because of its failure to be a credible opposition. Labour's basic strategy of government had become untenable. Labour post 1945 had adopted the dual role of manager of the mixed economy and orchestrator of the welfare state. It derived its main ideas for its role in government not from 'socialism' but from two leading Liberals, John Maynard Keynes and William Beveridge. Anthony Crosland had welded the two together in a convincing 'revisionist' package in *The Future of Socialism*, published in 1956. Crosland's vision of Labour's role became the reality of Party policy, even for those who belonged to the opposing camps of the left. Government would manage the mixed economy, and ensure through Keynesian macroeconomic management both full employment and economic growth. The welfare state would remove the uncertainty and hardship associated with old age, unemployment and sickness – offering a comprehensive range of benefits and services. A growing economy would provide the space for an egalitarian strategy, redistributing a growing national cake through welfare and taxation measures without directly penalizing the well-to-do. Growth would make growing equality of opportunity possible and equal opportunity would promote growth.

Crosland's vision ran into trouble in the 1970s. Britain's economic failure undermined a strategy founded on the success and growth of private industry. When private industry failed to deliver the goods the social liberalism that was the essence of Labour's strategy for government became impossible. Crosland assumed that private firms would make the right decisions in an expanding economy; the policy left it to private industry to organize production and distribution. The failure of Britain's manufacturing sector threatened not only prosperity but Labour's conception of government. Inflation and the rapid growth in public services made wage determination and taxation battlefields. In 1974 a weak Labour government had come to power in the teeth of an economic crisis. It had one asset to offer – its close link with the trade union movement. Labour could govern the economy because it, and only it, could ensure the support of organized labour for the necessary policies of economic adjustment. Mr Heath had failed to tame or to win the collaboration of the unions. Labour did manage to exploit that asset. It *did* cope with the economic crisis created by the failure of the Heath–Barber boom and the crisis of governability created by the 1972 miners' strike.

Labour combined an incomes policy with an austerity policy. It managed to reduce inflation from over 20 per cent in the first year when it took office to 8.1 per cent in 1978. It managed to staunch the foreign exchange crisis and it tried to check the exponential growth of public expenditure. Labour combined its link with the unions with orthodox and quasi-monetarist economic policies. It put stabilization before redistribution. Croslandite policies predicated on sustained growth were abandoned in the face of a stagflationary crisis.

Keynesian policies could not tackle the combination of economic depression and high inflation. Labour was forced to retreat to orthodox deflationary economics based on tightening credit and the money supply and reducing public expenditure. One should remember that it was Heath's rash dash for growth combined with the oil crisis of 1973 that produced the spectre of runaway inflation, of a permanent industrial relations crisis as unions chased galloping price rises with endless and ever-larger wage claims, and of a financial crisis of the public sector as costs escalated ever upwards and pulled taxes after them. One should remember that it was management in private manufacturing industry that failed to invest, to remain competitive and to maintain domestic market share against foreign importers. Labour paid the price of a crisis largely of others' making.

Why did 1979 come to be a crisis of modern social democracy rather than of the Conservatives and the private sector managers who had the largest part in British failure? The answer is because that failure destroyed Labour's post-1945 social–liberal programme of economic and social governance, and because Labour failed to put a credible strategy in its place. Labour's crisis management from 1974 to 1979 rested on an ideological vacuum – Labour was politically bankrupt in May 1979. Labour's election defeat was not inevitable, however. A decision by James Callaghan to go to the polls in October 1978 would probably have led to a modest Labour victory. But what then? Labour's short-term successes in incomes policy, in controlling public expenditure and in economic austerity measures generally in the previous few years had rested on expedient agreements and short-term fear, not on a lasting programme of economic management. Pent-up frustration could not be checked once the depths of the crisis had passed.

The main reason Labour failed to check intense worker frustration at the grassroots in the 1978–9 'Winter of Discontent' was that it relied on voluntary union compliance in a national incomes policy without changing union attitudes toward wage bargaining, creating new organizational forms, or changing the unions' relationship to management and the state. The unions regarded national incomes policy as a temporary emergency strategy and in no sense as a permanent new relationship which transformed the 'normal' practices of free collective bargaining. The Trades Union Congress (TUC), the unions' collective leadership and, in the language of political science, the 'peak' organization in the pyramid of representation of organized labour, was unable to guarantee the compliance of its lower-level member organizations to policies agreed with the government. The national union leaderships were unable and unwilling to control pressure from members for wage rises above the national norms proposed by the government. Private sector unions were unwilling to accept a permanent incomes policy that tied them to the public sector, and public sector unions rebelled against the pay implications of public expenditure controls. It is as well to remember that public expenditure 'cash limits' were introduced by Labour.

The 'Winter of Discontent' undermined both Labour's authority as a government and public perceptions of its ability to guarantee union consent in a national economic policy of austerity. Labour could no more govern the economy and control the unions than could Mr Heath. Labour's greatest asset in 1974 became its greatest liability in 1979. It was stuck with its intimate link with the unions, despite the fact that it had sought to control them. It simultaneously alienated many union members and also those members of the public who saw the unions as too powerful and a threat to both economic stability and governability. Labour had abandoned both Keynes and Beveridge in 1974–9, practising both deflationary policies and public expenditure cuts. It had thrown away its hard-won revisionist synthesis in the face of economic necessity and yet it had found no new and lasting economic policy to replace it.[3]

As the crisis of manufacturing and the British economy deepened in the 1970s, the unions came to be seen as Britain's economic Achilles' heel. Union pressure, strikes, inflationary wage rises were all highly visible. Management's failures were more subtle and largely unseen by the general public. Labour lacked any credible way of tackling management failure and staked all on the unions' collaboration in solving the crisis. It emphasized the unions' role, whilst lacking an industrial strategy that would put the heat on management and, if not expose management's deficiencies, at least overcome them. Labour abandoned demand management in an inflationary crisis in which that strategy could not work, yet it had no viable supply-side policies. The left's policies were rejected, rightly, as economically unworkable by the Labour cabinet. But there was no alternative to put in their place. The government carried out an ad hoc programme of nationalizations and quasi-nationalizations of failing firms, and it offered state subsidies and a holiday from corporation tax. It lacked any convincing strategy for building business confidence or increasing the rate of manufacturing investment. It built no more lasting institutions of collaboration with private management than it had done with the union rank and file.

Labour was perceived to have presided over a period of economic chaos and rapid rises in direct personal taxation. Many manual workers entered the income tax system for the first time under Labour. Public expenditure was simultaneously squeezed and yet perceived to be beyond control and to be a brake on economic growth. The public sector was no longer the benign distributor of growing wealth as part of a strategy of social equalization and economic modernization. The public sector took from the nation's declining wealth and crowded out private industry and private enterprise.

Labour entered the 1979 election with every major part of its post-war social and economic strategy undermined, and with a history of the recent failure of its new and ad hoc expedients in economic management. It could hardly expect to win either on its immediate record or on its long-term capacity for economic management. Labour's failure in 1974–9 was more deep-seated than mere contingency, hard times and bad luck. Mrs Thatcher, who had looked so unelectable in 1976, had become a serious contender for power. Labour had been forced to abandon Keynesianism and to introduce proto-monetarist policies. Mrs Thatcher's new gospel of economic liberalism based on free markets seemed an alternative to Labour's failed social liberalism based on a managed mixed economy. Mrs Thatcher's tough and uncompromising monetarism appeared more effective than Denis Healey's half-hearted essays in this direction. Free markets and monetarism together offered a new strategy of economic management that made cooperation with the uncontrollable unions unnecessary.

The Conservative Party thus offered in the May 1979 election what appeared to be a coherent remedy for Britain's economic failure and industrial discontents. What had appeared partisan, doctrinaire and impossibly right-wing in 1976 became practical politics in 1979, and largely for reasons not of Mrs Thatcher's making. Mrs Thatcher had changed little in those years and she had enjoyed little success up to 1978. Conservative policy had become less unpopular because Labour policy had become very unpopular. The Conservatives offered employed manual workers the dual promises of tax cuts and an end to restrictive incomes policies – those who could bargain would be free to do so. Union power was to be curbed by legal controls, offering the unorganized and un-unionized freedom from paralysing strikes. Inflation was to be tackled by tight monetary policy. Industrial competitiveness was to be restored by tax cuts that would give incentives to enterprise and by the defence of private industrial managers' freedom to manage. Inefficient state monopolies were to be broken up and de-nationalized. Public expenditure was to be rigidly controlled and the exponential growth of the public sector checked so that private industry could find the room to expand. An economic liberal policy would control inflation, reduce unemployment and lead to rapid growth once the economy had been restored to health.

The Conservative victory in 1979 depended crucially on the defection of large numbers of skilled and semi-skilled workers from Labour. Those groups have remained with the Conservatives in 1983 and 1987, giving them more of the skilled and semi-skilled workers' votes than Labour. The Conservatives could now claim to be the party of the industrial working class in the private sector. Labour lost a key constituency and has not regained it. Mrs Thatcher succeeded with this constituency not because she achieved some new 'ideological hegemony' over it but because she offered opportunistic prosperity-oriented policies and because those groups had long been opportunistic voters who put personal benefits first in making political choices.

Mrs Thatcher's governments since 1979 have blended the new economic doctrine with opportunism. The victory of Mrs Thatcher over Mr Heath was less an unparalleled break with Conservative tradition than a mutation in which one of the two traditions of Conservatism came out on top. Modern Conservatism has always been Janus-faced. Conservative doctrine and practice are a combination of economic liberalism and a 'one nation' opportunism based on an appeal to the common people. These two have always co-existed in tension, and one or the other has predominated depending on the conjuncture of factors. Mrs Thatcher has certainly made little play with 'one nation' patrician Toryism: how could she? But she has remained a flexible and opportunistic politician, and she has kept the two traditions of Conservatism in a creative tension. The virtues of the free market and the sovereignty of the private firm, the hostility to nationalization and the nationalized industries, the opposition to high taxes and a willingness to cut public expenditure, and the preference for sound money and a strong pound have all been consistent factors in Conservative thinking and rhetoric since the 1920s. With the demise of the old Liberal Party in the 1920s, the Conservatives became the sole inheritor of the Gladstonian virtues of economy in government and low taxes. The Conservatives became the main economic liberal force in opposition to Labour interventionist, collectivist and welfare thinking.

Mrs Thatcher drew on a long tradition of Conservative free market and anti public spending doctrine when she sought to re-cast Conservative thinking into a direct challenge to Labour. The Conservative-led National governments of the 1930s followed orthodox fiscal and monetary policies in the face of prolonged and severe depression. During the Second World War Kingsley Wood as Chancellor of the Exchequer consistently opposed Keynes' views on economic management and Beveridge's schemes for social insurance. The Conservatives under Churchill resisted nationalization as hard as they could during the 1945–51 Labour governments. Even in the 1950s, the supposed heyday of Keynesian consensus, Macmillan sacked Peter Thorneycroft as Chancellor because the government would not countenance public expenditure cuts. This led to the resignation of the whole Treasury front bench team in 1958. The Heath government of 1970–4 (a leading member of which was none other than Mr Nicholas Ridley) began with a programme containing substantial elements of economic liberalism. What made the 1970s different was the linking of the deep-seated prejudice in favour of restricting public spending with the new economic doctrine of monetarism. But even monetarism was primarily a new technical argument in an overwhelmingly Keynesian context for the old pre-Keynesian traditional ideas of a balanced budget and 'sound money'.[4]

Yet Mrs Thatcher threw away monetarism, the apparent core of her ideas in 1979, when it became a political liability. She did the biggest 'U' turn of any modern Conservative politician: proving herself at once more pragmatic than Stanley Baldwin and more cynical than Harold Macmillan – both hard acts to follow. Conservative economic policy between 1979 and 1981 very nearly failed. It produced an unprecedented rise in unemployment, a wave of industrial bankruptcies, an overrated pound and galloping interest rates. It radically reduced public expenditure on goods and services whilst leading to a vast rise in welfare payments as a result of unemployment; overall public spending, therefore, did not fall, in contradiction of a central 1979 policy goal. In 1979–82 the Conservatives followed a far more pragmatic industrial policy than their rhetoric of ruthless economic liberalism might have led one to suppose – aiding rather than sacrificing lame ducks. After 1981 they followed a more pragmatic and expansionary economic policy, and after 1983 a strongly expansionary and growth-oriented policy. Mrs Thatcher staked her claim in 1979 on the prospect of greater personal prosperity for voters and an end to economic strife. She abandoned much of the substance of her economic ideas in order to seek the pragmatic goal of prosperity – how she did it we shall see in chapter 4. The Conservatives engineered a consumption-based and credit-fuelled boom. For the beneficiaries of this boom it has indeed become the case that they 'had never had it so good' – in 1987 they voted with their pocket books.

This should give the lie to the myth of 'Thatcherism', to the idea of Mrs Thatcher as an ideologically motivated rather than pragmatically motivated prime minister. Prejudices she has aplenty, but 'Thatcherism' is a mirage: the closer you approach policy, the image created by political rhetoric vanishes. In many ways she has far more in common with Harold Macmillan than she would ever dare to consider. In many ways too the problems of her government since 1988 are like those of previous eras of expansionary policy – the Macmillan era and the Barber boom of the early 1970s. I shall return to this in chapter 4, but it is worth noting here that Mrs Thatcher has followed an expansionary policy and one strongly emphasizing domestic private consumption. Some Iron Lady!

A revolution in attitudes?

Central to Conservative rhetoric in 1979 and to the myth of 'Thatcherism' was the claim that Britain needed a revolution in attitudes. Dependency on the state had been fostered by decades of collectivism and welfarism. Workers were passive and expected their firms to provide undemanding paid employment. What was needed was an 'enterprise culture' in which individuals would take the responsibility and the risk of wealth creation themselves. In such a culture enterprising and successful individuals should enjoy the rewards of their efforts and they should be able to make provision for their own needs. Taxes should be cut to allow individual incentives, and efforts made to encourage private provision for health, education, pensions, etc.

The revolution in attitudes hoped for by the government simply hasn't taken place. It is a large part of the myth of 'Thatcherism' that the Tories appeal to a new more fluid, more individualistic and consumption-oriented society. If so, attitude surveys and opinion poll data are severely at fault. Many commentators have noted that public attitudes have obstinately refused to conform to the supposed success of the Thatcher revolution. Voters are unwilling to follow Mrs Thatcher on issues like health, education and welfare, even if they are willing to choose the Conservatives as the government. The reason, of course, is that you can choose only *one* government. If a voter feels that no other party is competent to govern, then he or she has to choose all the policies of that party along with it.

The survey data presented in the Fifth Report of *British Social Attitudes 1988* shows, for example, that there is no large-scale support for the extension of private education, that support for the principle of a universal National Health Service is overwhelming, and that respondents are willing to see public expenditure rise to support public services. In 1987, for example, a mere 3 per cent supported the proposition that taxes should be reduced and less spent on health, education and social benefits, whilst 50 per cent favoured higher taxes and more expenditure.[5] Moreover, the proportion of respondents favouring greater spending has grown in every year from 1983 to 1986. The message is clear: the public, including Tory voters, want a satisfactory level of collective provision of health, education and welfare.

Attitudes toward business show no more evidence of a shift toward 'enterprise' values or of a new legitimacy for the actions of company managements. When asked by the British Social Attitudes survey to 'suppose a large company *had* to choose between: doing something that improves pay and conditions for its staff; OR doing something that increases profits', respondents showed a shrewd and yet damning estimation of firms' priorities: 80 per cent thought the firm would choose to increase profits, while 69 per cent of respondents would choose to improve pay and conditions for staff.[6] The British Social Attitudes survey demonstrates that while public opinion is not anti-profit it has a clear perception that profits should be used to secure the long-term prospects for employment and national wealth. On the other hand, it expects firms to put the short-term interests and incomes of shareholders and managers first: 52 per cent of respondents thought that profits should go to investment, whereas only 42 per cent expected this to happen; only 3 per cent favoured benefits to shareholders and managers, against 34 per cent who expected firms to give an increase in dividends and 21 per cent who expected a bonus to top management.[7] This is directly contrary to Mrs Thatcher's continual insistence that it is for shareholders to decide what is in a company's interest and for managers to manage its affairs, subject to suitable incentives. The public do not see things this way: they want companies to serve the nation and profits to be used to sustain national prosperity. The public persist in treating the firm as a public body with social obligations. They are well aware of the vast discrepancy between what they think *should* be done and what they expect companies *will* do. There is no legitimacy for a nakedly 'enterprise' attitude in which a company's business is making money and its business is exclusively its shareholders' and managers' own business.

Yet Labour has been unable to exploit this advantage. The reason is, of course, that it was perceived as anti-business and that its policies were seen to be inimical to both profitability and national prosperity. Labour has been identified with nationalization and over-powerful trade unions. In the early 1980s it was dominated in public perceptions by a strident and incompetent manifestly anti-business left. Voters had no clear choice of a party that both supported private enterprise and profit and yet was determined that firms be managed and profits used in the interests of society. If Labour can convincingly accept that message – rejecting its anti-business image and yet proposing credible policies to revitalize manufacturing – then it could once again begin to be perceived by voters as a party of government. Public attitudes make it clear that the radical reform of company law and business regulation to make companies more accountable and socially responsible would not be unpopular.

These public attitudes toward business are not to be lightly dismissed. Not only do they make a mockery of Thatcherite 'ideological hegemony' but they also contradict basically and flatly the most fundamental beliefs of Mrs Thatcher herself. These attitudes also show that a government that tried to build a consensus for the revitalization of manufacturing industry and asked the public to put investment before current income would not meet an inherently hostile response. This is important for, as we shall see, my argument depends on such a consensus being possible and being articulated by a coalition of governing parties.

The pessimism of electoral sociology

The thesis of Thatcherite 'hegemony' supposes that Labour has been left behind by social change and that its values no longer resonate with important sections of workers who used to be part of its traditional constituencies. There is enough evidence to make this credible on a first reading. The political portrait of Labour drawn by many of the analysts of the elections of 1983 and 1987 is of a party supported by the failures in Mrs Thatcher's new order. Labour is the party of the northern traditional working class, of unskilled and public sector workers, of the health, education and welfare 'salariat', of council tenants and welfare recipients. Far more skilled manual workers and subaltern white-collar workers vote for the Conservatives than for Labour. It is argued that prosperity and a growing population in the South, the continued expansion of owner occupation, and the increase in individual shareholding with privatization all threaten to confine Labour to shrinking regional and social bases of support. On this diagnosis Labour can never hope to unseat the Tories, let alone form a majority government.

Moreover, this gloomy diagnosis claims to predict the future too – it will be worse for Labour as these social trends continue to develop. This sociological prognostication depends on a highly questionable assumption, that is, that there is a natural affinity between certain classes of voters and a particular political party. This assumption is not a new one, but it used to be made by the *left* and was seen to favour the left; that is, the working class will naturally support the party of labour. Now it is seen to favour the right: the affluent and successful – skilled workers included – will support the party that rewards individual achievement.

To put the case for a natural affinity in a caricature form, it implies that what parties say or do can have little effect on who supports them. This violates the basic assumptions of all electoral politicians; they must believe that what they say and do in a campaign makes a real difference. It cannot all be a matter of changing class structures and basic attitudes. Well, 1987 appears to offer support to the electoral sociologists. In terms of the Conservative vote, the election might never have happened – support remained steady despite a very poor Tory campaign.

It is unclear, however, in what the postulated natural affinity consists and why it should be with one party rather than another. It cannot be a simple perception of one's place in the occupational structure or status hierarchy. One would expect the university-educated to cluster overwhelmingly at the upper end of the occupational ladder and the unemployed to cluster toward the bottom. Yet only 34 per cent of the university-educated voted for Mrs Thatcher in 1987, whilst 32 per cent of the unemployed voted Tory in 1983. If voters do try to follow their interests in identifying with parties, then those interests cannot simply be read off from one's occupational or status position. Rather it is a matter of perceptions of parties' positions in relation to one's conception of one's interests. Few people have a single and unambiguous 'interest' – occupation, housing tenure, geographical location. Non-occupational associations and interests can conflict with and counteract one another even from the standpoint of that abstraction of electoral sociology, the rational calculating agent. People have to invent their interests and in doing so they take note of what political parties, among other sources, do and say. A campaign will seldom transform voters' perceptions of their interests, but a long period of political campaigning and argument can do so. If there were a rigid natural affinity between occupational classes and parties how would one explain the shift of skilled workers from Labour to the Tories?

There is comfort and heartache for Labour here. Policies, positions and images obviously do matter in voters' perceptions of parties. But Labour's policy image still frightens off many manual and office working-class voters. It seems reasonable to assume that many skilled manual and subaltern white-collar workers vote Conservative instrumentally. That is, they have no fixed 'ideological' identification with Toryism; rather they perceive Conservative government as best for their living standards. This is hardly Thatcherite; it is a product of post-war affluence and the Macmillan era. Labour itself throughout the 1950s and 1960s helped to promote the image of a full-employment economy with steadily rising real wages. Affluent working-class voters in the South have voted Conservative because, for them, that *is* the condition of the economy. Even if those voters felt sympathy for the unemployed in the North, they did not trust Labour with their own prosperity. Far from there being a natural affinity, there is a very calculating marriage of convenience between Conservatism and the southern affluent worker.

There is no doubt that it will be very difficult for Labour to recapture the southern skilled working-class vote. The issue is, however, more complex than a straight switch of successfully employed workers in the South from the Conservatives to Labour. Let us accept for a moment that the thesis of a natural affinity between these groups and the Conservatives is not proven. Voters may not simply identify with the Conservatives and stick with them through thick and thin. That type of unquestioning traditional loyalty has declined for *all* parties, not merely Labour. Many voters are defectors to Conservatism and have voted on the basis of pragmatic rather than ideological grounds. They may desert the Conservatives on such grounds, if there is a viable alternative. That alternative may not be the Labour Party, but giving up the Conservatives implies that voters are not implacably hostile to Labour.

To vote for the Social and Liberal Democrats or for the Social Democratic Party (SDP) is not just an anti-Conservative act (outside, that is, of a by-election in which voters wish to register their dissatisfaction with the ruling party's performance). In a general election, voting Democrat or SDP is voting for a party that either can only govern in coalition with Labour or will let in Labour as the largest governing party. Voters have to feel safe with Labour even if they do not vote Labour. Labour, therefore, has to appeal to affluent employed workers in the South even if it does not expect to get their votes directly. Unless voters in the South either switch directly to Labour, which seems less than likely, or switch to another opposition party, no non-Conservative government can be formed. If Labour wants to regain office, it has a vital interest in disproving the thesis of a newly formed identification between certain social groups and the Conservative Party. If the support of these groups for Conservatism is pragmatic and conjunctural, capable of being broken by Conservative failure in government and a credible appeal by the opposition parties that address that failure, then Labour can at least hope to participate in government.

The pessimistic thesis, implied by the notion of 'Thatcherism', makes this shift appear virtually impossible. This is the reason that the thesis of 'Thatcherism' presents Labour with its greatest difficulty. If it were true, then Labour could survive as a potential party of government only by converting itself into a wholly new type of radical party fundamentally committed to individualist and consumerist values. That, of course, is the basic implication of the fashionable new ideas proposed by the Young Turks of *Marxism Today*.[8] The thesis that we are living in 'new times' and that social change has undercut traditional Labourism threatens to render the aims of even the Labour Party's modernizers obsolescent.

Marxism Today sees Britain in the 1980s as shifting away from a traditional industrial society based on mass production and a relatively undifferentiated working class toward a new 'post-Fordist' society based on individualism, consumerism and the service sector, and involving fluid and rapidly changing social relationships and identifications. A new radical party must reflect these changes away from collectivism and class membership to individualism, and from large-scale manufacturing industry toward a more diffuse and differentiated occupational structure. Such a party would combine issues that affect all members of society as individuals, like the environment, and issues that affect specific social groupings and incline them to radicalism, issues of discrimination and equal rights. It would be a union of common individualist and consumer concerns and the agenda of what is called the 'new social forces' (Blacks, women, gays, etc.).

The problem is that, in making a case against a traditional socialist politics founded on a homogeneous mass 'working class', the new Marxist critics overstep the mark. The traditional socialist case is obsolete, but then so it was when Crosland wrote *The Future of Socialism* in the 1950s. There have indeed been rapid social changes in the 1970s and 1980s, but Britain has not changed into a post-modern, post-Fordist society. In chapter 4 I shall show that Britain has been slow to adopt the new forms of manufacturing organization, and is behind other countries in moving away from large-scale assembly-line production. No case for a new politics can be based on forms of economic change that simply have not taken place here. I should add that 'post-Fordist' is an inaccurate way to characterize the changes in manufacturing in Britain's most advanced competitor countries (the reasons are highly technical and need not concern us here). Such new patterns of manufacturing are based not on a fluid and highly individual-istic society but on social relationships that emphasize the co-hesion and cooperation of social groups. Far from being 'post-modern', the societies of Britain's more industrially flexible competitors are actually rather conservative.

As in the case of social change, so in the case of attitudes. The evidence given above shows that the British public have not embraced individualism and consumerism as fully as either Mrs Thatcher would like or *Marxism Today* supposes. The public remain conservative about forms of collectivist welfare and social service provision, and they are far from enthusiastic about 'enter-prise culture'.

The Yuppie utopia implied in the claim that we are living in 'new times' is only the latest part of *Marxism Today*'s case. If their claim for social change does not quite fit the bill, what about that earlier and still widely canvassed thesis of the 'hegemony' of Thatcherism? Stuart Hall, the Marxist sociologist, is the origin-ator and leading exponent of the notion of 'Thatcherism'. Hall has the major virtue, along with Martin Jacques, the editor of

Marxism Today, of having realized from the early 1980s that Mrs Thatcher was a lasting phenomenon, not just another prime minister. Yet they have overblown that perception, using the ideas of the Italian Marxist Antonio Gramsci (1891–1937). In an election post-mortem in the July 1987 issue of *Marxism Today* Hall argued that the new Conservatism had come to exert 'hegemony' over people's attitudes and aspirations. Thatcherism had seized ideological hold of the affluent working class,[9] which had become part of a 'social bloc', an alliance of social groups under Conservative leadership.

But why on earth consider the Tory's 42 per cent of the electorate as a 'social bloc', rather than a ramshackle coalition of instrumental interest groups, potentially highly unstable? Why consider the Conservatives as displaying consummate ideological skill, as being in tune with and able to manipulate public opinion? On the contrary, the Conservatives can be crassly incompetent and inept at either gauging or handling public opinion, as the growing disasters over the poll tax, water privatization and National Health Service reorganization show. Why treat Mrs Thatcher as ideologically inspired and in tune with ordinary voters' aspirations? Mrs Thatcher is more pragmatic than she is consistent, and yet she is very much out of touch with ordinary people. Far from being a great asset, she is unpopular even with many Tory voters.

The Conservatives did not campaign as a 'hegemonic' party in the 1987 general election. Even though they called the election and had been preparing for it for some time, they got off on the wrong foot. They behaved like an opposition party propelled into an election in a hurry and they took time to adjust from being the government to being just another party in the rough and tumble of political campaigning. Half way through the election the effect of Labour's defence policies, its confusions on taxation and its very vague economic programme began to tell. An initially competent Labour campaign flagged and the Tories were home and dry.

It is thus surprising that Stuart Hall's analysis treats 1987 as a victory founded on Conservative ideological skill, rather than as a testament to Labour's continuing weakness in projecting itself as a party of government. Given the choice, voters might well have preferred a more centrist and accommodating Toryism, but that choice was not available. Voters can only choose between a small number of parties, warts and all. To vote Conservative is not to endorse every government policy or approve of every action of Mrs Thatcher.

Hall's conception of 'ideology' over-politicizes the attitudes voters bring to the matter of electoral choice. He is right to emphasize that voters choose party images rather than detailed policy programmes. Voters do construct their interests through background sets of ideas, but these seldom correspond to an articulate political outlook. If we are to explain voters' mental sets then we should use a different framework from the one utilized by Hall. If anything, the ideas of the English sociologists John Goldthorpe and David Lockwood, first put forward in their famous study *The Affluent Worker* published in 1968–9, have far more explanatory power than the ideas of Antonio Gramsci.[10] Workers judge politics and political parties apolitically, in terms of the expected benefits to themselves and their families. We have to recognize that private consumption and individual choice in life and leisure are not phenomena of the Thatcher years but go back at the very least to the post-war boom.

Labour modernizers like Bryan Gould, in emphasizing the need to appeal to voters as individuals rather than as members of a class, to recognize a radical shift in popular expectations about politics, are merely echoing a long-established theme. As consumers, affluent working-class voters expect a government to promote economic success *and* to provide the necessary public services to a high standard. Voters generally are both individualists and collectivists; affluent workers are little different in this respect. Manual workers place a high premium on personal prosperity for the very good reason that they are neither so well-off nor so secure as to take it for granted. They depend very directly for their living standards on the performance of the economy and they know they can suffer in a severe recession. Good economic management by a national government is vital to them and they will not see it compromised. This told against Labour in the 1980s, but it could equally tell against the Conservatives if the performance of the economy and perceptions of their ability to manage it both begin to fail. Affluent workers are instrumental in their approach to politics and they can switch allegiance on pragmatic grounds. Well-to-do socialists and members of the middle classes should not despise them for this. People whose position is secure and who have long enjoyed the privileges many workers have only recently come to expect – their own home, foreign holidays, a private pension – should not judge others too harshly.

A qualified individualism and a desire for prosperity have been assets for the Tories, but they are not secure assets. Paradoxically, the instrumental individualism and the strong orientation to economic success of the affluent worker, which are not new trends but ones well established in the 1960s, offer Labour a chance to campaign against the Conservatives on what might seem to be their strongest ground. It has been distrust of Labour's capacity to deliver economic success that has been crippling. Enough voters, just, believed Harold Wilson's claims for economic modernization in 1964 – these voters were disappointed. In 1991 Labour will have to convince the key voters that it can do better than the Conservatives. Labour has a big job in this respect: it must overcome the perceptions of 1974–9 as a period of economic chaos and the early 1980s as a period of its domination by an authoritarian and impractical left. To do this it will need to do more than just drop the old policies that made it unelectable; it will have to show that it can govern in the national interest.

How then to counter the marriage of convenience between Conservatism and the southern skilled worker? Not by policies aimed at them exclusively or at their narrow short-term economic interests alone. Labour cannot buy votes by appealing directly to the pocket book. Few people are pious in the privacy of the polling booth and the Conservatives will always be better at a purely cynical and opportunist appeal if they have half the chance. Labour can address such workers only as members of a social and economic community, who suffer or prosper in direct relation to the collective fortunes. If Labour can show that the decline of manufacturing industry exposes even the currently affluent in the most favoured regions to insecurity and potential poverty, and that it has a viable strategy of national economic revitalization, then it may win the argument. To do this it must behave as more than a single party, relying on purely party solutions and purely party support.

A real national crisis requires a different kind of government. We have seen that Labour needs to convince southern voters that choosing the opposition candidate in a general election will not let a purely sectional Labour Party into office. How better to do that than to claim with justification that it will not be an exclusive party government, that it will work with the other opposition parties and any social and political force willing to cooperate to revitalize manufacturing industry and with it the whole economy? Voters are not pure individualists: they want a welfare state, and they view industry as part of the community and serving the community; although they want personal prosperity, they want it to be secure and for the less fortunate to share in the social wealth we all create. Labour can offer them both private wealth and a tolerably fair and stable society. The British people have rejected mere individualism and purely private gain, but they have been unable to give expression to that rejection in a government of their choice. It is up to Labour to make that possible.

A tale of two dissidents

The 'boxes' in this book are intended to provide a sideways look at some issues that are not covered in the main text. Several of them were written to illustrate what a ludicrous and yet vaguely sinister society we have become. No tale can indicate this better than the contrary fates of two Czech dissidents: the playwright Václav Havel and the philosopher Julius Tomin. Havel's situation is simple and desperate, but easy to comprehend. The Czech government is determined to shut him up and is sending him to prison for his part in organizing public demonstrations. Havel is deemed an outlaw by the regime, and yet he has a clear place and function within Czechoslovakia. He may be poor and harassed, but he can be in no doubt that he is valued by most Czechs and that the regime's threats are an index that they know this.

Consider Tomin, however. When he held philosophy seminars in his Prague flat he represented a beacon of dissidence and a threat to the regime. People freely discussed philosophy and even if their discussions centred on Plato, dead for over 2000 years, for the authorities that would never do. Tomin was got out to England, with the good offices of some English philosophers. Suddenly he vanished from public view. He didn't choose to play the role of the active and strident political émigré: he just wanted to study philosophy, and went on reading and talking about Plato. In modern Britain that is close to insane. Several so-called 'universities' have closed their philosophy departments, and philosophy jobs, though under-paid, are like gold dust. Tomin is not a careerist, nor is he young, and his philosophical ideas are not fashionable. No philosophy lectureship or research fellowship for him. Julius Tomin winds up on the dole. After a while the Oxford DHSS decides it will not subsidize dissident philosophers. If Tomin will not train as a bricklayer or take a job as a short-order cook, then he can starve.

Enter one of the few characters who makes one feel some hope for England: the landlord of a pub in Swindon. Having read about Tomin, he decided to forgo a brand new car and hire a philosopher instead. He gave Tomin a contract to lecture in his pub. Because he is a robust character, with imagination and little concern for social stereotypes, the landlord gives us hope. He has secured Tomin a living where all the universities in the country have failed. He has supported a man fêted by the British government when he was in his native land, but who was then thrust aside to starve when he came here. The landlord shows a liberty of thought and action that disgraces vice chancellors, Foreign Office ministers, and MPs alike.

The landlord's customers also give one cause for hope because they show that enough ordinary people want to talk, to think and to argue. That they should do so in a pub, with a good glass of beer in their hands, more closely resembles how the Greeks argued – in private company drinking wine – than any university seminar. Lobotomized consumerism will never triumph while there are ordinary public places like pubs full of people who want to hear philosophers or poets. Perhaps a future government should give a fraction of the money it spends on universities to sponsoring quiz contests, poetry readings, and philosophy circles in pubs. It might then achieve the first duty of education, something schools and colleges do badly: getting people to despair of ignorance and enjoy knowledge.

CHAPTER 2

The Constitutional Crisis

THE BRITISH POLITICAL SYSTEM is in deep trouble. In the 1960s Britain was regarded as *the* paradigmatic stable democracy. Westminster continued to think of itself as the 'Mother of Parliaments'. Foreign commentators offered Britain as the best example of an effectively functioning two-party system within a large, well-governed and homogeneous nation state. Successive crises have destroyed that image and have led to the questioning of the most basic political institutions by a wide spectrum of informed domestic and foreign opinion.

Just to list the problems is a lengthy job in itself. The 1960s ended with a renewal and intensification of the Ulster question. The Province has continued ever since to be virtually ungovernable. Nationalist terrorism has proved unconquerable. It has also infected the politics of the whole British state; the state of emergency in Ulster has leeched out into the whole political system. Anti-terrorist legislation has undermined civil liberties in the UK, giving the police unprecedented powers in peacetime. Internal exile has become a possibility in a supposedly liberal state. Political parties, notably Sinn Fein, are denied access to press and broadcasting. The prospect of a political solution, despite recent hopeful talks by the legitimate political parties in the Province, seems remote.

In the early 1970s mainland Britain edged toward ungovernability. The opposition to the 1971 Industrial Relations Act, the 1972 miners' strike, and the 1978–9 'Winter of Discontent' all appeared to demonstrate that the unions had the power to frustrate and defeat central government policy. Since the Conservative victory in 1979 this 'ungovernability' has been ended by decisive state action and a series of anti-union legislative measures. But the result offers no stable model of how industrial relations are to be conducted in a free society. The unions, from being alleged to be 'outside the law', are now so hobbled by legal restrictions that they cannot decide by their own procedures how to conduct their own internal affairs; this conduct is prescribed by government and subjected to legal penalties in the minutest detail. No sensible person would deny that the unions' actions should be subjected to legal limit; that they should be denied some of the most basic rights of free association is, however, inconsistent with the workings of democracy. The Government Communications Headquarters (GCHQ) affair, the withdrawal of teachers' negotiating rights, and the Dover seamen's strike all show unions reduced to impotence by what amounts to active state suppression. It has become possible for the state to deny unions negotiating rights without any kind of constitutional check. Even critics of the unions ought to fear the long-run consequences of such a policy.

In the 1970s Britain's homogeneity as a nation state was challenged not only by Ulster, but also by the Welsh and Scottish nationalist movements. Both the major political parties have tried to sidetrack or derail any effective progress toward greater autonomy and regional self-government for Wales and Scotland within a federal United Kingdom. Labour tried to forestall the Scottish nationalists in 1979 by an artfully contrived referendum on an assembly with ambiguous status and powers. Mrs Thatcher has simply excluded the issue from the agenda, seeking to reduce even those elements of a distinctly Scottish administration that exist under the present constitution and to subject Scotland to a programme of 'reforms' (like the poll tax) inspired in London and for which there is negligible Scottish support. Scotland is to be a centrally directed province, despite the fact that the Conservatives have no real legitimacy in Scotland, in terms of either national elections or local government. The Conservatives, driven into utter marginality in Scotland at the last election, are straining the fabric of the 'United Kingdom' to breaking point by imposing bitterly contested policies north of the border by means of the parliamentary sovereignty of Westminster. Sensible and intelligent Scots are now speaking a political language only previously heard on the lips of leaders of independence movements in Britain's colonies.

Also in the 1970s Britain entered the EEC. The depth of political uncertainty over the EEC, a political hot potato for Labour like devolution, led to the issue of British membership of the Community being put to a referendum. Two major referendums in the 1970s, an unprecedented event in British politics, showed how far the constitutional issues in Britain had moved away from being coped with by the traditional mechanisms of elected party government and how little cross-party consensus there was on the shape and nature of Britain's constitution. Pro- and anti-marketeers could be found in both the major parties. A pro victory in the 1975 referendum has not settled the issue of Europe, since the Community has continued to change and develop. Active opposition to the Community has declined, to be replaced by grudging and unconstructive membership. The performance of the Conservative government since 1979 in Europe has been a consistent seeking of narrow national interest and an increasingly negative stance toward greater economic and political integration. The Conservatives signed the Single European Act and have made a great deal of fuss about the creation of a single European market in 1992. They have stressed the free market aspects of the new developments whilst ignoring or denying the new agenda of social interest consultation, the new 'social' programmes, and the deepening of common governmental institutions.

Mrs Thatcher is now the main obstacle to the further development of the Community. Her grounds for opposition to political integration within the Community are exactly the same as those that anti-marketeers gave for saying 'no' to membership of the Community – that it will undermine the 'sovereignty of Parliament'. Mrs Thatcher is determined to cling on to one of the worst features of Britain's constitution, precisely because it allows her unchallenged rule at home. That sovereignty is now threatened externally and in a way it will be difficult for her to gainsay. Britain is no longer strong enough or independent enough to impose an alternative agenda on the Community. Britain will be dragged reluctantly into common European policies, imposed by majority vote, and it will be the main loser if it tries to sabotage the more progressive of those policies. Britain will be exposed to more intensive economic competition within the Community, whilst failing fully to benefit from the new programmes designed to ensure that wealth and investment are not simply concentrated in the most favoured regions. Britain under continued Conservative rule stands to benefit least from the long-run possibilities of progressive change in its central government institutions and from the prospects of enhanced regional government offered by the new Europe. A much-needed shake-up in Westminster and a much-needed process of decentralization can be diluted and denied by obstructive British policy. This would be the greatest lost opportunity to reshape British government in this century and that at a time when the need for a powerful external stimulus to institutional change has never been greater.

The two-party system has now broken down irrecoverably, but no new stable system of party competition in elections has come to replace it. Many commentators have regarded a stable two-party system as the foundation of the modern British political system and as the condition for the effective working of parliamentary democracy. It would not be exaggerating to say that the two-party system is the most important unwritten annexe to our unwritten constitution. The British system gives a majority party government undisputed control of legislative and executive power, so much so that it has been called an 'elective despotism'. For checks on that power to be effective government must feel challenged *outside* of Whitehall and the Commons, since the constitutional constraints on a legitimate government are few. That threat was always seen as the opposition, an alternative government that used the Commons as a platform with an eye to the next election. Such an opposition is a threat to the party in office because it offers a credible prospect of electoral defeat. This limits the ruling party's actions and constrains it from adopting unpopular policies. The existence of two strong national parties, each with a solid core of the vote, each threatened when in office by relatively small marginal shifts in electoral support, ensures that there is stable succession to office, a clear and simple choice for voters, and a real check on the actions of the party in office. Britain's first-past-the-post electoral system is only effectively representative of voters' choices if there are two roughly equal national parties.

This system worked even when a ruling party spent a long time in office, as did the Conservatives from 1951 to 1964. Two-party politics was never as complete and equal as the mythology suggests – Labour was weak in the 1930s, for example – but the system survived because the governing party could not feel certain that it would not be defeated. In 1951–64 the Conservatives were forced willy-nilly to let much of the 1945–51 Labour legislation stand, because a good deal of it was too popular to challenge.

This constraint has been removed from Mrs Thatcher's government. The 1979 election was an old two-party one that Labour lost. Neither election since has been so. With the demise of the two-party system Mrs Thatcher has faced no serious electoral threat and has twice won against a split opposition, on a mere 42 per cent of the vote. She has enjoyed an unassailable majority in the Commons. The parliamentary opposition to her government has been ineffective because no party can impede a 100-seat majority – speeches and challenges in Parliament only work if they are part of a credible electoral threat. Mrs Thatcher has been steadily emboldened by the discovery that she faces no opposition. The demise of the two-party system, something outside her control, has allowed her the space for authoritarian solutions. It is unfortunate that the drift of Labour to the left and the splitting-off of the Social Democratic Party occurred when the Conservative Party lurched far to the right and did so under a leader sufficiently determined to drive through policies irrespective of their popularity in the country at large.

It seems certain that the old two-party system is wrecked beyond repair. Labour is unlikely to be able to capture the middle ground so completely as to marginalize the two competing centre parties nor is it likely to be able to recover enough seats in the South to form a majority government under the present electoral system. If opposition party support divides as it did at the Epping and Richmond by-elections, then the Conservatives could form a majority government on no more than a third of the national vote. Yet Labour remains opposed to proportional representation (PR) and an electoral pact between the three opposition parties would be difficult to devise even if there were the political will for it. If something does not change, the Conservatives could rule for a considerable time whilst being very unpopular with a majority of electors. That would gravely weaken democratic institutions in Britain.

Britain is a highly centralized state and it has become more centralized during the Conservatives' ten years in office. Thus there are no strong regional governments with the fiscal base and the autonomy to counteract central state policies. The autonomy of local government has been relentlessly diminished by Conservative legislation and administrative action. There is no constitutional check on the powers of central government in respect of local authorities and they have no constitutional rights, even to exist. This is shown by the abolition of the Greater London Council (GLC) and a whole tier of local authorities, essentially because the GLC had tried to compensate for central government policies with new strategies of its own. Britain has moved toward centralism at a time when even countries like France are trying to enhance the powers of local government and when strong regional governments have become recognized as an important part of local economic development strategies.

Lastly, a radical government without genuine legitimacy for many of its more unpopular measures, like the poll tax, or water industry privatization, or NHS reorganization, faces no serious constitutional check. Neither the House of Lords nor the judiciary can effectively challenge a Bill passed by a majority in the Commons. This means that the 'rule of law' is gravely threatened in Britain. The test of lawfulness is purely formal – that a Bill has passed through the Commons by the appropriate procedures. Legislation cannot be challenged and administrative action is subject to few legal checks. Other countries have far stronger systems of constitutional checks and balances to ensure that government action and legislation meet more than merely procedural standards of appropriateness: individual rights and principles with which to judge legislation are written into constitutions; constitutional courts can review legislation according to these standards; strong and elected second chambers can scrutinize and reject legislation proposed by the lower house; and administrative law is highly developed, so as to subject the actions of officials to scrutiny.

An honest person comparing the constitution of Britain with that of, say, the Federal Republic of Germany could only conclude that the latter was superior. Britain is very clearly a 'second best' democracy, no matter how much the politicians may bluster.[1] Only some of the more intelligent politicians in the two centre parties are willing to accept this verdict and to put constitutional change high on their political agenda. Labour and the Conservatives have shunned the issue. For Mrs Thatcher democracy means no more than a periodic plebiscite which selects *who* shall rule; it has little or nothing to do with *how* they should rule. A 'mandate' from a general election should allow the governing party to do virtually whatever it likes; it should not be forced to submit to discussion, consultation, judicial scrutiny or constitutional check while in office. Why should she listen to those she has beaten, let alone accept they might have the constitutional power to check her? In Mrs Thatcher Britain has found a politician to expose the nakedness of the constitutional checks and guarantees to public view. She has helped to puncture our insular and incorrigibly ignorant view of ourselves as the premier democracy, and helped to show the need for a break with our political history, with the institutions and traditions that we have celebrated to the point where we have ceased to think about them.

Britain's political system may have moved into crisis in the 1970s and 1980s but that does not mean that it functioned in the past as the myths say it did. For example, in 1910–14 Britain faced a series of acute constitutional and political crises: the struggle over Lloyd George's social insurance legislation between the Liberal majority in the Commons and the Tory-dominated House of Lords; the condition of near civil war in Ireland over the Home Rule issue; the bitter labour disputes and syndicalist agitation; and the suffragette campaign. Other examples could be cited in addition to 'The strange death of Liberal England' – most notably the 'great fear' among orthodox politicians about revolutionary agitation and the influence of Bolshevism in the period immediately after World War I, the General Strike of 1926, and the defection of a section of the Labour Party to form a National government with the Conservatives in the 1930s.

The myth of political stability does contain an important truth, however. The continuity of the British state has not been broken by war and occupation, or by revolution, since the seventeenth century. Political crises there have been, but no fundamental recasting of the state, as in the French and American revolutions, or as in the case of Germany and Japan after defeat and occupation in 1945. Democracy was thus added slowly after 1832 by successive extensions of the franchise to an existing parliamentary system. Modern political parties and modern party government developed *pari passu* with the rise of a mass electorate. However, the basic constitutional powers of Parliament changed but little. *Parliament is a pre-democratic institution.* Politicians and electorates have thought of Britain as a democracy – politicians claiming to derive their power from the 'will of the people'. But that is not where Parliament derives its power in strict constitutional law.[2] Parliament enjoys the powers that it has because it is sovereign. The Queen-in-Parliament is sovereign and illimitable. The Queen, Lords and Commons together, if they give assent to legislation, can pass any law they like without constitutional or other legal check. In theory Parliament can by a simple legislative act change its own procedures for elections or even suspend elections indefinitely. Democracy is in a sense dependent on Parliament, not Parliament on democracy. The core of Britain's constitution thus pre-dates ideas about constitutional limitation of the powers of the legislature that one finds in the American constitution and all constitutions derived from it.

The danger with such a system is that unlimited legislative sovereignty is now, since the rise of mass democracy, placed in the hands of a party government. Parliament has long ceased to be an assembly of semi-independent notables, and the majority party's MPs are subject to the discipline and the power of patronage of the leadership. Legislative power is thus concentrated in very few hands and, given party discipline, subject to virtually no check – given a majority. Eminent constitutional lawyers have long seen the theoretical danger of a contradiction between the unlimited sovereign power of Parliament and the rule of law. They have generally supposed the danger to be remote because Parliament was broadly representative of the nation and politicians would not attempt to pass legislation which fundamentally damaged the rights or interests of a large section of the population. Both these saving conditions have now collapsed: a party representing a minority of voters has acted with extreme partiality and has used its control and sovereign legislative power without regard to widespread opposition. The political crisis may be recent but it was a crisis waiting to happen. The way Britain's constitution has evolved has placed minimal restraints on an essentially pre-democratic legislature.

This is not the only defect of Britain's pre-democratic inheritance. British government has long concentrated and centralized power, treating it as a property or exclusive possession. David Marquand in *The Unprincipled Society* has produced a damning indictment of what he calls the 'Westminster model' of government. Marquand is concerned to refute fashionable views of twentieth-century Britain as suffering from a growing dose of three diseases: collectivism, corporatism and consensus. On the contrary, he argues, British governmental institutions have prevented a constructive dialogue with the major organized social interests and the mutual harnessing of the energies of the state and the major economic agents. Britain thus failed to develop what Marquand calls a 'developmental state', one capable of mobilizing society for economic change by both active intervention and the orchestration of cooperation by the major social groups. Three features of the 'Westminster model' prevent this: one I have discussed above is the unlimited sovereignty of Parliament, which puts a premium on party government and majority rule, and not on collaboration and dialogue; the second is the appropriation by the executive of the prerogative powers of the monarch, another pre-democratic inheritance which gives to ministers the advantage of acting as agents of the 'Crown'; and the third is the doctrine that civil servants are no more than executors of their ministers' will and that ministers alone are answerable to Parliament. The latter two features severely restrict the accountability of administration, since ministers are answerable in all substantive matters only to a Parliament where the ruling party has a majority anyway.

Modern British democracy has emphasized 'win or lose' politics with Westminster and Whitehall as the prize. The electoral victor enjoys all the assets of legislative and executive power. Such a conception of office as the chance to exercise one's will without impediment exerts an irresistible influence on politicians. Westminster is a means of acting on the wider society. 'Reform' means the actions of a party government, determined by party policy. The idea that Westminster itself might be in grave need of reform is something quite new to politicians and still resisted by them in the main. Resisted in particular are any measures that would diminish the powers and prerogatives of an exclusively party government.

Moreover, this can hardly be blamed on Mrs Thatcher. She has driven the 'Westminster model' close to the scrap heap, but only by carrying to extremes the in-built tendencies of the political system. In a way Mrs Thatcher is the first politician to play the game for real, doing what others have merely talked about or hoped to do. The Labour left has consistently urged that the power of Parliament should be used to force through fundamental reforms. This has been a familiar litany from the 1930s to Tony Benn. Political change is secondary for Labour radicals to economic and social reform delivered through Westminster. 'An irreversible shift in power and wealth in favour of working people' never meant a more democratic constitution and more accountable government. Tony Benn always called for the sweeping away of restraints on the power of a democratic House of Commons that he saw in the House of Lords.[3] In fact Labour, like the Conservatives before Thatcher, has never been a ruthless reforming party using the power of a parliamentary majority to the full. Labour has twice enjoyed majorities as great as Mrs Thatcher's, in 1945 and in 1966. In 1945 it carried out a substantial programme of social reform, but its most radical *political* reform was to abolish the Universities' and Business Votes in 1947. Westminster was to remain, and Whitehall too was largely undisturbed.

The Labour left has never had its way because by and large its policies were electoral liabilities; until, that is, the fatal period of the early 1980s when it was indeed allowed to make Labour unelectable. Political reform was not on the wider agenda because in the 1950s and for much of the 1960s government appeared to face few structural problems and the economy was booming. Labour thus never used its periods of office to introduce constitutional reform. Parliament was taken for granted and many of the leading members of the Labour Party, like Herbert Morrison or Michael Foot, have been slavishly addicted to the rituals of Parliament and to its traditions.

Harold Wilson in 1964 and Edward Heath in 1970 both

attempted radical programmes of economic modernization. Both failed dismally, and not merely for technical economic reasons. Neither was able to win the collaboration of the major social interests in creating the conditions for sustained growth. In both cases good intentions were defeated by the limits of the 'Westminster model', not too much corporatism and consensus, but too little. Neither politician could step outside of the structure of party government, and neither found a structure of workable institutions for facilitating inter-party and inter-interest group collaboration toward common goals. The effect of politicians treating governmental power as an exclusive possession and of regarding other parties only as electoral competitors was to cut the ground from under the development of a political culture in which dialogue, collaboration and bargaining were possible. Mrs Thatcher, with a bleak if short-sighted honesty, has drawn the lesson that dialogue, collaboration and bargaining are futile.

She succeeded a government that staggered from crisis to crisis because it could not create or cement a collaborative political culture, even when it ruled by a pact with the Liberals. Had Labour conceded PR in 1974–9, had it seen the need to deepen its collaboration with the Liberals, had it sought *institutional* changes to make the 'Social Contract' an ongoing reality, then it could have prevented the Thatcher years. For it to have done so, even though the political crises were visibly accumulating around it, would have involved breaking with the habits of a lifetime.

Mrs Thatcher has often publicly despised 'consensus' and she is in turn criticized by others for her one-sidedness and partiality. It is often said that she has ignored the need for balance and impartiality in public appointments, using her powers of patronage and her prerogatives ruthlessly to favour her own candidates. This seems to me the least of her faults, and one shared by many previous prime ministers. The difference is that *their* cronies were not possessed of an explicit ideology and expected to act like 'one of us'. Mrs Thatcher has promoted her own people, often without regard to talent or appropriateness. But what makes them different is that 'her' people are part of a wide circle of socially conservative free marketeers. Harold Wilson was no stranger to the practices of patronage and preferment, but 'his' people had no aims.

What Mrs Thatcher has revealed is that there is no longer a stratum of 'neutral' public worthies, any more than there are 'neutral' institutions. The BBC, the universities, the Church, etc., are all objects of either explicit and interventionist government policies or of Conservative ideological disapprobation. Yet surely in a way Mrs Thatcher is right. Given the character of the 'Westminster model', semi-autonomous institutions like the BBC or the University Grants Committee that are dependent on public funds are a contradiction in terms. In truth the problem is that the existence of such institutions must be fragile given the sovereignty of Parliament and the absence of any effective constitutional guarantee for their independence. Mrs Thatcher has clearly recognized that an unwritten constitution is no restraint at all if you have a secure majority. Lamenting her lack of 'restraint' is silly; we should lament the lack of institutions and rules that restrain her.

I have emphasized a growing constitutional crisis since the 1960s and the long-run and inherent deficiencies of British parliamentary institutions. The reason for this is that far too many critics lay the problems primarily at the door of Mrs Thatcher. There is no doubt that Mrs Thatcher's period in office has brought concern about Britain's political institutions and the state of civil liberties to a head. But many of these problems pre-existed her. Mrs Thatcher is not the first prime minister to encourage economy with the truth or to practise selective leaking and news manipulation. Harold Wilson could hardly be regarded as a saint in this respect, nor could Harold Macmillan. Was not the austere and old-fashioned William Beveridge the tutor to all subsequent manipulators when he leaked his famous report on social security? Mrs Thatcher's obsessions with security have been carried to extremes. But she inherited and did not invent a system of closed government. Labour had ample opportunity to reform the Official Secrets Act. In fact Labour gave the greatest fillip to British obsessions with secrecy and spying when it decided in 1946 to build a British atomic bomb. James Callaghan in the 1970s allowed the Chevaline programme to develop in the greatest secrecy – a modernization of Britain's nuclear warheads that dwarfs the Zircon affair in both scale and the degree of deception of Parliament. Harold Wilson used MI5 to spy on political opponents, and successive governments allowed the intelligence community to remain an unaccountable state within a state.

We cannot pretend that pre-Thatcher politicians were innocents nor can we imagine that the powers of ministers and the privileges of closed government were not exploited by Labour in the past. Britain was not a model democracy in 1979, much as many of the more conservative politicians in all parties continue to regard it as a golden age brought to an end by Mrs Thatcher's authoritarianism and extremism. It is not a mere matter of political honesty that we must view the defects of British government and the British 'constitution' in a perspective that stretches back far beyond 1979. British institutions can be effectively reformed only if they are approached with a degree of objectivity and in terms of a commitment to democracy that goes beyond the seeking of narrow party-political advantage and point scoring.

The Charter 88 solution

In late 1988, Charter 88 was launched, seeking to bring just such an objectivity and a cross-party spirit to the issue of democratic reform. Charter 88 enjoys broad cross-party support. It includes among its signatories, for example, Lord Scarman, as well as more obvious figures of the centre like Des Wilson, Richard Holme and David Marquand. The depth of concern for constitutional reform can be seen from the subsequent mushrooming of support, with tens of thousands of signatories across a broad political spectrum.

Charter 88 is a call for a 'new constitutional settlement'. It proposes that such a settlement would:

> Enshrine, by means of a Bill of Rights, such civil liberties as the right to peaceful assembly, to freedom of association, to freedom from discrimination, to freedom from detention without trial, to trial by jury, to privacy and freedom of expression.
>
> Subject executive powers and prerogatives, by whomsoever exercised, to the rule of law.

Establish freedom of information and open government.

Create a fair electoral system of proportional representation.

Reform the upper house to establish a democratic, non-hereditary second chamber.

Place the executive under the power of a democratically renewed parliament and all agencies of the state under the rule of law.

Ensure the independence of a reformed judiciary.

Provide legal remedies for all abuses of power by the state and the officials of central and local government.

Guarantee an equitable distribution of power between local, regional and national government.

Draw up a written constitution, anchored in the idea of universal citizenship, that incorporates these reforms.

I must confess to being an initial signatory of the Charter and hardly a dispassionate observer in the matter, but I shall try to step back and view the document from the perspective of, say, a politically aware American who had not kept up with recent developments in British politics beyond the odd article in the *Washington Post*. The American is likely to be stunned that such a document could appear in an old-established democracy. Charter 88 is asking for a constitutional settlement that is the norm in most modern democracies. Most of these demands were clearly understood by the founders of the American constitution in 1788 to be the precondition for lawful and accountable government, and for the protection of the citizen from executive power. Having suffered British rule and being well aware of the limitations of British institutions they formed a constitution that deliberately limited sovereignty, divided power and subjected both law making and the executive to judicial review. Charter 88 is asking for ideas about government that were well established in the eighteenth century and are now commonplaces of constitutional law throughout the democratic world.

Charter 88 and our innocent American provide useful confirmation of how pre-modern and pre-democratic British institutions are. Yet, in the British context, Charter 88's constitutional settlement is little less than revolutionary. Lord Scarman is an unlikely Robespierre, but such a written constitution represents a fundamental break with the institutions and practices of the British state. Charter 88 cannot be a matter of piecemeal reform since it strikes at the heart of the unlimited sovereign power of Parliament and the present position of the executive.

Charter 88 is revolutionary, and yet rather timid. It fails to address some of the central issues that have arisen in Britain since the 1970s. It is non-committal on the issue of Irish, Scottish and Welsh national autonomy and appears to envisage a unitary state. It is silent on the issue of European integration. It explicitly raises the issue of regional government and yet ignores the issue of federalism, the only way that both nationalist aspirations and the autonomy of strong regional governments within England can be ensured. It evades the question of the precise status of the monarchy under the new written constitution. What is the position of the Crown if parliamentary sovereignty is to be limited, if the prerogative powers exercised by the executive are to be curbed, and if political power is considered to arise from the wills of citizens rather than that democracy and civil liberties are privileges granted by the Queen-in-Parliament to her 'subjects'?

Obviously, Charter 88 is a compromise and these are thorny and divisive issues. But they won't go away. They are a central part of the present constitutional crisis. The drawing up of a written constitution has to be by a special Act of Parliament. It is a central part of current constitutional law that the current parliament enjoys unlimited sovereign powers and, therefore, that no Act of Parliament can bind a successor. Even if such a Constitutional Reform Act were passed, it could be repealed by a subsequent parliamentary majority hostile to the legislation. A new constitutional settlement, therefore, depends on something more than a bare parliamentary majority in favour; it depends on a broadly based political conviction that such a change is desirable and will be binding. The major parties would have to endorse such a settlement and agree to set up a constitutional convention in which the details of the constitution were settled by political agreement before it passed into legislation.

This is where the problems start. Charter 88 covers a wide spectrum of opinion – it draws on political activists in all three opposition parties, eminent judges and lawyers, leading figures in the arts, prominent academics and leading writers. What it does not have is the support of the leadership of the Conservative and Labour parties. This represents an insuperable problem since these parties command the support of over 75 per cent of the electorate.

One would expect the Conservative Party to be hostile. Such a constitution would undermine the possibility of the Conservatives holding power as they do under current electoral circumstances and it would severely inhibit their use of power even if they could form a government under a system of proportional representation. It is just what Mrs Thatcher would expect of the 'chattering classes' and her opposition to it will be implacable. Labour is another matter. Labour's response has come from the leadership. Roy Hattersley wrote an emphatic criticism in the *Guardian* and Peter Kellner floated the leadership's view in his column in the *Independent*.

Hattersley's argument is that such a constitution would prevent a strong reforming Labour government. It would diminish legislative and executive power and would, therefore, weaken the capacity to reform powerful vested interests in society. PR is unacceptable both because it would deny Labour a chance of a majority and because it would break the direct relation between an MP and a specific constituency. Hattersley defends the existing form of parliamentary sovereignty and the existing electoral system. He is definitely not hostile to the legal entrenchment and protection of civil rights.

Kellner cleverly tried to drive a wedge through the Charter 88 agenda, pleading with its signatories to drop PR in the interests of consensus among the opposition parties. PR is for him a narrowly party-political issue, a key policy plank of the centre parties and of direct benefit to them. The implication is that Labour would be sympathetic on the other constitutional issues. But, as we can see with Hattersley, this is not exactly the case. In fact it is very difficult to separate PR from the broader issues. It is difficult to see how we could have a broadly representative national assembly without PR, and only such an assembly could be an effective means to extend and entrench individual rights and constitutional guarantees. A purely party government acting on its own intiative will lack the degree of consensus and the legitimacy to do so. On the other hand, contrary to Hattersley's view, if unlimited sovereignty were to be retained the case for PR becomes overwhelming. A. V. Dicey, the most eminent British constitutional lawyer of the twentieth century, understood that the unlimited sovereignty of Parliament and the rule of law were compatible only if the Commons were broadly representative of the British people.[4] The present electoral system combined with multi-party politics has shown that the Commons is no longer so representative, and that extremely partial legislation can be driven through on the support of the minority of the electorate.

It is Hattersley and Kellner who are pleading a narrowly party-political case. Labour is hoping for a majority that opinion polls and election results show it does not really possess. Even if recent shifts in opinion poll support in February and March 1989 strengthen the Labour Party, they still do not offer it the prospect of strong majority government. Labour must be 10 per cent ahead of the Tories to obtain the sort of landslide needed to recapture key Conservative seats in the South by its own efforts alone.[5] Tory support is shrinking back toward the level of the last general election. Unfortunately, given a split opposition, hard-core Conservative support needs to crack and voters switch directly to Labour to ensure a general election victory. Labour is unlikely to benefit from such a switch on any terms, but it is also unlikely to get back into office unless it can appeal to the interests of successfully employed skilled workers in the South. In a period of radically diverging major party objectives, for one major party to directly succeed another in office implies a radical shift in the preferences of the electorate and a big change in their attitudes. There is no longer the common ground between the parties that made the switching of votes a relatively easy matter for many voters. Indeed, Labour's growing support seems likely to strengthen the very illusions about the possibility of majority government that may deny it office. Labour has to outflank the Conservatives with a new strategy if it is to shake hard-core Conservative support. Central to that strategy is that it should act in opposition as something more than a potential single-party government tied to the traditional social interests that provide its own hard-core support. An opening to the other opposition

55

parties, not a formal pact, may make it easier for hard-core Tory voters to shift support to these other opposition parties, without the fear that they will be 'letting Labour in' as an exclusive single-party government.

It is frankly incredible that a senior politician in the Labour Party should defend the present electoral system on the grounds that it allows decisive reform. The myth of 1945 dies hard. Labour has not been a decisive reforming party, tackling and overthrowing major vested interests. Its periods in office have generally been marked by situations of crisis and retreat from its stated reform goals. This may have been completely unavoidable, as in 1974–5, but it is a fact. There is little evidence that the current Labour Party could act as a radical reforming government on the basis of Labour support alone. It is more than arguable that Labour cannot even win a workable majority in the present state of electoral politics. Hattersley's stance is like that of an animal who is choking to death but cannot bear to disgorge the offending morsel because it likes the taste of the food. Far from being a principled and valid opposition to Charter 88, a genuine disagreement from opposed premises, this is an attempt to defend the indefensible and to protect illusions. It shows how far Labour still has to go before it can stake a real claim to leadership of the opposition and do more than sit on its existing assets as the second largest party. It is likely to remain the also-ran for ever if it goes on like this.

Labour's support for political reform is crucial. Only the combined weight of the three opposition parties, together with the support of Tory dissidents, could give constitutional change the 60 per cent majority it needs to be justifiable and legitimate against determined Tory opposition. Labour is losing a great chance to become a *national* party, rather than a regional and socially sectoral party, by dodging the issue of constitutional reform. It is an issue that can shake the Tories' own solidarity and can marginalize them in defence of the indefensible. It is an issue on which the three opposition parties could build a solid ground of cooperation that goes beyond narrow electoral pacts.

Democracy beyond the constitution

Charter 88's proposals would transform the British political system and it would need a massive change in party attitudes to accomplish them. Let us suppose that, by some miracle we cannot foresee, a constitutional convention in 1992 did lead to a Constitutional Reform Act. Britain would then find itself in the same state as most other advanced democracies. But it would also share their problems. Countries with constitutions like that proposed by Charter 88, notably the United States, still face grave problems of democracy and political accountability. Legally guaranteed civil rights, judicial review, a system of checks and balances, a Freedom of Information Act, all go a long way to check abuses of governmental power, but they leave important problems of democratic influence and the effective scrutiny of governmental action unanswered. This is not the old game of trying to out-revolutionize the revolutionaries. Charter 88, revolutionary as it is in the British context, represents a bare minimum of democratic accountability. It is an essentially eighteenth-century solution to the problems of control of government. Governmental power has evolved far beyond the minimal state of 1788. In all modern large-scale industrial societies we face the problem of 'big government'. Government has become a ramified and multiform complex of public service agencies, responsible for a vast amount of services and activities, and with many functions from macroeconomic management to the provision of social welfare, from energy policy to environmental protection.

'Big government' will not go away. Yet a constitutional solution to accountability hardly touches this mass of agencies and functions, it barely comes to terms with the. complex issues of public policy and the control and coordination of government action over a wide range of issues. This cannot be simply left to governmental agencies to control nor can it be regulated from 'outside' alone, by legal requirements and legal reliefs for harms against the citizen. That involves perpetual firefighting after the event, intervening when harms have been done, exposing and correcting abuses.

One solution is quite clearly impossible. That is to turn the clock back to the mid-nineteenth century, to turn big government back into small government. The 'nightwatchman state' is gone beyond recall. It rested on a self-regulating economy of small economic units trading on open markets. But the economy of the late twentieth century is just too interdependent. Its division of labour is too complex, its economic actors are too big and too powerful, and the demands the public place upon government have changed irreversibly. Health, education and welfare are publicly provided in some form or another in most large modern states. Big corporations and major organized markets, like those in securities, cannot be left to police themselves. The provision of trained manpower, employment policy, the provision of necessary social infrastructure, and the protection of public health and the environment are all tasks that government agencies must supervise even if they do not provide all these services directly. Inevitably modern industrial economies are 'mixed economies' in the sense that public regulation and public services are essential to the workings of private production and distribution. Free self-regulating markets are a mirage – even big private corporations need and generally want such regulation and such services, even if only to protect them from the anti-social actions of their own kind.[6]

Ten years of a government allegedly directed toward 'rolling back the state' have not turned big government into small government. The tasks and the scope of modern British government remain vast – despite an intensive programme of privatizations, cutbacks, plain neglect and the favouring of the government's friends. Indeed, these very actions have led the Conservative government both to make new interventions and to respond to inescapable public demands for action. Privatization has created a parallel need for the regulation of the new corporate utilities; the Conservatives could only make privatization palatable at the price of creating public regulatory agencies, however ineffective. Neglect in public spending has led to a public outcry that cannot be dodged at the price of political disaster. The crises over food standards, the environment, the declining state of public transport and the general fabric of the cities are driving the government into panic measures. Every disaster leads to a public inquiry, with consequent damning conclusions about neglect and pressures for additional public spending.

Outside of the utopias of the ultra-right, the case for the public service state remains unarguable. But so too does the case for its public control and accountability. What does 'democracy' mean in this context? It must mean more than fair multi-party elections. It must mean more than formal accountability to a parliament or the possibility of judicial review. It means that public influence and scrutiny penetrate *inside* government, that governmental policy is subject to a competition for influence over policy decisions that goes beyond parties competing in elections to get the chance to govern. The issues in elections are simple and the competing parties few. The issues of public policy are far more intricate than can be settled by party platforms at elections, and the range of bodies with an interest in those decisions goes well beyond the political parties themselves. The only way to make the heterogeneous issues of policy over a wide range of complex and often technical areas open to democratic discussion and to widen public influence is to make government open and responsive to the influence of a plurality of non-governmental organizations and institutions with an interest in those policy areas – not just the Confederation of British Industry (CBI) in the case of the Conservatives or the Trades Union Congress (TUC) in the case of Labour.

To see this fully implies bringing together two perspectives. One is to take the positive message of classical liberalism, but to separate it from the advocacy of the small state and the free market.[7] Classical liberals were sceptical about government. Government has a tendency to become a conspiracy against the citizenry, and should be subject to constitutional control. Formal democracy needs to be linked to a set of means to ensure the benefits of open competition for political influence and to ensure that government actions are publicly scrutinized. If this happens government is likely to be both more efficient and more equitable. Open government is more efficient because policy is based on adequate information, and on thorough and open public discussion which covers the available options, and in which the relevant interests are both consulted and are expected to lobby openly and responsibly. Closed government is inaccessible only to some; it is open to powerful and covert lobbying by vested interests favoured by the party in power. Open government is more equitable because it gives a more even chance to a wide range of opinions and interests to try to influence policy. Classical liberalism saw both the need for government based on discussion and the need for the state's actions to be known in order to be accountable. To think in this way is to recognize that the machinery of government would behave very differently if it is not subject to such constraint. It is to recognize that large-scale continuing government is not a mere device for executing the 'will of the people', as all too many naïve radical democrats hoped and believed. If we recognize the rightness of classical liberalism's fear of governmental power then we can see that the meaning of 'democracy' must be far broader than free elections and multi-party systems. Representative democracy and elected officials are only one part of democratic governance; a whole set of mechanisms that allow wider political competition, public scrutiny and public influence that constrain government is an essential 'supplement' to electoral democracy.

To achieve this supplement under modern conditions we must move beyond the ideas of the classical liberalism of the nineteenth century. Despite the excesses of the current Conservative administration and the defects of the constitution, Britain remains a democracy. Why? Certainly not because the electoral system is fair or because British government is open and self-limiting; nor because of the simple fact that we have a multi-party system. Britain is a democratic country because political organization and political influence are not under state control and because in the wider society there are numerous bodies that campaign against and contest the ruling party's perceptions of the issues.

This is where my second perspective comes in. That perspective has roots in the nineteenth century, in the ideas of the French political thinker Alexis de Tocqueville, but it has been modernized to cope with twentieth-century phenomena by a school of American political thinking called 'pluralism', the leading exponent of which is the Yale political theorist Robert A. Dahl.[8] A process of plural political competition by a number of organized political bodies is a precondition for effective representative democracy, as is the commitment of these bodies to a political culture in which such open competition is possible. Parties view politics as an open competitive game; they do not seek to use an electoral majority and political power as a ladder to monopoly control, a ladder they kick down when they get to the top and thus deny to others the chance of succeeding them. When parties behave in this way (like the Nazis), they destroy both electoral democracy and the wider processes of plural influence that sustain it.

Pluralism thus supposes that there is effective and active political competition by a large number of independent organized interests in the wider society, not just political parties, to influence the decisions of government. Such interests not only lobby government but control and organize important areas of social life independently of government. A society in which government is overwhelmingly responsible for most social activities cannot long remain a democracy, even if it has a multi-party system and elections. Social organization and social control must be pluralistic, not just the contest for governmental power. The process of political competition is thus effective between elections and sets the issues that underlie electoral contests. The parties both draw support from and are forced to make concessions to the organized interests.

A system of political competition will have winners and losers just like the economic competition between firms. Those with greater resources – wealth, education, spare time and organizational skills – have a far greater chance of influencing decisions and controlling affairs than those with fewer. A democratic society is compatible with the existence of economic and political inequality, and with social classes. Such a system will tend to reinforce inequality if nothing is done about it, compounding wealth and social power with unequal political influence. To the extent that a significant proportion of political actors accept and sustain the 'rules of the game', however reluctantly, the results of such a democracy confer a certain legitimacy on the inequalities of resources that produce such unequal outcomes. Pluralism does not contend that political competition gives everyone an absolutely equal chance, but it does require that organizations are not systematically excluded from the setting of the political agenda. If this happens then the process of political influence becomes closed and oligarchic and can ultimately undermine the social foundations of an effective democracy. Formally democratic societies can fail to be fully democratic, and democrats must try to prevent unfair processes of exclusion and marginalization of important social interests.

Britain remains a 'pluralistic society' and, therefore, an open democracy. But it is not an equal society nor do the competing plural interests have equal influence. It remains, however, a society with a rich diversity of organized interests and of the social groups and associations on which these interests are based. These vary from very large and powerful interests like the CBI, to small and active campaigning organizations like Friends of the Earth. Influence is unequal but it is not fixed. Even in such an unpropitious political climate as that created by the present government, organizations that start with few resources and appear marginal, like the groups in the environmental lobby, can change and shift the political agenda. Big polluters are now under pressure, even if they have an inside track of access to sympathetic officials and ministers. Groups like Greenpeace can shake and threaten the powerful, shifting the concerns even of hostile governments as politicians come to fear the impact of their campaigning on public opinion.

The major political parties draw support from associations and organized interests. Political parties would be very restricted in their appeal if they were forced to rest on one social constituency or exclusive ideology, given the wide diversity of groups and ideas in society. If the Conservative Party drew support *only* from big business it would be a negligible electoral force. In a politically and organizationally complex society political parties have to appeal to multiple constituencies of interests if they are to be electorally strong. The major political parties are umbrella organizations that put together complex coalitions of those organized interests with which they have an affinity. In this way they build pyramids of support to give themselves wide electoral appeal. The payoff is that they have to pay attention to the interests within their constituency both when campaigning in opposition and when in power. The Labour Party draws support from a wide variety of such constituencies, like the unions, Black activists and anti-poverty campaigners. The Conservatives likewise get support from major companies, anti-immigration groups and supporters of private health and education provision. It is only by the aggregation of what would otherwise be small minorities that the parties can hope to win broad-based electoral support. Parties are vote-getting machines that simplify the voters' choice, but they cannot do all the work of building public support on their own. They are able to reach out into society through the groups associated with them and it is these groups that do much of the campaigning on the issues between elections.

Even a party that wins an electoral majority rules as a *de facto* minority grouping. Parties may have a massive majority of seats, like the Conservatives, and yet be in a minority position in terms of votes, opinions and political support more generally. An overwhelming majority of wider support for one party is a most unusual event in a pluralistic political system. For a pluralistic system to be healthy, parties have to recognize this fact, accept that they rule as *de facto* minorities, and be at least willing to listen to interests beyond their own constituency. The more exclusive and partial they become in government, the more they weaken both the broader processes sustaining democracy and also ultimately their own base of support.

For such a system of 'minorities rule' based on the pyramiding of interests by political parties to survive, enough political actors must feel secure enough that the ruling coalition of minorities will obey the unwritten rules of the game and that they in turn will have a fair chance to win in the future. If this does not happen then the wider foundations of democracy start to crumble. It is at this level, rather than at the formal constitutional level, that the Conservatives have endangered democracy. The British system, as we have seen, favours exclusive party government. Despite its inherent defects it worked well enough while the major parties kept to the principles of pluralist competition. It was this self-limiting behaviour of the parties, aside from their rhetoric or their formal understanding of the system, that made Britain a tolerable democracy. Mrs Thatcher's governments have thrown away these self-limiting constraints and have played the game by its formal constitutional rules. The result is to expose the formal defects of Britain's institutions that make it a 'second best' democracy.

Mrs Thatcher has behaved as if her 'mandate' rested on an overwhelming basis of genuine support. Her very partial legitimacy has been used for highly partisan policies that have severely strained democratic legitimacy in the wider sense than a majority of seats in the Commons. She has also tried to shut out from influence organizations and interests that are not 'one of us'. She has used legislative power to undermine the basis of organizations in the wider society she disapproves of, like the trade unions. The Prime Minister believes that there is one legitimate set of values, her own. She has acted as if other plural political and social organizations are illegitimate and ought to have neither influence nor the right to exist. She has stated her aim to be the elimination of 'socialism' and claimed that it is 'alien to our British way of life'. She believes that only one party is really fitted to rule, her own, and that there is only one justified way of organizing the wider society, the free market. Strong interest organizations not committed to the free market are thus enemies of the good society. The influence of such organizations can only be pernicious and, were she logical and possessed of enough power, she ought by rights to suppress them completely. She is, of course, not as logical, as powerful and as tyrannical as her pronouncements would lead one to believe. But she has acted and thought in such a way that in the long run would reduce democracy to the bare formal minimum: to national elections that would be little more than a plebiscite to decide who should rule. The victor should then rule exclusively and partially, as a narrow party government.

Mrs Thatcher is a bad democrat because she is no pluralist. Of course, she recognizes the need for free and fair multiparty elections. She is not a dictator. But she has such a restricted meaning of democracy that hers is a doctrine unfitted to the governance of a complex and plural society. If political pluralism – the open competition for influence and parties aware of the need to respect that competition when in office – is the principal way to make modern societies properly rather than just formally democratic, then Britain is in grave need not only of formal constitutional change but of a change in political attitudes and political culture if it is to be a first-class democracy.

The new democratic left

The pluralist view of democratic politics has never found favour with the left. In part this is the fault of incautious pluralists, notably in America, who have taken the analysis of the conditions for open political competition to be a description of the state of affairs in the USA and the 'Free World'. Left-wing critics have not found it difficult to argue that power and influence are in fact unequally divided and they have linked this fact with the inequalities of capitalist society that they see as inevitably giving rise to a skewed division of political power in favour of the wealthy and the business class.

If pluralism is seen not as description but as advocacy, as some of the more intelligent pluralists have argued, then some of this criticism falls to the ground. Some, but not all. Pluralists have to show that inequalities can be overcome by organization and advocacy on the part of the disadvantaged. They have some considerable evidence on their side, as my example of the ecological movement shows, and so too does the rise to power of trade unions and labour parties in late nineteenth-century Europe, when the hitherto powerless and excluded built up strong forms of countervailing power and influence using both the democratic ballot box and the freedom of association guaranteed by classical liberalism.

The problem for the traditional left is not only that the pluralists can show the rise to influence of the underdog, but that most left-wing socialists have sought an exclusive monopoly of political power for the 'working class'. Socialists have treated the working class as if it was both homogeneous and the overwhelming majority of society, whereas neither of these claims is the case. Organized labour has always remained a large but minority interest. As such it can claim no right to, nor can it in fact succeed in gaining, a monopoly of political power. The political appeal of radical socialism has always been to no more than a small minority of the electorate, whenever the voters have had a free choice. Radical socialism, and Marxism in particular, has developed no doctrine of governance suitable to a large, complex and pluralistic society. Where radical socialists have captured a monopoly of political power, democratic institutions have perished. Where democratic institutions have been strong, radical socialists have never captured a monopoly of political power. The legacy of Stalinist communism has fatally undermined the radical socialist left's credibility as a democratic force.

Parliamentary socialism has been successful only where it has accepted democratic institutions and where it has confined its programme of social change to a set of reforms far short of the thoroughgoing expropriation and conversion to public ownership of 'the means of production, distribution and exchange'. The Labour Party has been able to govern in Britain because it never attempted to put Clause 4 of the Party's constitution, which sets out this goal, into practice.

Parliamentary socialism has always been a hybrid, one in which a willingness to accept modern democracy has prevailed over formal socialist objectives. Radical socialists have seen this as 'betrayal' but they have always lacked a credible political alternative to it. Revolution is simply never on the agenda in a working democracy, however weak and compromised it may be. When parliamentary socialist parties have failed to 'win' in the democratic game, as the Labour Party has done since 1979, then not only pragmatic socialist politics but socialism itself has moved into crisis.

In the 1980s a new generation of democratic socialists has sought to answer this crisis by changing the content of socialism so that it comes to mean radical democratization. But in doing so, by and large they have rejected the conclusions of pluralist political thought and have relied more on changes in formal democratic institutions. Some of the supporters of Charter 88 are drawn from this new democratic socialist left. Charter 88's constitutionalism is compatible with their ideas of a new democracy based on 'republicanism' and 'citizenship'. I have made it plain that although I support Charter 88, yet I see its formal constitutional aims as both too little to ensure a working democracy and also revolutionary in the British political context.

The major party politicians reject both currents of political reform. The intelligentsia has rallied to Charter 88, although not to the new republicanism. The new consensus for democratic change among intellectuals of the left and centre is penned in by a wall of silence on the part of major party politicians and also the wider public. Despite the wide disquiet about Britain's failing electoral system, major constitutional changes are not yet part of the mainstream political agenda nor are they likely to be if they remain at the level of formal political reform.

Why is this? Because most voters put substantive social and economic issues first on their own political agendas, and, provided they are secure and prosperous enough, are willing to take the existing political institutions for granted. Most voters are neither political activists nor well informed about public affairs. They confine active participation in politics to a vote in periodic national elections, and a substantial section of the adult population is not even interested enough in politics to do that. Given their limited knowledge and participation, most ordinary voters believe they live in a perfectly adequate democracy. Democracy means a chance to choose the government, and that is just what they get. Undemocratic countries are those where the ordinary citizen does not have this choice. The advocacy of democratic reform and the claim that the system is undemocratic largely pass them by. This is not a political apathy peculiar to Britain; rather such limited participation is a commonplace fact of all Western representative democracies.

This poses a serious problem for the Charter 88 proposals and for the left advocates of the 'new republicanism'. The radical advocacy of political reform operates at two levels – the campaigning for specific institutional changes, like PR or the constitutional guarantee of civil rights; the promulgation of a new republican ethos based upon active citizenship and increased participation in common core democratic institutions. What is missing from both is a doctrine of democracy that addresses the problems of modern representative government and proposes a solution to them that takes account of limited mass participation. Constitutional reforms are panaceas that fail fully to address the first issue, and the advocacy of participatory citizenship fails to tackle the second.

I have tried to show why Charter 88's programme, while admirable, is both too much and too little in the way of democratic reform. Let me spend some time on the 'new republicans'. The reason for doing so is not that they are likely to succeed or are very influential, but because the failure of their alternative shows why the pluralist argument offers the best chance of enhancing and deepening democracy in Britain.

A long exposition of the new republican ideas would be tiresome and the interested reader can find a brief presentation in Chantal Mouffe's essay 'The civics lesson' in *New Statesman and Society* (4 October 1988).[9] The term republicanism here does not mean that the advocates of such ideas wish to replace the monarchy with a republic – many of them already live in republics like the USA. 'Republic' here is used in the sense of *res publica*, a commonwealth in which the members share common responsibility and for which there is a common good. What this body of ideas tries to do is to highlight the notion of 'citizenship'. A democracy needs the active participation of individuals who are regarded as equal citizens with rights stemming from their membership of a political community. Citizens decide, through the political process, those things that are needed for the common good, and citizenship implies that those rights and resources necessary to full and active membership of society are equally available to all. It is the antithesis of the free market view of common goods as minimal and the private pursuit of self-interest as the desirable goal. This current of thought tries to restore the Greek and early-modern classical republican view of the polity as a common 'public sphere' in which all citizens can be and are active, and can play some part in the workings of government. Citizenship supposes 'civic virtue', a public-mindedness and willingness to participate. The new republicanism draws on an old tradition of pre-nineteenth-century political thinking that it seeks to modernize and adapt to new concerns. But the basic assumptions of this tradition not only pre-date but also cut across those of modern mass representative democracy.

Modern representative democracy is a creation of nineteenth- and early twentieth-century political reform. Throughout this century, representative democracy has been challenged by radical political forces that saw it as 'bourgeois', partial and obsolete, most notably communist and fascist movements. Representative democracy has survived this challenge and gained in legitimacy from it. Far from offering more democracy, such movements replaced representative institutions with more or less oppressive forms of tyranny. These challenges cloaked dictatorship in an entire language of Orwellian newspeak aiming to make it appear a higher form of democracy. We all know the names of these variants on 'less is more': 'People's Democracies', 'Socialist Republics', 'People's Republics', 'Führer-demokratie', 'Guided Democracy', and so on. Trying to criticize representative democracy root and branch thus raises the spectres of Hitler and Stalin.

Our modern democratic socialists are not trying to persuade us that 'truth is lies'. They know that direct criticism of representative democracy and the advocacy of some other political system is simply suicidal. They are political realists and so are careful not to propose institutions other than a plurality of political parties competing for the popular vote in periodic national elections with mass universal suffrage. The dominance of representative democracy poses real problems, however, for the new democratic republicanism, which is centred on more active citizen participation and heightened civic consciousness. The radicals cannot but accept existing institutions, and yet want to add to them elements of a tradition alien to representative government and which harks back to small republics of actively participating citizens. They want to adapt eighteenth-century radical republicanism of thinkers like Rousseau and Tom Paine to twentieth-century states.

The problem is that representative democracy with universal suffrage involves both mass participation, but also minimal activism, by the masses – millions cannot be directly involved in the political process. The individual voter cannot be very influential, just one vote in millions. The ordinary citizen has to become extraordinary to participate directly in politics other than by voting. Activism is the choice of a small minority who involve themselves in running political parties at the grassroots and participating in issue and interest organizations. It is difficult within the representative ethos to re-create the 'civic virtues' because they stem from common active participation of citizens, whereas minimally involved voters are minimally committed to politics. The advocates of active citizenship are hostile to such institutionalized apathy, which they see as bad for democracy (and not without reason), and yet are unable to supplant the institutions that give rise to such apathy. Democracy is compatible with a mass electorate but only if one does not make unreasonable assumptions about mass participation.

Parliamentary democracy *is* in need of enhancement and renewal. The actual forms of real public influence on and control over government outside the elections in a mass democracy are best appreciated through the ideas of the pluralists. Yet the new radicalism tends to downgrade them. These forms are the competition of organized interests for political influence and the processes of lobbying and corporatism that go along with them.[10] Individual citizens can pursue their specific interests in a mass democracy only by associating with others and organizing to have particular influence.

Interest organizations involve, at least formally, far more citizens than political parties – bodies like trade unions, pressure groups, clubs and associations. Individuals can be associated with such a group and yet, as with parties, leave its day-to-day work to activists. This the radicals see as yet another variant on apathy and they often see such organized interests as breaking up the 'public sphere', balkanizing political influence into the self-seeking lobbying of particular groups. Some of them recognize organized interests, but only in the sense that they see them as springing from an active 'civil society' outside of the state. An activist 'civil society' is good, but not limited participation in interest organizations. For this threatens once again to undermine widespread participation on the basis of active common citizenship. They seek an ideal 'civil society' as much as they want an ideal 'public sphere'. Organized interests with specific goals and limited participation on the part of their members are influential to the extent that they achieve their own narrow ends. These ends are different from and subvert the collective sovereignty of citizens and the common good of all members of the political community. Rousseau, their mentor, wanted to abolish all such bodies if possible since they undermine the 'general will'. Modern republicanism doesn't go this far, for it is wedded to the ideal of 'civil society'. It does, however, have a strong suspicion of corporatism and lobbying, and the privileged political influence that such processes give to major organized interests.

If institutionalized apathy is an inevitable by-product of mass democracy, then it is virtually impossible to introduce a republican ethos, to create an active and involved citizenry participating as a mass in the major political institutions. 'Citizenship' in this active sense is what modern democracies discourage. This is a simple structural fact, rather than a conspiracy by politicians to exclude the people. There is no alternative to representative democracy in a large and populous state. A mass electorate implies just a few major parties that both compete for and also organize the national vote. Parties simplify the voters' choice by encouraging voters to identify with the party's political image and its leadership. Parties are hierarchical and they too tend to limit the participation of the ordinary member. Representative democracy is confined to choosing parties, the electorate chooses and endorses who shall govern. Such a democracy simply cannot provide direct participation and involvement in government. Representative democracy is not 'rule by the people', but the choice of who shall rule them.

Corporatist democracy

The limitations of representative democracy to a democrat are all too obvious. Yet its institutions can neither be supplanted by participatory democracy nor supplemented by a citizens' activism. How then does one advance the cause of greater democratization within the minimalist institutions of representative government? The only available answer is a long-term one: to seek to strengthen the role of organized social interests in influencing government and to democratize as far as possible the internal governance of those interests themselves. It is to see the future of democracy in building a more explicit and effective system of pluralist political competition for influence on government and also in the construction of corporatist networks of dialogue and bargaining between these competing interests. Open competition is necessary for democracy, but so is the corporatist coordination that enables the competing interests to cooperate in attaining major social goals.

To make pluralist influence more democratic the range of interests with influence needs to be extended beyond powerful 'lobbies', like the road haulage industry and the farmers, to give interests with fewer resources and less immediate bargaining power with government a real say. This can only be done by a government willing to develop the range of pluralist influence and to institutionalize it. For such institutionalized pluralism to work, the processes of government decision-making and of lobbying to influence them need to be made more open. Democratic decision-making functions best when there are effective flows of information about the consequences of a decision and when there is organized public support for its implementation based on the fact that it has been openly and fairly arrived at. Democracy can best be considered as an ongoing dialogue and a process of mediation between government and the organized interests representing society. Such a dialogue is more broadly based than one based exclusively on political parties. Such dialogue and mediation can best be achieved through the building-up of corporatist forums in which interests are represented as widely as possible. These forums permit an exchange between government and the social interests – an exchange of influence on government policy decisions in return for the consent of the organized interests in the implementation of those decisions.

When such a two-way process works satisfactorily, government decisions tend to be both more open and yet more authoritative. For such corporatist forums to work properly, organized interests need to be more inclusive of their potential memberships. Exclusive and highly partial organizations lobbying for special interests undermine democracy. Inclusive organizations bargaining with government and other organizations in open forums will tend to enhance it. It is only when organizations are impelled by such open processes of dialogue and bargaining with others that they begin to take heed of the needs of others and to accept the need to keep to agreements. Mrs Thatcher is not the only person to recoil from this: everyone knows 'corporatism' is the dirtiest word in her political lexicon. By 'corporatism' Mrs Thatcher means any attempt at a collaborative political culture, any attempt to consult and involve the major social interests. Mrs Thatcher is opposed to corporatism not merely because it gives influence to the trade unions, but because it undermines the possibility of purely party government based on the sovereignty of Parliament.

But there are others for whom corporatism is no less abhorrent. Trade unionists of the left and right like Ron Todd and Eric Hammond also reject corporatism out of hand. The reason is that they would lose out in a collaborative political culture based on dialogue. Yet this shows that the corns of the powerful are being trodden on, that open corporatism may undercut both authoritarian government and self-interested and unaccountable lobbying on behalf of the powerful.

If the corporatism of bargaining by organized interests is the best way to secure influence on government and for government to attain its objectives without compulsion, then the processes of bargaining need to be inclusive, formal and open. Corporatism has had such a bad press in Britain because these conditions have not been met. The 'peak' associations representing labour and capital, the TUC and the CBI, are unable to control their members. Many people are left out of interest organizations like the unions – notably the unemployed, pensioners and non-unionized workers – and they use the ballot box to punish unfair sectional lobbying and bargains that are not kept. Bargaining is often informal and agreements voluntary rather than binding, as with Wilson's 'Social Contract'. Bargains and commitments to honour them have been seen as one-off concessions rather than as the normal and open way of conducting affairs. The politics of corporate bargaining and private interest lobbying in Britain in the 1960s and 1970s shows that a working set of extra-parliamentary arrangements was never developed to counteract the defective formal political system.

Self-interested lobbying is the norm of pluralistic societies that do not attempt to organize and systematize the process of competition. The politics of private interest lobbying in the USA offers a good example of the triumph of highly exclusive groups seeking purely selfish benefits from the state.[11] But modern societies cannot give rise to a 'general will' in the way that classical republicans like Rousseau hoped for; they are inescapably plural. The nearest such complex societies can get to a general will is a social pact between the major social interests to further certain common goals that they have arrived at by a process of bargaining and mutual accommodation. Such a pact requires a governing party or coalition of parties strong enough to act as a social leader and get the major interests round the table, but not so strong as to dominate the associations through its control of the state and simply enforce its own version of a 'bargain'. This is a difficult balance to strike but it is not impossible. It requires a source of leadership capable of proposing and negotiating a social pact. Typically this will be a political party with the drive and popular support to make the process credible and attractive enough to the major social interests. Developed systems of corporate bargaining have generally begun with a social pact made in order to cope with economic crisis or some other emergency, like war mobilization.

A democracy strengthened by processes of open corporate bargaining between inclusive associations enables the social interests they represent to be mobilized effectively to secure common commitments to economic performance. It is the extension of electoral democracy and party government by such corporatist bargaining that has assured the economic success of states like Austria and Sweden, and to a lesser extent West Germany. It has enabled them to achieve these results with a low degree of coercion. Successful corporatism links the demand for greater democratic influence and the needs of social mobilization to secure economic growth. Britain has lacked such a system of corporatism to orchestrate its own inchoate process of political pluralism. It has also lacked a first-class system of formal democratic accountability. It has suffered in consequence a more coercive and less democratic political system, and a less successful and more divisive economy than some of its more successful European neighbours.

The best prospect for introducing a corporatist extension to representative democracy is provided by the possibility of serious economic difficulties as the Conservatives' push for economic modernization reveals its partial and inadequate nature. The Conservatives have reduced the accessibility of government for those social interests they dislike and they have promoted a divisive scramble for economic benefits in which the strongest alone prevail. Yet they have not assured sustainable growth. Labour is more likely to be taken seriously by voters as the Conservatives' economic miracle unravels if it shows itself to be capable of functioning as the orchestrator of a 'one nation' social pact. The possibility of a new social strategy for economic development will justify incremental change in a corporatist direction. Politicians of the Hattersley stamp and the wider public, who do not sign Charter 88, may tolerate political change if it offers a sustainable regime of economic regulation and delivers the goods. Political reform will become part of the mainstream political agenda only if it can piggyback on the concerns of citizens in their private life, notably economic concerns. It will be accepted by pragmatic politicians only if it offers some definite payoff. Corporatist bargaining offers both secure public influence through inclusive organizations and also a new regime of macroeconomic regulation to replace Keynesian management by state officials as the basis for a sustainable expansionary policy.

A purely political argument and one that involves radical changes in existing democratic institutions is unlikely to capture the politicians or the electorate. Charter 88's diagnosis of the formal defects of the British political system is compelling, but its problem is that its changes are exclusively political, hitched to no specific social and economic goals, and also extremely radical in the British context. Radical political and constitutional changes are almost always the result of war and revolution. Defeat and occupation, and revolution in the aftermath of war, are the ways in which the continuity of existing states has been broken in this century. Pure revolutions in political affairs sanctioned by electoral victories are rare. Social pacts in periods of economic crisis to secure the conditions for better economic performance, but which lead on to greater democratic influence through the enhancement of organized interests' access to the state, are much more common – Sweden in the 1930s is the classic example.

If political change is to happen in Britain, we must hope that the Labour Party comes to see the need for such a social pact and to recognize that it can survive best as the leading party in a corporatist developmental state. Through a social pact wider and more formal political changes could become possible. Dialogue between the non-Conservative parties and the major social interests to create the conditions for sustainable growth could lead to the possibility of more radical formal constitutional change. Without some other common ground between the parties, without a prior stimulus to consultation and discussion, then the level of support needed to make formal constitutional change sufficiently legitimate to be successful and to survive will not be available. Moreover, the implementation of a purely political reform programme would still leave us with grave problems of ensuring democratic accountability and public influence on government decisions.

Paradoxically, it is the answer to the problems that formal constitutional reform does not solve that also makes formal constitutional reform possible. A corporatist extension of representative democracy is likely to be a by-product of a strategy for coping with economic crisis through a social pact. And as a by-product of that by-product, a dialogue between the parties, the conditions for constitutional change may be created. A new constitution will only grow out of a new collaborative political culture. That culture will only develop because of a necessity outside of party politics. In chapter 6 I shall return to the arguments for a social pact, outlining the economic necessity for collaboration between the parties and the social interests in order to create the conditions for sustainable growth. The sources of many of Britain's economic problems are political, but Britain will only reform its political system and develop a new political culture if it fully understands the gravity of the economic problems facing it and the costs of not undertaking such reform.

A pluralist state

I have concentrated here on the national level of politics. Britain is now so centralized and so dependent on central government action that regional and local changes can only follow from a new political spirit in Westminster. However, the solutions to the problems of the non-English nations within the British Isles and of the need to decentralize and devolve power to regional governments in England can only be aided by the cooperation of social interests and their dialogue with governmental bodies outside of Westminster. Regional governments will become large and remote bureaucracies, repeating many of the difficulties of national government, if they are not brought into close dialogue with the groups and social interests in their areas. National forums of corporate bargaining will be too remote and too generalized, unable to do much of the day-to-day work of consultation and scrutiny if they are not doubled by and linked to regional and local bodies. A large state like Britain cannot mediate interests if they remain at the 'peak' level alone. Lesser interests and groups are then always faced with being swamped by the influence of the big battalions.

In chapter 6 I shall argue that regional and local regulation of the economy is crucial to a fully working 'developmental state' and that regional and local economic strategies are crucial to a programme of revitalization of manufacturing. Such regional and local regulatory bodies are common in Britain's more econom-ically successful EC partners – like the more active *Länder* (regional state governments) in West Germany or the governments of Italian regions like Tuscany or Emilia-Romagna. Britain is behind the EC in this respect and it will suffer if it does not develop regional governments capable of participating in the new 'social' Europe. Active regional governments would come to see their local Members of the European Parliament (MEPs) as national advocates, building policy links with them and strengthening the British role in the European Parliament. At present, MEPs are simply a consequence of Britain's national membership of the EC and are marginal to the main political processes. A semi-autonomous Scotland and Wales would find its MEPs a distinct channel for advocating regional policies. English regions like East Anglia or Humberside would quickly learn the lesson and the advantages to be gained from such links.

The development of a regional and local system of self-government would help to push Britain in the direction of a formally federal constitution. However, just creating such auth-orities as yet another tier of government, without developed social strategies, would not do this. Federalism has to be built up out of real local units and objectively 'federal' relationships. Centralism is so much the principle of British politics that we find it difficult to see how levels of authority and governmental functions can be distinct and yet compatible one with another. Federalism implies a plurality of political authorities each with

77

its own powers and constitutional prerogatives. Only by decentralizing authority in fact and cementing that division with a formally federal constitution can we finally overcome in the long run the problems of 'big government' that are so obvious in the UK. A logical development of giving greater voice to plural social interests at the national level is the building-up of a state whose constitutional structure is pluralistic. In the early twentieth century Britain had influential and acute advocates of a 'pluralist state' – intellectuals like the widely respected Anglican clergyman J. N. Figgis, or the prominent socialist political thinkers G. D. H. Cole and Harold Laski.[12] We need to listen to those voices once again. The Labour Party has ignored such voices and has remained wedded to Westminster centralism.

Such plural and federal authority, giving distinct powers and constitutional guarantees to regional governments, for example, is the best long-run solution to the overbearing 'sovereignty of Parliament' and its accompanying excessive centralization of executive power in Whitehall. Britain is the exception among the democracies in this respect, a consequence of its own peculiar political development. Charter 88's aim of an equitable distribution of power between local, regional and national government guaranteed by a written constitution implies such federalism. A federal constitution implies not only rights to local autonomy but a constitutional defence of those rights against Parliament and, therefore, a constitutional supreme court able to adjudicate between the claims of national and local legislative and executive bodies. Such a constitutional power of judicial review and such a plural 'settlement' of political authority involves nothing less than sending the 'Westminster model' to the constitution breakers and replacing it by a more modern model derived essentially from foreign sources. We import all too readily foreign manufactured goods, but rigidly embargo foreign institutions.

To become socially and institutionally less insular will only become possible if we decide to copy the social and political sources of our competitors' economic success, and adapt them to our own needs. I shall return to this once again in chapter 6, but the point needs emphasizing. Political change will only happen if we can build a broad enough consensus for economic change, and that consensus entails the conversion of parties and social interests to a new political culture. Such a culture requires more than slogans from the parties and social interests; it requires the kind of objectivity necessary for them to work together. Objectivity is a commodity in short supply and it implies a capacity to act together singularly lacking in ordinary electoral politics. Electoral politics inevitably divides the parties; each seeks a distinct and exclusive party image, and each seeks to appeal to a distinct constituency of interests. Such adversarial politics cannot be ended, but it must be mitigated if a collaborative political culture and viable process of corporate bargaining are to be built.

The reality of open corporate bargaining is that it involves bringing all relevant interests, by pressure if need be, to an inclusive forum with an open agenda. Partial consultation and partiality to certain interests inevitably defeats the purpose of such corporatism and violates the basic principle of trust on which it must be built. Mrs Thatcher has shut out the unions and shown her own inflexibility and partiality. But Labour has too often done the same, if on a less exalted level. Certain Labour councils have made much of consulting and involving the 'community' in policy making, inviting community representatives to be present at policy committees in areas like housing or race relations. The 'community' in question and the organizations representing it have been as partial as Mrs Thatcher's solicitous consultation of business interests. Labour groups have consulted only organizations from their own constituency, treating these as the representatives of a genuine 'community', and in doing so ignoring representatives of local business or excluding the often bitter and resentful local white working class. This is a strategy for subverting dialogue while appearing to encourage it and is not part of the process of open corporatism advocated here.

The 'local state', Labour and Conservative, is all too often a bleak reflection of the faults of national politics. Closed and exclusive Conservative councils that drive through policy in semi-secret committee meetings and then rubber stamp it in main council meetings with guillotined agendas and restrictions on debate and access for the public are a worse reflection of these faults than Labour's 'loony left' councils, for the latter are too shambolic and incompetent to be effectively undemocratic. In any case, the 'loony left' is in full-scale retreat. It is among Labour local politicians that one can find a willingness to adopt strategies of even-handed consultation and pragmatic cooperation with local interests. In this respect many Labour local councillors are ahead of the Party in Westminster and the Walworth Road headquarters in embracing corporatism.

To talk of objectivity in approaching social problems and of trying to bring often opposed and competing interests together to make common policies may seem naïve and unpolitical. It certainly goes against the spirit of politics as a struggle and competition between competing groups and parties. But sustainable competition cannot exist without cooperation; carrying political struggle to its adversarial limit one winds up in Beirut or Belfast. To imagine that political conflict and competition can be ended is naïve. But it is also naïve to imagine that many of the most important questions facing government today can be settled by competition between conflicting interests, with the victor taking the spoils. Only an idiot would apply such a model to problems of the environment, letting polluters and Greenpeace fight it out and see who gets the most influence. A definite objectivity is needed in such issues – if the ozone layer is being destroyed then we must do something about it. Such objectivity also helps to build consensus and it can be forced on the most adversarial of politicians, like Mrs Thatcher. A large part of the tasks of 'big government', its role as a public service state, likewise fall into the category of issues that need to be approached objectively. When they are not, when simple-minded ideology and the schematic thinking it encourages are applied to complex problems, then we see the results: the Central Electricity Generating Board parcelled out despite all logic because of the call for privatization; crumbling sewers and filthy streets; cities ruinously choked by uncontrolled traffic, and so on.

To advocate objectivity, dialogue and cooperation in politics is not to be 'wet' and unpolitical, it is to point out how tough and demanding are many of the problems that face us. They are problems that require management through political action, but they are resistant to solution through the more simple-minded forms of adversarial politics. Many problems require study, the active cooperation of the vast majority of political actors involved, and a consensus about a lasting and consistently applied solution.

The increasing alienation of many ordinary people from politicians and the growing cynicism about the political process occur primarily because electoral politics diminishes the possibility of such dialogue and cooperation. The doubling of electoral democracy by corporatist bargaining and consultation would provide a new impetus to cooperate, allowing electoral politics to break free from the narrow search for party advantage. In an increasingly complex and problematic world, that would not be the least of its merits.

The Tories' Charter 88

I have never suggested that freedom is dead in Britain. But it has diminished, and a principal cause of its impairment has been, in truth, the absolute legislative power confided in Parliament, concentrated in the hands of a government armed with a parliamentary majority, briefed and served by the professionalism of the Civil Service, and given a more than equal chance of self-perpetuation by the adroit use of the power of dissolution. When such a government is indoctrinated with the false political doctrine of mandate and manifesto, or when it is perpetuated in office until a suitable moment for dissolution occurs by an unprincipled bargain by another party equally threatened with electoral defeat, the expression 'elective dictatorship' is certainly not a contradiction in terms, though it may contain an element of meaning of where we are heading rather than statement of despair at where we have arrived.

(Lord Hailsham, *The Dilemma of Democracy*, 1978)

It is a striking fact that many of Charter 88's objectives were first proposed by the *Conservatives* when last in opposition. It was Lord Hailsham who gave current popularity to the phrase 'elective dictatorship'. He thought an unrepresentative and partisan *Labour* government might interfere with the fundamental right of private property through large-scale nationalizations. Hailsham proposed encoding that right and other individual liberties into a Bill of Rights. Other Tories argued for PR as a way out of unrepresentative Labour rule. Politicians may be cynical, but this more advanced Tory advocacy was at least politically intelligent: it recognized that democratic institutions are never even-handed or consistent in their effects on political parties. When the balance of advantage swung back in their favour, the Conservatives, ever pragmatic, instantly dropped the 'principles' that had been used to advocate the now unnecessary reforms.

CHAPTER 3

Defence – an Absurd Debate

BRITAIN IS UNIQUE among Western democracies for the degree of divergence in public and political attitudes toward defence. This is so great as to amount to national schizophrenia on this issue. Britain has a very strong pacifist and anti-nuclear movement, centred on the Campaign for Nuclear Disarmament (CND). It is strong in the sense that it has been able to impose divisive and electorally damaging policies on the Labour Party. For over thirty years, since the battles between Gaitskell and the left, CND has been able to chain the Labour Party to the 'debate' on unilateralism. Britain also has an exceptionally strong commitment to retain all the trappings of a Great Power, chief among these being an 'independent nuclear deterrent'. This delusion has affected members of all the major political parties, but in recent years the Conservatives and Dr David Owen seem to have cornered a virtual monopoly in it. It is popular with a certain jingoistic flag-waving section of the population. Moreover, nuclear modernization has been tenaciously and silently pursued in Whitehall for over forty years.

Britain is not a Great Power. Britain is militarily the weakest of the three medium-sized powers in the European Community. France has a *genuinely* independent nuclear force – if less effective than Trident, at least it does not depend on American technology. France has a larger army, and an airforce and navy comparable to Britain's. West Germany has a much bigger conventional army and airforce. Britain is also the weakest of the three in that it spends a higher percentage of a lower GDP on defence and it maintains a research and development (R&D) establishment bloated beyond all relation to the size of its armed forces.[1] In a country starved of skilled scientific and engineering personnel by a backward and restrictive education system, military and atomic power R&D soaks up a very high proportion of such workers. There is some evidence that military R&D 'crowds out' civilian research and commercial research, both by offering major firms the soft option of defence contracts and by diverting public funds from civilian applications and education.[2] The effect of Britain's Great Power delusion is not, therefore, confined to military spending but has disturbing effects on the whole economy.

Britain's nuclear forces are neither genuinely independent nor effective as a deterrent. The missiles (first Polaris and then Trident) are provided by the USA. So is, on the quiet, much of the intelligence necessary to the targeting and control of the missiles. Britain depends on American goodwill and on the Nassau Treaty signed by Macmillan and Kennedy in 1962. The treaty gives Britain access to US technology, but it also gives the US both a long-term and an immediate constraint on British policy. The long-term threat is not to renew missiles or supply spare parts if Britain acted contrary to American interests. The immediate constraint stems from the vast disparity of the two arsenals. The British force – even after modernization with Trident – is but a small fraction of the American strategic nuclear forces. No one seriously imagines either that the USA would allow Britain independently to threaten the USSR with its missiles or that the USSR would accept the fiction of an independent British force.

The major argument for a British deterrent is that the USA will not launch a generalized nuclear war in order to stop Soviet forces if deterrence fails and a shooting war breaks out in Europe.[3] Would Washington commit suicide to keep the Soviets out of Bonn or London? Most unlikely. But the USA, with its large nuclear arsenal, has options well short of suicide. It can engage in limited actions while retaining forces large enough to deter a generalized nuclear attack by the Soviet Union. The idea that American unwillingness to act can be insured against by a British deterrent is much more unlikely than the proposition that US deterrence will work. The idea that the USSR would cease operations to avoid clashes with Britain or France simply because they have 'deterrents' is incredible. Remember that, in this scenario, deterrence has already failed in that the balance of nuclear terror between the two superpowers has not prevented one side from launching large-scale conventional military aggression. The

USSR, having not been deterred from entering the war by the threat of the US nuclear arsenal, having already seen the USA refuse to intervene with strategic nuclear weapons, is most unlikely to be deterred by Britain's nuclear forces. The USSR, therefore, persists in military action. British deterrence has now failed in a 'background' sense. Britain has only one option left, a specific nuclear threat. The choice facing the British government is stark: it has given an ultimatum and at the end of the period set it must either launch its missiles, in effect committing suicide and provoking a general nuclear war at the same time, or submit. If the USA were not willing to fry for Bonn or London in the first place, it would not passively let London drag it into the pan by making nuclear threats. At this point it would be *London* that would pose most threat to the USA rather than the Soviets. A policy that relies on the willingness to commit mass suicide in a situation of military defeat and without altering the outcome – and in open defiance of the USA at that – is no policy.

The logic of Britain's deterrent strategy, in so far as it can be reconstructed, is quite different from that of the 'intermediate nuclear forces' until recently stationed in Europe. These US forces, Pershing II and cruise missiles, have now been negotiated away under the new superpower agreement. The aim of the intermediate weapons, proposed initially by European leaders like Helmut Schmidt, was to offer specifically 'theatre' nuclear forces, separate from the main US strategic deterrent. It was to prevent the 'credibility gap' that the US strategic deterrent would be used in the case of Western Europe being threatened by Soviet victory. These weapons were to serve as a direct counter to equivalent Soviet systems – SS20s – and, if used, were pointed at intermediate targets in Eastern Europe; they were *not* a main deterrent against the Soviet Union. Many commentators, not only those on the left, perceived them to be provocative and ineffective systems, likely merely to trigger a generalized nuclear exchange.

But Britain's 'deterrent', if independently used, is not a theatre force in this sense; rather it is intended directly to threaten the Soviet homeland with retaliation in the case of an attack or threat of an attack on the UK. The UK is unlikely in any scenario to be subject to 'nuclear blackmail' first. The most realistic scenario is the one sketched above of a successful *conventional* attack threatening the UK. The Soviets simply don't need nuclear blackmail, just to persist with conventional action. It is Britain that then needs the nuclear blackmail. But Britain does not have enough nuclear forces both to launch specific attacks on selected targets as a threat and also retain a general deterrent capacity. If Britain's deterrent were used as a theatre force then there would be nothing left to counter subsequent Soviet nuclear threats. From a US perspective, given a developing *détente* with the USSR, such weapons as the British and French deterrents ought to be viewed as a disaster for Western defence policy, since they could only be used to pre-empt American strategic decision and trigger a nuclear war.

With nuclear strategies as irrational as the British appears to be, one has to be grateful that the superpowers' strategic positions make more sense. The above might be construed as an argument against nuclear weapons. It is nothing of the kind – it is an argument within nuclear strategy against *British* nuclear deterrence.[4] Actually the argument is predicated on the viability of nuclear deterrence. Deterrence can only be understood and seen to be effective in the wider context of the Western Alliance. Deterrence between the superpowers inevitably works in a very crude way, since they share no common doctrine, but it works. It works at the gut level of paralysing action by fear, and is quite unlike the sophisticated doctrines evolved by nuclear strategists. The very scale of the mutual nuclear threat, the very superfluity of weapons on both sides, means that neither side could be sure of eliminating the other's forces by a surprise all-out nuclear attack and would be devastated by the opponent's surviving missiles in turn.

Deterrence is neither stable nor foolproof: it can be undermined by changing technology; it is prey to political error. No sensible person would like to rely on deterrence lasting decade after decade in a period of mutual hostility and cold war. But the very uncertainty and threat implied by intense cold war is politically insupportable. We are now in our third 'thaw' since the early 1950s, and they get warmer all the time. Even a leader as initially bellicose and as intransigent as President Reagan could see the need for *détente* when it became possible. Deterrence may not be certain, but it is fairly robust. It works, at least in the medium term, even in conditions of intense mutual hostility and with leaders of no more than minimal rationality. The superpower stalemate, plus the fear of 'what would happen if', not only paralyses the use of the nuclear stockpiles, it paralyses action more generally. This fear leads both of the superpowers to keep out of diplomatic or military adventures that might lead to direct military action between them, and to make their major allies do the same. The Europe settled at Yalta in 1945 remains largely as the superpowers divided it. It is the risk of error, and the incalculable consequences if error happened, which counsels extreme caution in the superpowers' interactions one with another.

The USSR, for example, could not *know* what Washington would do in the case of an aggressive Russian conventional campaign to revise the frontiers in Western Europe. Maybe it wouldn't commit suicide for Bonn and would accept the sacrifice of 300,000 American servicemen in Europe? But can the USSR rely on mere optimistic suppositions about American rationality and self-interest when taking what may be an incalculably dangerous course of action? The risk is known – extermination – and it cannot be eliminated. The prize is infinitely less than the risk. All the time in this we accept the warped logic of military hypothesis. Clearly, the USSR has enough trouble with *Eastern* Europe without wanting to gobble up the rest of the continent. It is true, however, that until recently it did plan for a pre-emptive attack in a crisis where it feared attack in turn. The Soviet military have had one imperative graven into their skulls at staff college – never, never repeat 22 June 1941.

If deterrence works it is because of uncertainty about the opponent's actions and the scale of the risk if one miscalculates. However, once we assume a war *has* started, then the pressures of nuclear deterrence on action lessen and conventional military operations move out of tight central control. The logic of action has changed. The whole point of the military adventure once started is to test out the resolve of the enemy by pursuing military objectives and pushing the enemy up to the point where a generalized nuclear exchange becomes a serious possibility. Threats of nuclear action alone will not stop them, since they were implicit *before* the war began. The odds are that this process of escalation cannot be terminated except by firm superpower *political* action at the highest level; in this Britain could only tag along. If Britain tried to stem the process by a *nuclear* response, it would in all probability provoke an uncontrolled nuclear exchange. Its threat would have been incredible. Britain has nuclear strength sufficient only to provoke disaster.

The consequence is that, set alongside the US nuclear arsenal, British (and French) nuclear weapons add nothing to Western deterrence. The best analogy is that if deterrence were to fail and the two sides entered into a generalized nuclear exchange, the British forces would be equivalent to a small boy armed with a penknife rushing to the aid of a large man armed to the teeth. Incredible as an independent deterrent, British nuclear forces are also an unnecessary complement to the vast American arsenal. Britain's Trident submarines are, quite literally, pointless.

This can be argued whilst accepting, with caveats, the logic of deterrence and from a perspective of the Western Alliance. It implies no commitment to an anti-nuclear stance. You can find generals and admirals saying it *sotto voce*.[5] Much of the unilateralist and CND case, by contrast, assumes Britain can leave the world of power politics and alliances by a mere act of will based on moral convictions.

Britain at present and for the foreseeable future is a nuclear *target*, willy-nilly. It is on Soviet targeting plans as you read – Mr Gorbachev notwithstanding – and, probably, in certain well-explored and highly secret US contingency plans, it would become a target for *American* nuclear weapons too. Britain relies on its not really becoming a target on a mixture of Russian policy, which is to avoid war at all costs, and on the 'umbrella' offered by the US deterrent. The US deterrent operates independently of Soviet goodwill. Britain cannot avoid being under the US nuclear umbrella, whether it wants to or not. It is strategically simply too valuable to the USA. The umbrella makes futile both the striving for nuclear independence and that for non-nuclear (and non-target) status. Both sides in the schizophrenic debate on national defence adopt positions that are militarily indefensible. Both sides do so because of a refusal to face the hard choices imposed by military–political realities not of Britain's making. The unilateralists, on the one hand, cannot opt out of a world of power politics and they cannot opt out of American hegemony – in the last instance the US nuclear umbrella is not there for our benefit and it will not go away because we have moral objections to it. The advocates of nuclear weapons, on the other hand, cannot face the fact that Britain is a second-rate and declining power within a US-dominated 'Atlantic Alliance'. The fact that the US nuclear umbrella may not actually protect us, that it might not be used in a crisis in Europe, is irrelevant. It is 'over' us, like it or not, until it fails. This is what US hegemony and British subaltern status ultimately mean. We are no longer a Great Power, and should view the world with the degree of objectivity and realism that is necessary to lesser states.

When did Britain cease to be a Great Power? There is no easy answer to this question. Let us try to specify more closely what is implied in it. When Britain ceased to be able to defend all its major global interests and commitments by its own independent military means? The time when it could do so probably never existed: British hegemony after 1815, often called the Pax Britannica, existed only where naval power could have effect and rested less on real British strength than on the absence of any powerful challengers to it. By 1900 Britain faced just too many serious competitors and ones whose industrial strength was superseding its own, like Germany and the United States. Britain suddenly found it could not protect its interests in the North Sea, the Mediterranean and the Far East at the same time. In 1902 Britain ended its 'splendid isolation' with the Anglo-Japanese alliance. With the 1904 'Entente Cordiale' it made friends with an old enemy, France, in order to face a new one, Germany. Britain became just another power, rather than the world hegemon, the better part of a century ago. But the reality of its decline was far from immediately apparent.

Perhaps a better test of the loss of Great Power status is to ask when Britain ceased to be able to match or contain its major rival. Obviously, Germany was Britain's major foe in this century. Britain defeated Germany in the 1914–18 war and was the major partner in the anti-German Alliance. British troops faced the strongest part of the German army for much of the time from 1916 onwards. In 1918 Britain had won a major continental war, but at what it deemed an unacceptable cost in lives and economic disruption. This conditioned British responses for twenty years. Through the 1920s and 1930s the British government abandoned any pretence to determine world affairs by its cheeseparing economy in defence spending and a foreign policy that was a mixture of vacillation and craven cowardice. In 1922 at the Washington naval arms limitation conference, Britain conceded parity in warships with the USA and threw away its alliance with Japan. It then proceeded to appease Japan, Italy and Germany as each of them in turn threatened the international order.

In 1939 Britain blundered into a war with Germany that it could neither hope to win, even with French aid, nor afford to lose. In 1940 Britain was humiliatingly defeated along with France, and was left to await partners who could win its war with Germany for it. The Battle of Britain merely stopped the conquest of the British Isles in 1940. It could not represent a turning point in the war, until Britain acquired allies powerful enough to fight Germany directly. Unlike in 1914–18, the British in 1939–45 never fought more than a tiny fraction of the German army. Moreover, the British were staggeringly incompetent and ineffective at waging war on land. Britain was saved by American largesse in Lend-Lease and by Russian blood: 20 million Russians died in their war with Germany, against 450,000 Britons.* The figures speak for themselves. Without American industry and Soviet sacrifice Britain would have been powerless to defeat Germany. In 1945 Britain was no longer a Great Power. It could, to an honest observer, be no more than a second-rate but loyal ally of the Western superpower.

Yet in 1946 the Labour government began in great secrecy to build a British bomb, and the illusion that Britain could buy Great Power status by its membership of the nuclear club has continued ever since. Even the nuclear disarmers of the 1950s shared a version of the illusion, since they imagined that a unilateral 'gesture' by Britain would make a difference. They too

---

* Both figures include civilian deaths, and the British figure includes deaths in all theatres of war, including combat with Italy and Japan. This comparison is not intended in any way to diminish the sacrifice of those Britons who died nor to question the rightness of the cause in which they fought. We should be glad we were spared Russia's agony, but also be grateful for the Russian peoples' sacrifice.

dealt in myths of British greatness, but for them it was in *moral* rather than military strength.[6]

Until the British reassess their role in the twentieth century and come to accept their current military and political marginality in world terms, then defence will continue to bedevil British politics. Midgets on either side of the debate will try to play the roles of Churchill and Bertrand Russell. Britain's Great Power legacy drove it into the Falklands War. Next to Thatcher playing Churchill, the most nauseating sight was Michael Foot playing Churchill on the Saturday in 1982 when news of the invasion first reached Britain and a set-piece debate took place in Parliament. No sensible person would want to stomach the Galtieri regime, nor were Argentine claims to the wretched islands of any greater substance or point than the British. Once begun, that futile war followed its own inescapable logic and the driving necessity of Conservative political survival. Mrs Thatcher benefited far less from the 'Falklands factor' than is supposed. Had Britain *lost* the war, however, her leadership and political credibility would have been gravely weakened. The Falklands War fed the central British illusion of Great Power status and reinforced it by a (touch and go) victory.[7]

It is time we *all* grew up – Tory jingoes and moralistic CND'ers alike. If the Labour Party leadership were to wake up and see that British nuclear weapons simply don't matter, it could then ignore them and get on with the properly political business of winning elections. Westminster is worth suffering a Trident force for – after all it can do no damage if the government has no intention of using it. The most real form of unilateral nuclear disarmament is the one that takes place in the head. One leaves the submarines at sea and waits until they become irrelevant, perhaps sooner rather than later if superpower disarmament talks bore fruit. But that, horror of horrors, is called 'multilateralism'. For Labour politicians to be cowed by abstract moral arguments about the wickedness of nuclear weapons is a sure sign that they are not serious about politics. Politicians can think sensibly about weapons, nuclear and otherwise, only in *political* terms, that is, in terms of the conditions imposed upon their actions by international power politics and by domestic electoral politics.

Labour politicians, union leaders and CND activists are all

utterly ill-equipped to look at the position of Britain in the world. If the UK is a declining medium-scale power within an alliance and under the hegemony of a superpower, then politics should start from that fact and not from the moral vaporizings of CND and Labour Party conferences. The world is not a *tabula rasa* to be re-made as our morals dictate. These conferences are festivals of the provincial and the blinkered, whose moral chauvinism cuts them off from any vision of world politics. Britain cannot escape from the Western Alliance and the American nuclear umbrella. The irony is that a neutralist Britain would become a potential target for *both* superpowers. The British Isles are a stationary aircraft carrier which threatens both the Soviet route to the Atlantic and the route for US reinforcements to Europe in the case of war. A neutralist Britain is a fantasy, since it would unhinge the US strategy for containing the Soviet Union. Britain is a key base for US bombers targeted at Central Europe and also the 'hinge' for a series of anti-submarine measures designed to block Soviet vessels in the Arctic Sea. It is just too important for the US to throw away.

All serious American politicians (Republicans and Democrats alike) start from the premise that the USA is a world power. They do not share the mawkish sentimentality of Britain's pacifist left and would, if necessary, put ruthless diplomatic, political and economic pressure on any neutralist-inclined government in peacetime. Given the very strong domestic support for the Conservative Party and its strong pro-American sentiments, there would be no need in peacetime to stage a coup like that which ousted Salvador Allende in order to get rid of a neutralist government. In a war emergency, the US would send in the Marines to secure US bases.

If one wants a non-nuclear and neutral Britain then one will have to *fight* for it. That fight would not be likely to be an open military conflict against NATO, it would be against domestic enemies, since sabotage and civil disobedience would have to be met by the riot police and jail terms. The sections of the left in Britain that espouse neutralism not only lack the political strength to make neutralism happen, they also lack the fire to fight for it if it did happen. CND is not a political movement in the sense that it will if necessary sweep its opponents away in order to obtain its ends. On the contrary, it is an *anti-political* movement. It simply ignores the realities of political struggle and prefers a gesture politics of moral earnestness, imagining that Britain can 'decide' to be neutral. Its members are willing to *suffer* for their beliefs, many of them are personally brave, but they are not willing to force others to suffer in order that these beliefs prevail.

CND's anti-political stance has for long rotted political thinking about defence in the Labour Party. Neil Kinnock has known for some time that the unilateralist commitment is a political liability, but for an equally long time he lacked either the ideas or the political will to counter it. The left has been possessed of a power of moral blackmail more effective on Labour policy makers than any nuclear blackmail – 'surely you can't be in favour of such evil weapons?' The sensible answer to such insinuations is that it really doesn't matter what you or I think. Mr Kinnock as Prime Minister could not alter the geo-political situation of Britain, whatever his policies or his morals. It is this absence of political calculation, this perpetual looking *inward* to Party opinion, that makes Labour look weak, incredible and provincial abroad. Kinnock's visit to Washington in 1987 had to be a disaster and to diminish his electoral prospects; not only because Reagan was determined to snub him, but also because he lacked the first precondition for appearing to be a statesman – a credible international position and a reliable domestic power base. He looked incredible to the rest of Washington, not just the White House.

What is striking is the prolonged and ineffective response of the Labour leadership to unilateralism. The feeble attempts to fudge the nuclear issue during 1987–8 were of no interest to anyone outside the Labour headquarters in Walworth Road or hardened circles of constituency activists. They were mere tissues of words made to appease the Party itself. Even then they often crumbled before opposition, as when Kinnock's mediocre and confused half-multilateralist 'something for something' formula was humiliatingly redefined away in response to growls from Ron Todd, Labour's Transport and General Workers Union block-vote supremo. Mr Todd seems currently to be being redefined away, silent as a lamb on what appears to have been a multilateralist trip to Moscow. But even if multilateralism does break out, the issue of American bases remains. Kinnock's position on this is now less clear than ever.

The USA is not really interested in whether Britain wants to keep Trident or not. Washington would have understood a decision not to replace Polaris with Trident on grounds of cost. Thatcher insisted on Trident under the terms of the Nassau Treaty, and the US at the time was hardly minded to cause a row with a key ally. However, times have changed and if the strategic arms limitation talks make serious progress then the USA would probably be very glad if Trident were out of British hands. If the strategic nuclear arsenals of the superpowers were radically reduced, say to 50 per cent of their present levels, then Britannia's Trident will matter in the balance of terror and the Soviets will press for it to be included in the American inventory. That will be totally unacceptable to the USA.

While the Americans may politely or not so politely ask us to give up Trident in the near future, that is hardly a relief for the unilateralists. What the US really wants of Britain in matters nuclear can be put in the form of three related issues. First, that Britain accept the American nuclear umbrella and therefore that the USA has the final power of decision in matters of nuclear war and peace. This is what American hegemony means. The USA has this power anyway but wants Western governments to recognize it and to accept it politically. A *political* refusal, explicit in unilateralism, would be a direct challenge to US leadership of the Western Alliance. Secondly, that the US has the use of bases on British soil and that it may keep nuclear weapons on those bases: tactical nuclear bombs, nuclear depth charges, etc., the essential technologies for a 'conventional war' in Europe. Thirdly, that Britain not render its own forces unable to meet modern conventional threats by an anti-nuclear fanaticism. If the Royal Navy has no nuclear depth charges, for example, its credibility as a sub-chasing force sinks dramatically and the US will not be able to count on it in planning for the contingency of an Atlantic war. To challenge the US on *these* issues is where the trouble starts. The problem will not be removed by Soviet troop reductions in Central Europe or by limitations on the movements of ground troops. These changes will make air and sea warfare all the more important and the Soviet Union is still modernizing its navy and airforce. In any situation short of the most radical demilitarization in Europe, which neither side seriously expects, these three conditions will remain vital to US defence interests.

Mr Gorbachev will not get us off the hook. Either we accept the Alliance as it is and the unequal power relations within it, or we enter into a politics of moral or military illusion. Mrs Thatcher and Neil Kinnock form a perfect couple: the one a flag-waving and posturing chauvinist, willing to waste large amounts of money on the Falklands garrison and on a pointless modernization of a useless deterrent; the other slowly struggling to free himself from the political albatross that is unilateralism – antagonizing the anti-nuclear faithful with his cynical attempts to put office before principle and yet still facing an uphill struggle to convince the electorate that he now knows and means what he says.

Readers of British historian Paul Kennedy's American best-seller *The Rise and Fall of the Great Powers* may well want to question a major premise of the argument so far. That is, the claim that the US is and can remain the hegemon of the Atlantic Alliance. Kennedy sees contemporary America as in a position comparable to that of Edwardian Britain – a weary Titan struggling under the weight of commitments that it lacks both the military strength and the underlying economic strength to sustain. The book's publication in 1987 fitted with an uneasy mood akin to that of 'Recessional' among American politicians and journalists. But we should not take moods for facts; the US has been worrying about declining since before the Sputnik. Kennedy's book informed debates in the US Senate, but the tone there was how to *retain* military and economic leadership, not to lament its passing.

One wants *evidence* that the USA is declining in military power and the capacity to assert its hegemony over lesser powers. Kennedy makes much of the relative economic decline of the USA, notably compared with the rapid growth of West Germany and Japan. Curiously, neither country sees things in this way: both are all too aware that their prosperity depends on export-led growth and that the USA remains the world's largest single national economy and the powerhouse of world demand. Japan and West Germany want a big share of the US civilian market, but in order to have that they know they cannot threaten American domestic prosperity too seriously or they will provoke a trade war. Japan and West Germany trade under a Pax Americana. The USA has done everything possible to sustain a liberal regime of international trade since 1945 and to act as military guarantor for the open world economy.

In Great Power terms, Japanese and West German *economic* success means little, since neither power can convert it into a proportionate military–political strength. Neither state desires to or can afford to re-play their respective bids for world power against the United States. In both cases military expansion would be at the expense of their civilian economy and there are other constraints too. Germany will be unable to man the existing divisions of the *Bundeswehr* given its ageing population and it needs to stimulate its own flagging economy, in which innovation and productivity growth are both slowing down. Given the *détente* with the East there is little pressure within the Federal Republic to divert greater funds toward defence. Japan's post-war political settlement would come apart under the pressures of rearmament and an aggressive foreign policy. The Liberal Democrats' forty-year-long rule would be threatened by any radical lunge to the imperialist right. Japan's politics are far more volatile than they appear on the surface and the ruling party cannot afford to lose voters frightened by a return to the past. The Liberal Democrats have been rocked by scandals in 1989 involving the Prime Minister, Mr Takeshita; eventually he was forced to resign. This is nothing new – corruption has been central to both Liberal Democratic rule and the Japanese 'Economic Miracle'. What is different now is that commentators are taking the opposition Socialist Party seriously as a contender for power. Japan desperately needs to expand social and welfare expenditures; housing is a major problem and, for a country with such a high GDP per capita, its welfare state is minimal. Moreover, Japan's geo-political situation is hardly propitious to the assertion of Great Power status. Japan has three very powerful potential enemies that make any bid for regional hegemony on its part futile: the USSR, China and South Korea all have very good reasons to fear a revived Japanese imperialism and they would have a strong common interest in resisting it – about the only thing they *do* have in common.

The other Asian states are either too small or too backward to become a serious threat to US hegemony. China is so backward in relevant technologies and so crippled by the necessity of feeding a still growing population by means of labour-intensive agriculture that its future as a third superpower remains far in the speculative future. All the talk in the business media about the challenge of the 'Pacific Tigers' is largely drivel in military–political terms and nothing to do with US hegemony. States like Taiwan and Singapore are militarily heavily dependent on the Pax Americana and they are absolutely dependent on the US home market. Most of them can be regarded as out-stations of the US economy and their prosperity would be threatened if the USA should suffer a serious and prolonged depression.

The problems of the US trade and budget deficits are familiar to anyone who reads the newspapers, but they also explain the structural position of the American ecomomy as the engine of effective demand that sustains the prosperity of the export-oriented states linked to it in an open international economy. Far from making the USA weak, it makes those states close to economic clients and trade policy captives of the USA. The US civilian manufacturing sector has certainly suffered from import penetration and de-industrialization. The civilian and military manufacturing sectors are, however, increasingly divergent and US *military* innovation shows no signs of drying up. The high-tech basis for military hegemony remains intact. The USA is moreover a major primary producer – enjoying a measure of self-sufficiency in raw materials and agricultural products that no other major state has.

That leaves the USSR – which is and will remain the second superpower. It is emphatically *not* 'Upper Volta with rockets'. This sneering phrase, current in the USA, reveals a streak of silliness, sheer vulgarity and wishful thinking in American re-sponses to the Soviet Union. The phrase is absurd because the USSR has a huge number of highly educated and technically skilled citizens. The sciences and mathematics are better taught in the USSR than in the USA: American pupils' illiteracy and innumeracy are a national scandal. The USSR can thus modernize if it can find means of mobilizing its resources (labour productivity is deplorable, for example) and if it can find both the incentives and the trust to let its skilled population act on their own intitiative.

But the USSR is massively behind in certain technologies and defence expenditure is acting as a major brake on civilian output and investment. Mr Gorbachev's policies, not least his disarmament gestures, stem from the fact that the USSR really does face a choice between guns or butter. The USSR also needs to slim down its defence establishment if it is to concentrate its declining defence expenditure on the 'guns' that matter. In information technology, robotics, lasers, new materials, optronics, and a host of lesser technologies, the USA has a decisive lead. This matters because non-nuclear defence technology is changing rapidly. The new 'emerging technologies' are not conventional aeroplanes, tanks or cannon, but extremely sophisticated missiles, remotely piloted vehicles and precision-guided munitions.[8] In this area the USA can hope to keep ahead of the Soviet Union at least till the end of the century. The Soviet tanks Mr Gorbachev has promised to withdraw from Central Europe are, even if they are modern, virtually death traps, made obsolete and at the mercy of tank-killing helicopters, clever artillery shells and sensitive mines sowed by rockets.

The USA thus remains in a different league from the supposed competitors for its position as hegemon. None of the major powers could usurp America's role as both guarantor and pivot of the international economy. But what of the relationship to lesser powers? The world is popularly portrayed as multi-polar and the USA as unable to prevail against strongly entrenched minor but regionally dominant powers. Since Vietnam and Afghanistan it has become fashionable to decry the capacity of both of the superpowers to prevail even in minor regional wars. But the defeats in both cases were substantially due to the military aid given by the *other* superpower in those conflicts – Soviet aid to North Vietnam, and US aid to the Afghan rebel guerrillas. Hegemony does not mean the capacity to prevail in *every* circumstance, simply the capacity to exert enough influence and to use power with a great enough frequency of success when needed to preserve the preferred international order of the hegemon and its allies.

We live in a post-colonial world. The test of effective hegemony must, therefore, mean something other than the capacity or the need to subject territories to physical and permanent occupation. It is interesting to reflect why European colonialism ended. Why were Western colonial powers unable to remain in and to govern countries like India or Algeria? The reason was by no means always because they were not 'strong' enough; for example, the French had in substance militarily defeated the National Liberation Front (FLN) in Algeria. The reason was as much that the metropolitan governments of the colonial powers were not willing to pay the price in domestic terms, both of military mobilization and of political dissent. The same was true of America's quasi-colonial war in Vietnam. The brutal truth is that from the colonizers' point of view, most colonial wars are no longer worth fighting long enough and hard enough in order to win.

Ultimately, the object of any colonial conflict nowadays is in fact a poor and backward 'Third World' country. Colonies no longer represent fabulous wealth – they are not like spice islands, trading posts or plantations in the earlier history of Western colonialism. What such countries represent in modern terms is liabilities, and their occupation is a net loss for the colonial power. What modern industrial state would want to be *directly* responsible for Bangladesh? Advanced industrial states trade more and more intensively one with another; that is where the profits are to be made. Tropical raw materials are of marginal relevance in an age of information technology and advanced electronic/mechanical products. Just as Bismarck said of a crisis in the Balkans that it was 'not worth the healthy bones of a single Pomeranian grenadier', so the increasingly cynical major powers, the USSR included, want to liquidate *direct* commitments in the Third World.

But that does not mean that they, and the USA in particular, have lost interest in exerting hegemony over these Third World states when they need to. Hegemony can be had cheaply enough in most cases. Moreover, even when the USA appears to have 'lost', just look at the current condition of the victors. Vietnam is politically isolated and its economy in a desperate state. It is boxed in by US allies, who (far from being 'dominoes') see Vietnam as a model not to follow. A minor power like Vietnam can be quietly left to rot, a lesson of just what you get if you leave the capitalist world. A state like Libya shows very clearly the workings of hegemony modern-style. The US raid against Tripoli in 1986 scared the Libyan leadership into relative conformity thereafter, downgrading their promotion of terrorism. The F111s were able to fly from the UK some 2000 miles away and at night. They were guided over the target by computerized street maps displayed in the cockpit and were able to bomb specific buildings. As a result Colonel Gaddafi's apartment was wrecked and his adopted daughter killed. This is but a foretaste of what the 'emerging technologies' will enable the USA to do. In the recent crisis, US sailors were reported as hoping the Libyans would 'make our day' and give them the excuse to show off the internally guided Tomahawk cruise missile.

What really marks the USA out as *the* superpower is its comprehensive system of satellite and signals intelligence and its effective world-wide communications system. No other power has anything remotely resembling it. Satellites can spot small targets, for example, easily identifying individual tanks. Signals intelligence can intercept telephone calls in Beirut from Cyprus and relay them to Washington. Technical intelligence is, of course, no substitute for the interpretation of the data gathered or political sense in responding to it. However, despite interpretative blunders, the USA now has an unmatched capacity to monitor all lesser powers and it can bestow intelligence favours on its friends in a way that gives it great influence and may enable its friends to prevail over their enemies. Britain in the Falklands and Iraq in its war with Iran both benefited from this privileged source. In both cases US intelligence may have decided the war.

It should not be imagined that the new *détente* between the USA and the USSR, inspired by the peace initiatives of Mr Gorbachev, will militarily weaken the superpowers in relation to lesser states. On the contrary, the reduction of the antagonism that has tied up most of their military strengths in mutual confrontation allows them to get rid of the obsolete and the superfluous weapons they have pitted against one another. In lessening the forces committed against each other they acquire the resources to pursue other goals – in the Soviet case, diverting investment and expenditure to domestic industry and civilian consumption;

in the US case, helping to hold down defence expenditure whilst pursuing the aims of military modernization through 'emerging technologies' and enhancing its capacity to intervene in the Third World.

When the superpowers agree, watch out. The superpowers' agreement on key regional issues enables them to cancel the unnecessary parts of their pursuit of global antagonism by proxy. Far from weakening the superpowers, this is but a new phase in the process of sharing the world between them that the US and USSR began at Yalta in 1945. Many commentators hailed the end of the Iran–Iraq war as if it were a great achievement for the cause of peace. The settlement was finally prompted by a change in Soviet diplomacy, which moved decisively against Iran and cut off some of its key sources of arms. The results are terrible: the reinforcement of the internal tyrannies of Saddam Hussain and Iran's mullahs. The victims are the Kurds and the Iranian opposition. The Kurdish victims of the gas attack in Halabja and the convicts buried in the rubble of Tehran's Evin prison learnt all there is know about the side-effects of superpower agreement. The poor devils at the mercy of Afghanistan's new civil war will go through a similar rapid learning process. In the superpower-sponsored settlement in Angola the victim in 'independence' for Namibia is the South West Africa People's Organization (SWAPO) and the main beneficiary is South Africa. One could go on and on – for example, with the Soviet foreign minister Mr Shevardnadze explicitly denouncing and disowning the communist guerrillas during his visit to the Philippines.

The USA and the USSR in concert may well be worse from a radical Third World perspective than the two of them at each other's throats. It removes both the space for independent actions and the possibility of seeking the sponsorship of one superpower against the other. The USSR will be glad to minimize its global commitments, to let Eastern Europe solve its own problems and to concentrate on domestic reform. It will confine its reaction to US adventures to schoolmasterly lectures and where necessary join the US in preserving international 'order'. Both will babble more and more about 'human rights', the talk neatly covering the gas-bloated corpses of Halabja and places yet to suffer from the new order of *perestroika* and global *détente*.

From a reforming Soviet or a Western perspective this is all pure gain – a 'lessening of international tension'. What it is *not* about is an end to US hegemony, particularly in the Third World. One might have thought that a left-wing party would be able to take in some of these lessons and respond to them with political realism. Peace is emphatically not breaking out; rather the superpowers are liquidating the absurdities of the second cold war. They are getting down to hard bargaining, continuing the explicitly Metternichian policy of Henry Kissinger that inspired the last phase of *détente*. Count Metternich, the architect of Austrian foreign policy in the early nineteenth century, perceived that Austria, Prussia and Russia could only be weakened by mutual antagonism but that united they could ensure the rule of conservative reaction in Central and Southern Europe. Prince Bismarck, the German Chancellor, saw the same thing a generation later. Mr Gorbachev has the wit to put into practice what cynical diplomats have long understood, and the US policy makers have had the sense to cash in on benefits that no amount of posturing about the 'Evil Empire' could give them.

In all too many ways the description of 'Evil Empire' fits *both* the superpowers. The pair of them have a long list of barbarous actions to their discredit which ought to make forfeit any right on their part to speak about human rights or to lecture others on international law. How can a power that has connived in the planting of murderous bombs in the crowded streets of Beirut or lobbed shells weighing 1 ton into defenceless villages in the Chouf mountains – to take but two examples from the US 'low-level' involvement in the Lebanon – dare to say anything? The answer, of course, is that it is better that the superpowers subscribe, however cynically, to human rights and international law than that they practise pure *Realpolitik*.

How should the British left react to this geo-political context and Britain's virtually compulsory membership of the Atlantic Alliance? Certainly not by a naïve moral revulsion or by an attempt to create an independent 'left' foreign policy. Accepting its close alliance with the US enables Britain to press for changes of US policy on certain issues or flatly to oppose its policy on others.

The basic lesson for the left is that it can best be influential in foreign policy through an institution it has largely affected to despise, the European Community. Britain can have some influence within the EC on a common Community policy on certain key issues, and a united and active European initiative has some considerable clout. Labour is no longer officially 'anti' the EEC, simply provincial and unenthusiastic about Europe. However, working to create unified EC foreign policy initiatives (for example, to put pressure on South Africa and to press for Palestinian autonomy) is about the most effective thing a British Labour government could do. Similarly the EC has the real leverage on Turkey to force it to settle the Cyprus problem. Without posturing, it would be possible to concentrate on certain issues, seriously neglected by Western opinion – for example, the Kurdish problem. As Britain is not a Great Power it should start to behave according to its circumstances. The British left would best start here by recognizing that Britain can have most influence by acting with others, and, therefore, that it must be both active and cooperative in EC policy making. The left remains as meanly Little Englander as ever, hence its wretched lack of realism about international affairs.

One thing that facing up to the fact of Britain's relationship with the USA could do for the left is to see that Britain can break with the illusion of a 'special relationship' without being anti-American. The Thatcher government has pursued a love affair with the USA. It has also pursued an obsession with 'security'. The two have gone together. Britain is desperate to preserve another trapping of Great Power status – its system of signals intelligence and information collecting built up since the WWII days of Bletchley Park. To do so it is willing both to invest large sums in hardware, witness the secret development of the Zircon satellite, and to ruthlessly enforce total silence on these matters both on the media and on security personnel. The suppression of unions at GCHQ and the Wright affair are both intelligible if we understand them as attempts to assure the USA that its joint intelligence activities and privileged sharing of information with Britain will not be compromised. The Wright affair is little short of insane on any other reading. There is no reason why the active *British* involvement in this whole business should continue. Zircon is a system appropriate to a world power, not to a second-rate regional power. Liberty in Britain should not be compromised to acquire information from US intelligence on privileged terms; in order to preserve this relationship, Britain imposes a degree of secrecy that would be impossible and intolerable in the US.

If the left accepts the fact of US bases and of nuclear weapons on them, then it can try to realistically revise the largely secret treaties under which the US forces in Britain enjoy quite extraordinary extra-territorial rights in peacetime and dictatorial powers in time of war. The USA desperately wants British bases. They are, as we have seen, important in the way that US airbases in, say, Spain are not (and yet the USA places intense pressure on Spain to keep them). Undoubtedly, the USA would pay a price to stay on terms that make military sense but that do not involve Britain behaving like a banana republic as at present.

In the matter of conventional defence policy Labour has fewer problems of appearing credible with the electorate. Indeed it could be regarded as too enthusiastic and optimistic. This comes from trying to compensate for its anti-nuclear position. Neil Kinnock and the Party's defence documents at the last general election promised to maintain and increase conventional defences. As if these were really effective against an attack! If an attack comes it will be because nuclear deterrence has failed in some state of crisis; conventional weapons are then unlikely to *deter* aggression unless they exist in such overwhelming numbers that an attack is deemed futile. Nobody really believes in building a conventional 'deterrent' of that kind – it is simply too expensive. Nuclear weapons are, by comparison, cheap. They are less labour intensive and have long lives at low recurrent cost once the initial period of capital spending is over. That will be the case with Trident by the early 1990s.

Conventional warfare under modern conditions would be, quite simply, ghastly. 'Conventional' explosives and weapons approach those of nuclear weapons for pure lethality, although they lack the lasting environmental effects. Conventional weapons are much worse than their predecessors in WWII and a war with them alone would convert much of Europe into a charnel house. Nuclear war would be unimaginably horrible, if it happened, but let us not treat conventional war as if it is a 'better' alternative.

Whatever happens, whether Mrs Thatcher returns in triumph in 1991 or some alternative government is elected, British defence spending will be under severe constraint. Britain will be in the middle of replacing several major weapon systems, notably tanks and combat aircraft, and capital spending will press hard on existing budget levels. In all probability lesser capital projects will have to be cut and the levels of existing forces will have to fall, even on the assumption of level constant value spending on defence. The surface fleet in particular will be a particularly likely casualty, having survived at its present level solely because of its Falklands 'reprieve'. Thus it is foolish for Labour to claim it will both strengthen and rely on conventional defence. It cannot afford to strengthen it sufficiently to rely on it.

Why not say that Labour will maintain at a basic minimum level those essential conventional defence commitments implied in Britain's membership of NATO? The logic would be to spend *down* to just above the point where British forces would become a political embarrassment within the Alliance, but *not* to advertise the fact in an election campaign. What kind of defence policy does this involve?[9]

First, maintaining an army in Germany (BAOR) committed to NATO. That does not involve either equipping it as it has been or developing new systems expensively by our own R&D. Britain cannot currently afford both to buy new tanks and to expand its army helicopter fleet, let alone get into modernizing with the 'emerging technologies'. In truth Britain would be better off buying new helicopters, developing a limited number of new missiles with export potential and otherwise buying other countries' advanced systems off the shelf. Shifting from a tank-based force to a helicopter- and missile-based force would not be a cheap and cheerful option, but it would not involve a large investment in obsolete tanks (something the Thatcher government is currently contemplating, having given a development contract to Vickers).

Second, buying just enough fighter planes to offer a minimum commitment to NATO and to offer some sort of air defence umbrella for the UK. Again, Britain is likely to be stuck with large investments in obsolete systems as a result of Conservative decisions. The European Fighter Aircraft (EFA) is a multi-billion pound project involving collaboration with West Germany, Italy and Spain. Whatever happens at the next election, Britain is stuck with the EFA. A Labour government has the opportunity to ensure, however, that the EFA is the last generation of complex conventional manned fighter aircraft. Conventional high-performance aircraft are desperately vulnerable because they use fixed runways, which are easily damaged by such weapons as conventionally armed cruise missiles. A single submarine cruising some several hundred miles away could launch enough cruise missiles to knock out most of the fighter bases in Britain. It makes much more sense to invest in offensive systems like cruise missiles or remotely piloted vehicles to attack an enemy's runways than it does to buy very expensive and vulnerable fighter aircraft to protect us against the airplanes that take off from these runways. Defensive preparations can be left to simpler and slower aircraft that act as carriers for relatively long-ranged intelligent missiles.

Third, the most effective and least vulnerable modern naval vessel is the nuclear-powered submarine.[10] Suitably armed with modern torpedos and missiles such ships offer both the best possibility of countering other submarines and a devastating weapon against surface ships. Armed with cruise missiles they can also attack land targets. The threat of British nuclear submarines kept the Argentine fleet in harbour during the Falklands War. It hardly left port after the sinking of the *General Belgrano* (a nauseating action in which Britain broke its own publicly announced rules of engagement, but effective none the less as a lesson to the Argentine navy and a guarantee that the war would be fought to the bitter end). Britain has a reasonable competence at building such ships and running them safely. They are cost-effective and they last a long time, so that with a modest annual outlay quite a large force can be kept up. They also have a major hidden advantage: they are of little value in anything other than a purely naval confrontation. Unlike big surface ships like aircraft carriers or amphibious transports, they cannot be used to dominate or occupy foreign countries. Unlike surface ships like frigates, they are incapable of acting as 'floating flagpoles' in the manner of the Armilla Patrol.

One might think them ideal weapons for a Labour defence policy, unarguably effective in a major war and yet keeping future governments' itchy fingers off playing at world policeman or engaging in imperial adventures. But the left has a violent opposition to nuclear power, let alone nuclear-powered weapons. It ought to swallow its principles in this case if it really does want to boost, as it claims, Britain's 'conventional defences'. There is no rigid divide between nuclear and conventional weapons. Strategic nuclear forces and some classes of battlefield weapons on land can be strictly isolated and delimited: their use involves crossing a nuclear 'threshold' of greater or lesser significance. At sea matters are different. Nuclear-powered ships, if sunk, will probably make nuclear explosions, whilst nuclear warheads aimed at other ships are regarded by most admiralties as normal and conventional weapons. Unlike the firing of a tactical missile in Central Europe, the firing of nuclear missiles at ships presumably would not be regarded as serious escalation. Concentrating naval spending almost wholly on nuclear submarines would be the best way of enhancing 'conventional' naval defence. If Labour cannot stomach this, a less cost-effective option is a fleet of conventionally powered submarines carrying missiles with conventional warheads. This, with a fair number of minesweepers, would still make better sense than the present motley collection of different types of ship.

In 1964 Labour entered power with Denis Healey as defence minister. Healey had a clear programme with definite objectives, objectives specified in terms of military logic. First, he sought to liquidate the British commitment 'East of Suez'. Secondly, he sought to cut an ambitious Tory programme of capital spending, thereby eliminating the new aircraft carriers that would facilitate foreign intervention and cutting out a number of very complicated aircraft projects, like the TSR2, that had astronomical development costs and were unlikely to succeed. Labour has no equivalent programme today, simply because it has no clear objectives. Labour has no settled position on Trident and its indecisive anti-nuclear stance leads it to make uncosted commitments to 'strengthening' conventional defence. It has no definite policy on the military content of such enhancement, and it therefore lacks clear military priorities that it could use when it found it actually had to *cut* defence expenditure.

One line of thought on conventional weapons which has had

considerable influence on Labour Party opinion but has yet to become official policy is that of 'alternative defence'. This view has many variants, from modernization strategies using 'emerging technologies' to create a defensive battlefield that would not be out of place in a NATO position paper (were it not for the non-nuclear stance of the proponents) to ideas that rely on mass militia forces to render occupation exceptionally costly to the attackers.[11] One has only to ask of those who adopt such positions (which they regard as an *anti-nuclear* trump card) what happens if deterrence fails? Nuclear deterrence is less likely to fail than conventional deterrence, since the risks are so great. Some degree of conventional defence, sufficient to make the military issue seriously contested and not a mere 'tripwire' to set off a nuclear exchange, is a condition for effective *nuclear* deterrence. But conventional deterrence is weak, even if the military forces that sustain it are quite strong, since the risk involved in challenging it is less. As we have seen, conventional forces have to be over-whelming to prevent a conventional attack by deterrence. No left government will create an overwhelming conventional superior-ity. Those governments that rely on militia systems plus orthodox military forces to deter an aggressor, like Sweden, Switzerland or Yugoslavia, are only able to do so because, as minor powers in secondary strategic locations, they are simply not worth the effort to an occupier.[12] Britain will never be in this position in a general war between the Warsaw Pact and NATO – it is the next target in priority after the most sensitive parts of the West German frontier.

If conventional deterrence fails, then the more radical alterna-tive defence ideas on the left have committed us to a very nasty war indeed. A militia army is a labour-intensive and low-skill force. Faced with efficient enemy forces, its casualties are likely to be massive and yet not able to stop the enemy reaching his objectives. A good idea of the nature of this war is the fate of the raw Iranian Revolutionary Guards thrown against the defences of Basra. The anti-nuclear obsession has led some sections of the left close to seeing a conventional bloodbath as a better alterna-tive. By a judicious mixture of nuclear weapons, multilateral arms reduction, conventional forces, and political confidence-boosting measures to prevent war mobilization, both a nuclear disaster and a conventional bloodbath can be avoided. But that involves accepting nuclear weapons for the foreseeable future and working within the existing system of alliances.

That may be a morally unacceptable position to many on the left, but then they must pay the price of political failure for the consistency of their conscience. Labour's implausible defence policy is just one nail too many in its electoral coffin. Changing defence policy alone will not win Labour the next election, but not changing it will help Labour to lose it. Few people really care about defence – it is low on their list of priority issues in opinion polls. Defence, like the sewers, is the sort of thing efficient governments are supposed quietly to get on with. Defence matters to Labour because most voters, Labour ones included, simply don't trust it quietly to get on with defence. Unilateralism is incomprehensible to most voters: abandoning nuclear weapons without a quid pro quo on the other side violates their idea of common sense. Opinion poll data show that voters' positive perceptions of the Gorbachev initiative are very much tied to his personal success and the continuance of reform in the USSR. They are impressed by Gorbachev, as well they might be, but *not* by the unreformed Soviet system. Trust for the USSR as such remains low, quite rightly. Defence and foreign policy cannot be predicated on the success of *perestroika*, even if it should do nothing to undermine it. The electorate is clearly not dewy-eyed about the Soviet Union, and presumably expects a long-run policy to be able to cope with both the success and failure of the reform. The electorate is not stupid, and Labour should not rely on the Russian leader's personal popularity to save it.

But even consistent and determined unilateralism on the part of Labour would create no worse impression than what really worries voters, which is perpetual debate, the shifty stance of the leadership, and the resulting indecisiveness and incoherence of policy. That leaves the Party's image in the hands of the *Sun*. Its very incoherence opens it up to manipulation.

During the 1987 election campaign, Labour's then defence spokesman, Denzil Davies, did the best he could with a wretched hand. He was helped by the Alliance spokesman being even worse and the Tory, George Younger, playing the jingo-chauvinist card for all it was worth. In the major televised debate on the issue

Davies was able to show that, faced with the success of the Reagan
–Gorbachev summit, Younger was forced to portray the Soviet
Union as if it were about to attack us tomorrow and the USA
about to decamp to fortress America, only plucky little Britain
standing in the Reds' way. If the voters *liked* what Younger had
to say they must be suicidal: alone against the Soviet Union they
might as well distribute cyanide pills. But Davies was stuck with
his Party's own equally mad anti-Americanism and he could do
little to check it, only paradoxically to rely on *American* goodwill
in disarmament negotiations with the Soviet Union.

If the USA is so willing to negotiate on strategic arms, and
if Labour relies so heavily on a favourable outcome of these
negotiations, then why can it not trust the Americans with bases
in Britain? Why be so willing to trust the superpower negotiations
that one is willing to persist with unilateralism, when Britain
might derive both influence and benefits from a tough multilateral
stance? In fact Labour's anti-American stance on bases is sheer
hooey. Labour is still relying on the US–Soviet *détente* to take
the heat off its own stance on bases with the Americans. Labour
as usual is trying both to fudge and to rely on policy being made
elsewhere.

Yet Labour needs to have a defence policy in 1991, not a 'wait
and see' policy, or, worst of all, a 'debate'. It needs to do a rapid
and thorough about-turn on two key issues. A U-turn on both is
necessary, as they are closely linked. First, it needs to abandon
unilateralism for an explicit multilateral policy. It is trying to do
this now and it may even succeed at the Party Conference in
1989. Strong efforts are being made to shift Ron Todd and the
TGWU and to include a multilateral position in the second phase
of the Policy Review. But for this to result in a credible defence
policy something more tricky is needed. Labour's second revisionist necessity is to ditch its feeble and implausible stance on
American bases. This may prove much more difficult, but it is
essential if Labour is to go into the next election as a credible
supporter of the Atlantic Alliance. That it hasn't done this already
is partly due to the fact that it is a strong sticking point for the
left, but it is also due to the indecisiveness of the leadership on
foreign policy issues. Its priorities remain in the areas of welfare
and economic issues, and it simply hasn't given full attention to

the severe electoral liability of anti-Americanism. Kinnock has let this issue simmer because his own perceptions of priorities lead him to hope it will go away. He would not tolerate an equally damaging commitment on domestic policy and would fight fiercely to suppress, for example, a Party Conference commitment to wholesale renationalization without compensation of privatized industries. He is too provincial to see that defence and foreign policy, while not high on the voters' agenda, are actually vital issues for someone who aspires to be prime minister. Mrs Thatcher has too many assets in this department for Kinnock to be able to afford to look weak against her. The issues simply cannot be left in second place because an election campaign can move them into first place.

The leadership now wants to ditch unilateralism, but it will not be allowed to do so on grounds of pure expediency alone. It cannot liquidate its commitments to unilateralism without a strong *argument* in favour of an alternative, or at least one stronger than that it would like to get back into Number 10. A multilateralist stance will still leave strong strategic nuclear forces in the hands of both superpowers. That is only acceptable if the logic of deterrence, tempered by confidence-boosting measures, is accepted. There is little sign that the leadership realizes this. Its left-wing opponents are too intelligent not to notice it. We are still in that sense back where we were when Gaitskell died. A merely opportunist fudge on the issue is unlikely to work, so Kinnock must be willing to suffer both a conversion and a tough argument with the left on nuclear fundamentals very soon. The unilateralists in the Party will not finally give it up without a hard fight and more than one decisive defeat. The issue cannot be quietly made to die. The Labour left and CND would be utterly spineless were that to be so. Pure expediency or the union block vote will not move them.

Unilateralism is a touchstone of political virtue for sections of the left; it is one of the key marks of tribal solidarity against the (healthy) wave of policy pragmatism in the Party. CND is founded not on pragmatism or policy but ultimately on a moral revulsion against nuclear weapons and on the belief that they have won the argument against deterrence. What is disturbing is that the Labour leader probably can't bring himself to tackle this issue, except at the level of expediency. He probably believes the CND case in his heart as much as he wants political power in his head. How finally to resolve Britain's schizophrenic debate on nuclear weapons will remain an open question while Neil Kinnock himself remains ambivalent on the issue.

Soviet reform and Western politics

The vast majority of the British public seem to like Mr Gorbachev. They evidently feel reassured because the Soviet Union has an intelligent and open leader. Mrs Thatcher and Mr Gorbachev get on well too. She is as likely, therefore, to benefit from the East–West thaw as is the Labour Party. The clear message of Mr Gorbachev's reforms is that Soviet-style socialism has failed. The one-party state and the command economy need to be transformed by democratic openness and market liberalism. This seems to reinforce Mrs Thatcher's message of the revitalizing effects of economic liberalism at home.

In Gorbachev the Soviet Union has found a leader who is willing to put the needs of the people before those of the state. The nineteenth-century Russian anti-Tsarist dissident Alexander Herzen foresaw a great deal of the Soviet experience, long before there were Marxists in Russia. He saw that the revolutionaries in Russia and also the revolutionary nationalists in Western Europe, like Mazzini, were prepared to make any sacrifice of themselves or of their people in the present to the future good of the nation. Such was the logic of Stalinism: work yourself to death to build a socialist future. Herzen recognized this as a life-denying barbarism and as a source of authoritarian rule. A truly democratic politics must seek to improve conditions here and now, never sacrificing the living present to an imagined future. In that sense Gorbachev is following an honourable Russian model of radical libertarianism and not simply deferring to the West.

Herzen was surely right, but a heedless living in the present at the expense of the future is no less of a fault. Paradoxically, while the Soviet Union needs desperately to find ways of meeting the immediate material needs of its population, Britain needs to find a way of not concentrating on short-term consumption and of looking to the future. We have failed to provide for a sufficient level of investment in capital goods and in training the labour force. To find means of securing the future we need forms of social cooperation, ways of coming together to discover and implement common goals. The free market and economic liberalism will not do this, but neither will old-style socialist rhetoric and exhortation to 'sacrifice'. The issue of investing in our economic future is quite different from the illusion of building a completely new and better society. If one can put the contrast like this, the aim is not to build the 'New Jerusalem', merely to renovate one of the suburbs of Tel Aviv.

If the Soviet Union and Britain face quite opposite economic problems, there is still something we can learn from the Soviet reform. *Perestroika* has involved the wholesale dismantling of illusions; that Marxism is a reliable guide to the modern world, that the Soviet Union is superior to the West, that socialism can economically out-perform capitalism, etc., etc. This the reformers have done with admirable pragmatism and openness, ditching the puffed-up pride and canting lies of the Brezhnev era. In Britain we need no less to ditch a number of illusions about ourselves; economic, political, cultural and military absurdities that will otherwise chain us to backwardness, decline and mediocrity. In doing so we need to ditch a social theory no less tenacious and no less schematic than Marxism, economic liberalism and its belief in the sovereign virtues of the free market.

CHAPTER 4

The Fading Economic Miracle?

BUDGET DAY 1988 was the crowning glory of the Conservatives' *annus mirabilis*. In June 1987 they had won a third election victory largely on the strength of people's experience of prosperity in southern England. Lawson's Budget capped that success with a programme of cuts in direct taxes on personal income, reducing the basic rate to 25 per cent and the higher rate to 40 per cent. The press, with few exceptions, hailed him as an economic miracle worker. Had he not presided over five years of rapid and uninterrupted growth, the most sustained performance by the British economy on record? No wonder then that the Labour Party had suffered in the June election from arguing a difficult and gloomy case, contending that the economy was in far worse shape than people's experience with their wage packets and in the shopping centres told them. A worker in the South whose wages had just gone up by 9 per cent and the value of whose house was rising faster than his monthly income simply could not believe or understand Labour's negative argument about the structure of the economy and the balance of payments.

Lawson cut taxes to honour an election pledge, but also as a gesture of pure bravado against the economic Jeremiahs. He was widely counselled before Budget Day, by the opposition parties and by the voluntary bodies concerned with welfare, to restrain the growth in domestic spending power and, given he had a surplus in public revenues, to boost public spending on popular areas like the NHS. The overwhelming balance of City and media opinion favoured Lawson's estimate of economic success. If one argued in the mid-1980s that the economy faced serious structural problems and a growing crisis in both the balance of payments and manufacturing performance, one faced a climate of disbelief. City economists, who represent the new economic consensus, simply denied such problems in the main. Lawson himself openly ridiculed, for example, the House of Lords Select Committee on Overseas Trade report of 1985 on the balance of trade in manufactured goods, which documented Britain's poor performance in meeting international competition and the growing balance of trade deficit. Even the Labour Party, shaken by a third defeat, came close to doubting its own unease. Many leading figures were arguing up to and even after the October 1987 stock market crash that Labour had to take account of both the new prosperity and the popular enthusiasm for the share issues in privatized companies.

The Conservatives made the following contentions in June 1987 and have stuck to them since: that Britain had the fastest growing and strongest economy in the advanced industrial world; that unemployment was falling steadily month after month; that British industry had benefited greatly from the Conservatives' deliberate shake-out of inefficient and subsidized firms between 1979 and 1982; that the manufacturing sector was fitter and leaner, now fully up to standards of international competitiveness; that Britain had turned the corner on productivity, and after a long period of stagnation the British economy could show an impressive rate of growth in both labour productivity and new investment; finally, that Conservative policies had overcome inflation and that Britain's international trading position was a strong one.

Mrs Thatcher and Nigel Lawson are not just cynical manipulators of the Big Lie. They honestly and fervently *believe* all these things, and they have been confirmed in that belief by a chorus of praise echoing from Fleet Street, from the economists' desks in City firms, to the High Street. However, with the exception of falling unemployment, almost every one of those loudly trumpeted election claims is substantially untrue. If an economic miracle has been achieved in Britain how *can* we account for the following facts?

In 1987, output in British manufacturing was back to about the level of 1979 and still below that of 1973. Five years of 'growth' from 1983 to 1988 have served to put the manufacturing sector back to roughly where it was at the end of the despised era of Labour 'mismanagement'. The overall growth of the economy hides a series of disturbing but crucial factors in the components of growth. Thus real output per worker has grown in the period 1979–87 less rapidly than in the periods 1951–64 and 1964–73.[1] The UK has therefore *not* departed from its long-run rate of growth in this crucial area. It is roughly the same as in the supposedly disastrous years of consensus politics and high public spending. That growth in real output per worker was slower in 1973–9 is hardly to be accounted for just by bad Labour policies. This was the period of the collapse of the great post-war boom and the inflationary effects of the oil price rise. *All* major economies faced difficulties in this period.

International comparisons are as sobering as those with previous periods of recent British economic history. On the measures of output per employee in manufacturing and real gross domestic product (GDP) per hour worked, Britain comes out most unfavourably compared to countries like France, West Germany and even the USA.[2] The evidence for productivity growth is complex and hotly disputed by economists,[3] but there is little actual sign of a domestic revolution in industrial efficiency and changes in working methods. Most of the evidence points to productivity gains from scrapping obsolete plant and cutting the labour force, and from working at full capacity, and not to the more efficient use of new plant or the introduction of new working methods.

As for investment: net investment in manufacturing was negative from 1980 to 1985, as more obsolete plant was scrapped than new commissioned. Later on, I shall argue in detail that both case studies and survey evidence show that British manufacturing today has not changed in some of its most basic failings since the mid-1970s. That this is so, that there has been no microeconomic revolution in the way firms are run, is shown by the accumulating evidence of macroeconomic failure.

Since statistics were gathered, Britain has always exported more *manufactured* goods than it imported. In 1983 the balance of trade in manufactured goods moved into deficit for the first time, and this is not adequately offset by positive balances in financial and other marketed services. Britain had a trade deficit in manufacturing of £10 billion in 1987 and a by no means pessimistic forecast of the deficit for 1988 of at least £15 billion. The balance of payments was in deficit to the tune of £2.7 billion in 1987 and the realistic forecasts for 1988 are in the region of £14–15 billion and for 1989 £13 billion. Nigel Lawson thinks this is a minor hiccup, easily financeable and a sign of Britain's strong growth in domestic demand. But domestic demand has a strong and unquenchable preference for *foreign* manufactures. Since the early 1970s Britain has been suffering from unprecedented import penetration in foreign consumer durables and capital goods, and the consequent 'de-industrialization' of its uncompetitive manufacturing sector. Britain has lost out not merely in relative terms as in the past but now in absolute terms too – British manufacturing industry registering major real falls in output and employment in sector after sector. There is no international or historical parallel for this in a major advanced industrial country.

This problem will not go away. Dampening domestic demand through high interest rates will cut back on current consumption. But foreign goods compete with the British ones largely on *non-price* terms: they are not cheap and shoddy, they can often command a price premium because they are better, and in many cases there are no British equivalents – try buying a British designed and made video cassette recorder! Britain also has to import a high percentage of semi-manufactures, industrial components and capital goods. As our domestic industrial base gets weaker we have to look for foreign suppliers of many components and advanced manufacturing machinery. Even if British industry were to continue successfully expanding and investing, it would have to suck in foreign goods.

Furthermore, when Mrs Thatcher came to power she inherited a great bonus that no other British government has enjoyed in the modern era, North Sea oil. In the early 1980s North Sea oil production was at its peak, and Britain could meet both its major energy needs and export oil. At some date in the 1990s British oil production will probably tail off and oil will start being imported again in gradually increasing amounts. If Britain faces balance of payments difficulties now, what will the situation be like then? The only answer would be to get British industry into shape *now*, to invest and to innovate to meet the challenge. But

Mrs Thatcher has chosen to use the bonus of oil to let the affluent among the British loose on a spending spree. Conservative policy has shifted the balance of national income dramatically from investment toward consumption. The household sector is now a negative net saver: households are financing purchases by borrowing on future income, buying on credit on the assumption that their money wages will rise steadily.

We can tell what the future is going to be because investment literally *builds* that future by the actions we take today. Britain's investment in *infrastructure*, the vital public facilities necessary for an advanced industrial economy like roads, sewers, etc., is disastrously low by international standards and has fallen dramatically during the ten years the Conservatives have been in power. Year after year of mean and pennypinching decisions on public investment have effects just as certain as similar decisions by a household – the beloved model for Mrs Thatcher. Spending on champagne while neglecting house repairs is a metaphor even grocers, let alone their well-educated daughters, ought to understand.

Even if firms *have* been investing more in manufacturing during the boom years after 1985, they have not been investing enough to meet the future challenge or even to meet the current standards of our competitors – our model should be Japan, not the dire levels of investment in the depression years of 1979–82. Moreover, British firms, as we shall see, utilize investments much less successfully than its competitors do. Mr Lawson's high interest rates will not only choke off consumer demand, they are a massive disincentive to industrial investment. There are already signs that firms are cutting back.

Far from having overcome inflationary pressures, the Conservatives' management of the economy since 1983 has done everything possible to stoke them up again. Inflation was running at over 7 per cent per annum in early 1989, while in 1978 (the last full year of the Labour government) it was 8.1 per cent. The Conservatives' acceptance of a free-for-all on private wage settlement has led to private sector wage rises averaging 9 per cent in 1988, above the rate of inflation and well above growth in GDP and in productivity. High interest rates will encourage those workers who can to go for even higher wage rises. High interest rates will probably lead to an overvalued pound and losses to dollar-sensitive exporters. The crisis of high interest rates and high exchange rates which crippled British industry in the period 1979–82 looks likely to be repeated, if on a less severe scale.

All these facts are readily available, many of them for some time. Yet when did you last see a City economist, the only sort of economist who appears on TV today, mentioning them and cautioning about the future? The answer is, of course, that the 'future' in the City has shrivelled to about three months. The ten-year time-scale needed for major industrial investments is inconceivable to such people, and the risks involved in working to that time-scale have become overwhelming for British industry. Yet that time-scale is commonplace in Japan.

The challenge before the opposition is both to get these facts onto the mainstream political agenda and to offer credible alternative policies for the future. In order to do so we have to look long and hard at the reasons for British failure – for such is the only word for it. Britain is failing as a manufacturing nation now no less certainly than in the 1970s. We have also to consider how the Conservatives managed the economy from 1979 to 1988 and how future governments could do better. But above all we have to look at the standards we must meet, the successes of our competitors and the secret of the success of countries like West Germany, Italy and Japan in manufacturing in the period since the crisis of the early 1970s.

A century of economic decline?

To do this we must first set British failure in its context. It has become a commonplace to argue that since at least the last quarter of the nineteenth century Britain has been suffering from industrial decline. The Conservatives have made much of this and of their success in turning the corner. Conservative remedies for decline imply that the sources of economic failure lie deeply rooted in our history and culture. Britain has suffered from a state-sponsored anti-business culture and from accumulating social rigidities that impeded the workings of the market. The thrusting entrepreneurial spirit of the industrial revolution began to wane in late Victorian England and at the same time collectivist solutions to social problems became increasingly fashionable, and competitive pressures on both capital and labour were weakened by the effects of regulation and welfare state measures. It is assumed in this explanation that other industrially successful countries have had free market economies and a culture open to 'enterprise' – which together allowed both the unfettered freedom and the financial incentives for successful entrepreneurs to innovate and invest. The twentieth century is supposed to have successively reinforced the trend toward collectivism with the rise of Labour and Keynesian state-interventionism. British enterprise has, it is claimed, been steadily and inexorably shackled by a combination of factors: by high taxes, by overpowerful labour unions, by a welfare culture that encouraged dependency rather than initiative in the labour force, by anti-industrial and anti-commercial values propagated by educationalists and endorsed by civil servants, and by the growth of big government in association with powerful vested interests set against change – in short, everything that Mrs Thatcher means by the despised word 'corporatism'.

Conservative policy thus implies a *social* explanation for the failures of British economic history, but the social factor plays a purely negative role – as the collectivism that stifles individualism, ambition and enterprise. The seminal text for this explanation is a book written by an American academic historian: Martin Weiner's *English Culture and the Decline of the Industrial Spirit*. This is often cited by the more thinking Tory ministers and publicists. (Weiner is not a Tory ideologist and he used left-wing sources for his book, notably the work of Eric Hobsbawm. An index of the popularity of his explanation is that some *Labour* politicians have adopted it too.) Weiner claims that later Victorian England rejected the robust individualism and commercial values of the earlier phases of the industrial revolution. The middle classes turned to ape the aristocratic ideal of the gentleman and of 'service', an ideal that rejected 'trade' as vulgar and preferred rural values to urban manufacturing. The new public schools disseminated this anti-trade outlook, setting the children of those who sought to convert wealth into social position against the careers of their fathers.

Correlli Barnett's *The Collapse of British Power* is a popular and influential right-wing classic. It is robust, readable and, it must be said, often telling on international affairs. Barnett again traces British decline to anti-industrial values in education and the public service. It reserves a particular animus for bleeding-heart middle-class do-gooders who sought to impede the laws of competition for essentially sentimental reasons and set out to build the 'New Jerusalem' of the welfare state.

Mancur Olson's *The Rise and Decline of Nations* is a more theoretically sophisticated work and one that has strongly influenced the international perception of the causes of British decline. Olson sees economic decline as the result of the gradual accumulation of social rigidities. A long period of political stability, such as Britain is supposed to have enjoyed, allows the accumulation of powerful vested interests, like labour unions, with great influence on government and the capacity to block changes that threaten them by getting the government to intervene in the workings of the economy.

The message from this history is that change in social values and a systematic demolition of all those institutions that impede the workings of the market are the remedies for this century-long process of decline. But what if the economic history is very different? A long and constant process of decline must have constantly acting causes; these cannot be short-run economic disadvantages but must be long-run cultural and institutional factors. What if Britain's century-long history of decline is an artefact, a phenomenon constructed out of a number of different declines with different causes and consequences? Britain has not been declining steadily and inexorably *in the same way* since the 1880s. On the contrary, Britain has suffered from several distinct conjunctures of decline and types of decline, these being punctuated by periods of industrial recovery and economic adaptation. It is the literature of anxious commentary that ties these periods together, as later writers returned to the anxieties of their forebears. Britain has been obsessed with decline; it also happens that its industries and institutions have more than once been able to innovate and adapt. Mrs Thatcher's is the latest in a long line of government-induced attempts at economic recovery. So far it seems to be one of the least successful.

We have to be clear about what we mean by 'decline'. Britain has, of course, suffered a steady process of *relative* economic decline since the 1880s. That is, Britain's share of world output and world trade has shrunk as other countries have industrialized. As countries like Germany and the USA became major industrial producers, Britain's relative share of world output simply had to fall, as a matter of statistical fact. Britain could not remain the sole 'workshop of the world' forever. At best Britain could have retarded this decline by being more competitive and growing faster, but it could never have arrested the trend.

Competitive failure and relatively slow growth have been the matter of a series of crises of anguished concern and public debate. The reference points have changed – starting with fear of Prussian efficiency in 1870 and continuing to the panic about West German and Japanese import penetration in the 1970s. What particularly exercised critics of British performance in the early 1900s was competitive failure and failure to innovate, relative to Germany in particular. Britain was suffering from import penetration in new products and advanced industries, like chemicals and electrical goods, and it was failing to match German productive efficiency in established industries like iron and steel.

In the open and highly internationalized world economy before 1914 Britain remained the major trading nation. It is important to remember that Britain was the leading commercial and financial power, the pivot of the international mercantile and financial system, to an extent that dwarfed its role in the world economy as an industrial producer. British industries and exports in this period were not technologically sophisticated: in fact Britain's biggest export in 1914 was a primary product, coal, followed by a relatively simple industrial product, textiles. British earnings from foreign investments, from financial services and from its vast merchant fleet (then still the major carrier of world trade) were a vital contribution to the balance of payments. Purely industrial considerations could never have first place in such an economy, nor was domestic industry the only avenue for profitable investments.

This pivotal position in the world economy was irrevocably lost during the First World War. Britain's commercial primacy rested on a virtually dogmatic commitment to free markets and to free trade. Having won the policy argument in the mid-nineteenth century, the free trade prejudice was unshakable despite strong protectionist agitation in the 1890s and the early 1900s; protectionism was politically unthinkable even if it might benefit domestic manufacturing industry.

In fact there are good reasons to believe that in 1870–1914 Britain failed to remain competitive and to innovate because markets were if anything *too* free and there was *too* little direct government intervention. Neoclassical economic historians challenging the thesis of entrepreneurial failure have argued that, in areas like iron and steel, British firms made the *right* decisions: they acted on market information and they tried to maximize profits.[4] This is only to show, however, that competitive markets and short-term financial information were not the best basis on which to develop modern industry. Without either direct government support or the long-run support of major industrial banks, entrepreneurs would find it difficult to build large new steelworks or chemical plants. British entrepreneurs were, furthermore, reluctant to leave the age of personal control and create giant professionally administered corporations funded on the stock market. If British entrepreneurs failed in this period it was because they put profits before long-run growth and because they preferred personal control to the rise of corporate management. In short, they failed because they behaved far too much like the ideal Thatcherite model of the entrepreneur. If the 'industrial spirit' did indeed wane in British culture, then this allegedly basic value change could not have had much impact on British businessmen, for they went on behaving as they always had – and that was the problem.

If there were institutional rigidities that prevented Britain from fully exploiting the technologies and production methods of the second phase of the industrial revolution they were those of the traditional *laissez-faire* market economy. Germany and America developed both corporate capital and modern centralized industrial finance, and these new institutions, combined with active state support in Germany and state indulgence toward tycoon capitalism in the USA, were vital to building new large-scale industries.

The First World War, while it undermined Britain's financial and commercial position in the international economy, provided a major stimulus to domestic industrial renovation. German imports were cut off and Britain needed to make import-substituting investments if it was to compensate. These investments were particularly in those modern industries relevant to war, like chemicals. During the war British industry thus enjoyed security from foreign competition and guaranteed home markets. With active state support it developed the foundations of some of the most successful large British firms like ICI. The war was thus a period of industrial renewal.

The new regime of relatively 'sheltered' domestic production inaugurated by the war continued, with interruptions, into the 1960s. The reasons for reduced foreign competition were distinct in the different periods, but they had the same effect – to give British industry relatively secure home markets. During the 1930s British industry was protected by tariffs, free trade having been abandoned for explicit protectionism and imperial preference. During the Second World War, industry was protected by the state monopoly of foreign trade and a non-competitive regime of all-out war production. After 1945, British industry enjoyed a considerable respite while its major competitors (apart from the USA) rebuilt their war-damaged economies.

After 1918, the British economy continued to be able to restructure and innovate. In the 1920s Britain was faced by an acute crisis of its traditional industries. The war had boosted demand for the old staples – coal, iron, textiles and ships – however inefficient these industries might be. The end of the war brought both a slump in this artificial demand and the return of stiff foreign competition. Coal and ship-building in particular were severely hit, with massive losses in both employment and industrial capacity. But even as the traditional staple industries contracted and painfully 'rationalized', other industrial sectors like motor vehicles, light electrical goods, etc., developed and prospered. In the 1930s there were two Britains as much as there are today and largely the same two, with the South East and the Midlands prospering while much of the North, Wales and

Scotland suffered profound depression and heavy unemployment. In the pre-Thatcher era, Conservative-inclined economic historians made much of Britain's capacity for industrial recovery, stressing this rise of new industries in order to counter the image of the 'hungry thirties'. For the Thatcherites this reversal of industrial decline has been downplayed. Britain needed to be re-made anew in 1979 and so the recent past had to be a failure.

After 1945 Britain's economic performance has been characterized by one commentator as 'very good relative to our own history but very poor compared to other countries'.[5] Until the early 1970s Britain's 'decline' remained essentially a failure to match the growth rates of key competitor countries like West Germany, France and Japan. But the economy was growing faster than in the past, output and real incomes were rising, and there was virtually full employment. Books like Michael Shanks' *The Stagnant Society* dealt with this new phase of relative failure in a period of unprecedented economic success.

The century from 1880 to 1980 is thus complicated, and at certain times in this period Britain was far from 'declining'. A complex and punctuated history of decline and renewal needs a more sophisticated and multi-conjunctural explanation than that offered by the decline of the industrial spirit and the accumulation of social rigidities. The most persuasive explanations for relative decline and competitive failure in the period 1870–1914 are those which point to classic features of free market capitalism: the pursuit of short-term profit on the part of British entrepreneurs and investors, and the persistence of industries organized around relatively small firms in intensely competitive markets into the era of big corporations and large-scale mass production. Britain failed to develop an interventionist state. In the 1960s, however, none of this was true. Britain had adapted to the corporate economy and since the 1930s it had widely copied American mass production techniques. The state was explicitly interventionist. Yet in the early 1970s Britain entered its most devastating period of industrial decline.

Industrial decline in Britain in a sense other than relative decline and competitive failure, that is, the *absolute* loss of output, capacity and employment in sector after sector, is very new. A good deal of it has occurred *since* the Conservative victory of 1979. The myth of a long period of decline, of the failed 'consensus' politics of the 1950s and 1960s, is a good cover for Britain's most rapid and disastrous period of retreat before foreign competitive pressure. British industrial decline, in the sense of 'de-industrialization' consequent on import penetration, is *recent*. The Conservatives' remedies for a century of failure are a good cover for their own failures but of no use in countering the problems Britain now faces.

In the late 1960s and early 1970s Britain was exposed to strong competition in an open international economy, the most liberal regime of world trade since 1914. The effects of the General Agreement on Tariffs and Trade (GATT) and of joining the EEC opened up British markets to competitors. In 1973 the entire industrial world suffered from the oil price rise imposed by the Organization of Petroleum Exporting Countries (OPEC) – an inflationary shock wave that threw world markets into a period of turmoil and extreme volatility. That instability and uncertainty persist. Britain has adapted much less well to the changed conditions than other countries like Japan or Sweden. It shifted from near full employment at the end of the 1960s into accelerating and virtually permanent high unemployment. Entire industries were eliminated by foreign import penetration, like motorcycle or TV tube manufacture, and others suffered serious loss of market share, like motor cars. Between 1966 and 1982 the manufacturing sector lost some 3 million jobs. The most dramatic rise in unemployment, from 1.2 million to 3 million, occurred between 1979 and 1982, when industrial output fell by 11 per cent. In other words, the most catastrophic and quite unprecedented period of industrial decline took place during Mrs Thatcher's own administration.

Few economies could take the grand slam blows by an over-valued currency, high interest rates and recessionary policies on top of already faltering demand. British industry was weak; it needed, and yet could not have, a protected environment. It could not cope with the disastrous combination of simultaneous exposure to foreign competition and damaging economic policies at home. British manufacturing failed to meet the crisis of the 1970s and it has not overcome its basic problems despite the

Conservatives' 'shake-out' in 1979–82 and expansionary policies thereafter.

Why was British manufacturing unable to meet the crisis of the early 1970s? Why has it failed to adapt and reorganize to meet the new competitive pressures of the 1980s? How have Britain's major competitors responded to the new conditions of competition in manufacturing and the fragmented and volatile international markets since 1973?

The causes of manufacturing failure

To answer these questions we must look in depth at the causes of recent British economic failure. British manufacturing industry has not suffered a continuous process of decline since the 1880s. It has, however, failed dramatically since the 1960s. From the 1930s onwards British firms caught up with the American revolution in manufacturing methods. Firms adopted the new mass production methods developed in the early twentieth century and they entered new technologically sophisticated industries. British firms embraced the managerial revolution, building up large corporate enterprises with hierarchies of professional managers.

Since the 1930s governments of both parties have encouraged industrial concentration. They saw fewer larger firms, able to exploit 'economies of scale' with long production runs for mass markets, as the key to industrial success. In the 1930s the Conservative-dominated National government supported the 'rationalization' movement and accepted the process of mergers and concentrations that had taken place during the 1920s. The merger boom of the 1960s was likewise not impeded by governments. Indeed, the Labour governments of 1964–70 actually encouraged industrial concentration. Labour created the Industrial Reorganization Corporation (IRC) with the explicit brief of building up strong firms with a major share of the market in their industry. The logic of industrial concentration, it was argued, required a few super-firms in each major industry that were to be the 'national champions', big enough that they could exploit the full efficiency of long production runs. Major firms like GEC and British Leyland were created in this period. Many of those newly created firms, built out of mergers, were shaken or laid low by the crisis of the early 1970s. British Leyland faced ruin and was semi-nationalized. GEC stagnated and kept its money in the bank.

The mid to late 1980s have seen yet another wave of intense merger activity. Firms are concentrating less to gain economies of scale than to protect themselves by the sheer size of their holdings against being taken over by others. The logic of industrial concentration has been replaced as the rationale for takeovers by the defensive game-playing of stock market obsessed tycoons.

Work practices and labour unions were perceived in the 1960s by both major political parties and most commentators as the major sources of Britain's manufacturing weakness. Unions were organized on obsolete craft and task lines, leading to multi-union plants where unions impeded production by demarcation disputes and the defence of obsolete divisions of labour. Full employment led to wage–cost inflation and a weakening of management's power of control. Poor productivity performance was, therefore, ascribed to the inflexibility of work organization and to less than optimal manufacturing units, the rationalization of plants being resisted by workers and their unions. Unit labour costs were too high and led to British products being over-priced relative to foreign competitors.

This diagnosis led, on the one hand, to proposals for reform of union structures, such as the 1966–70 Labour government's report *In Place of Strife* and the Heath government's Industrial Relations Act 1971, both strongly resisted by organized labour, and, on the other hand, to further proposals for industrial rationalization and concentration.

British labour unions certainly were often very obstructive, but there is a mounting body of evidence to show that labour resistance to change in working practices cannot of itself explain poor British performance on productivity. Productivity remains management's prerogative – work organization, investment and its utilization are all capable of change by management innovation. British managements did not put the transformation of productivity high on their agenda or fight hard for it. Labour resistance is as much an index of weak management pressure as it is of formidable worker strength. British managements failed to exploit or fully to utilize the production methods available to them. Labour costs are, moreover, a small proportion of total manufacturing costs – typically no more than 20 per cent. Halving unit labour costs, therefore, could at best reduce overall unit costs by 10 per cent, and such a target is virtually impossible to achieve. Reducing the holdings of stocks, for example, of things like components and raw materials, and increasing the efficiency of throughput of stocks in manufacturing – matters essentially in the hands of management's organization of work – could reduce costs by much more and far more easily.

Two studies dramatically illustrate industry's weaknesses in the 1950s and 1960s. S. J. Prais' study *The Evolution of the Giant Firm in Britain* challenged the prevailing ideas about the logic of industrial concentration. It pointed out that *plant* size is crucial to 'economies of scale'; that is, productive efficiency depends on the optimum size of manufacturing *plant* and not on that of the firm. Big British firms were much larger than the optimum size of plants and were often made up of numbers of plants of less than optimum size. Concentration of ownership did not of itself lead to industrial efficiency. Williams, Williams and Thomas' *Why are the British Bad at Manufacturing?* showed through detailed case studies that rigidities in labour organization and poor attitudes to work on the part of labour were not primarily responsible for poor productivity. This is not so much a pro-union argument as one strongly critical of the capacity of British managers to organize production. The low efficiency of utilization of labour was largely due to defects in the organization of production to be set at the door of management.

These studies and a number of others raise a series of dimensions of failure of British firms that cannot simply be dealt with in terms of poor productivity and restrictive labour practices. These can be summed up as follows.

First, productive efficiency is only relevant if what is made is both competitive as a *product* and properly sold. Many case studies show that British management at firm level has simply made the wrong decisions about the type of product to make, the type of markets to aim at and the appropriate marketing strategy to adopt. Firms in a wide range of industries – from motorcycles to machine tools to television sets – failed hopelessly in this respect in the late 1960s and early 1970s. Many were driven out of business. They failed principally because they neglected to design and effectively organize for production the right product ranges and to market them effectively, with proper investment in sales networks and after-sales service. Firms failed to keep abreast of research and development elsewhere, to spend adequate amounts on both new design and production engineering, and to integrate production and marketing.

These failures were suddenly and ruthlessly exposed by foreign competition as the whole international manufacturing regime changed. The late 1960s saw a dramatic increase in the internationalization of trade in manufactured goods as advanced industrial countries traded more intensively one with another. The most competitive firms no longer serviced domestic markets and then exported as a marginal bonus. On the contrary, their strategy was to sell in *world* markets, with the aim of a substantial market share in each of the major advanced countries' markets. Such strategies were strongly export-oriented and emphasized gaining a target market share as the key objective. To do this firms were willing to invest in marketing and sales networks world-wide. The Japanese and the West Germans are the key exponents of this strategy.[6] British firms were still thinking in terms of the boom years in a soft home market. They had been successful and profitable in the undemanding environment of growing home demand in the 1950s and early 1960s, when they were producing a capacity and could sell all they could make. They neglected export opportunities and even withdrew from foreign markets to concentrate capacity on the domestic market.

Secondly, price competition is not the crucial factor determining success in markets for advanced consumer goods where consumers have high disposable incomes, or in markets for producer's goods where the crucial criterion is not the initial cost but the productive performance and lifetime efficiency of the equipment. Domestic and industrial consumers will pay a considerable price premium if they can obtain a significant qualitative advantage from a particular product. Superior design, reliability due to high production and inspection standards and good after-sales service will lead consumers to pay more for a good. Firms like Audi and Sony established this reputation, and British firms lost it. British firms tried to compete on price, and, failing to be more efficient than competitors in the process of production, were often forced to squeeze both profits and labour costs in order to do so. Squeezing profits cut back on their capacity to develop new products from retained earnings. Squeezing labour costs was ineffective; it led to bitter labour disputes, and a disgruntled and less than efficient labour force. British firms' labour relations and employee cooperation were often worsening at a time when Japanese firms, for example, could offer their workers rising real wages, productivity- and profit-based bonuses, and improved conditions of service in return for active co-operation. In the 1970s British managements and government policy makers were frequently obsessed with price and particularly unit labour costs as factors in competition when other countries were moving to more sophisticated manufacturing strategies. They grossly misdiagnosed the sources of their competitors' success and laid failure at the feet of labour and the unions.

Thirdly, firms frequently adopted disastrous strategies to cope with foreign market penetration. Some firms, for example in the motorcycle industry, retreated from mass markets into the more expensive and complex end of the production range, hoping competitors could not follow. But the more sophisticated British motor bikes were not like those of BMW. They were just larger bikes built by the old methods and lacking many of the modern features. The Japanese followed into these product ranges and virtually eliminated British producers from the whole market.[7] Other firms retreated down-market, trying to compete with lower prices and correspondingly lower product quality. In areas like textiles and clothing, furniture, etc., this strategy led to abandoning the high-value end of the market to the Italians, the Swedes, etc., and leaving British manufacturers struggling to compete with low-wage Third World countries.

Fourthly, a common complaint on the left in the 1970s was that British managers were staging an 'investment strike'. There was little reason to suppose an explicit conspiracy, and both the left and the right oversimplified this issue. Apologists for British industry and for the financial sector have argued that, expressed in terms of percentages of GDP, British rates of investment were not so different from those of major competitors, and that there was no evidence that firms were seeking more finance from banks and being refused. Critics argue that British manufacturing has failed because of under-investment and that industry is starved of capital because property, overseas investment, etc., offer more lucrative possibilities.

There is no doubt that *external* industrial finance in Britain was dearer and given on more difficult terms than in, say, Germany or Japan. But in itself this need have made little difference, since in the 1960s and 1970s the main sources of investment were internal to the firm – consisting of depreciation allowances and retained profits. If firms had been successful enough they should have been able to renew and expand on a base of growing sales and profits. British failure in terms of investment is more complex than right apologists or left demonologists will allow. As the West German economy grew faster than Britain's, for example, not wholly dissimilar percentages of GDP devoted to investment hid the fact that in *absolute* terms West German industry invested far more than we did.

More important still than the level of investment is its appropriateness and the efficiency of utilization of the capital equipment acquired. In this respect Britain has failed badly compared to competitors: it has simply got less output from similar equipment or has misused equipment. For example, when British Leyland introduced a new production line at Longbridge to build the Metro it was dedicated to that make of car alone and new machinery was set up for one type of operation only. Thus, when the firm's projections for Metro sales were not met, the plant was forced to operate at below full productive efficiency and other models of car could not be built on the same assembly line.[8] Foreign auto firms like Toyota, for example, did not make this mistake and were able to build different models and variants on the same lines.

Failure to utilize investments effectively means that costs are higher and the equipment earns lower profits for the firm. Inefficient manufacturing methods combined with poor labour productivity due to bad organization of work eat into retained profits. Investments earn less and are less profitable. They also become more difficult to make or to risk on a declining market share.

The ailing firm is driven to seek expensive external finance if it wants to adopt a new strategy to recapture its market share. Far from their being involved in an investment 'strike', firms became both more constrained by the investment funds available to them and more risk averse. Non-industrial investments *were* more profitable, but mainly because of the poor performance of the manufacturing sector. The left's remedy – compulsory investment planning under threat of nationalization, proposed in the 1973 'Alternative Economic Strategy' – was therefore largely useless. If management had *liked* this strategy by some weird chance then public funds would have been poured into disastrous projects on a large scale, since the real problem was not the level of investment as such but the business strategies of firms.

How can we explain the overall poor quality of management decision-making that seems to have played a crucial part in Britain's recent industrial decline? Case studies cover many different industries and too many firms to make this a matter of happenstance. National culture – the 'anti-industrial' spirit – will not do. But nor will 'management attitudes'; this is simply to restate the problem. In fact, British managers from the 1950s through to the 1980s have been aware of the threat of foreign competition and, as that threat has intensified, have tried to meet it and match the best practice abroad. Laziness or incompetence alone will not do to explain managers' behaviour any more than they will for manual workers. Why then did and do managers get it wrong so often?

Industrial structure and the prevailing conception of the role of the firm explain a great deal. As we saw from Prais' evidence, large firms are much bigger than manufacturing plants. Most large British firms in the 1950s through to the 1980s have been multi-plant and multi-locational; they have increasingly become multi-industry too. The effect of merger waves, facilitated by stock market booms in the 1960s and 1980s, has been to create firms that are multi-industry conglomerate groups.[9] The top management of such firms is skilled in financial control and dominated by financial concerns. Accounting and marketing are the key routes to the top in British firms. Top managers are thus far removed from any knowledge of or an overriding commitment to product innovation or production organization in a specific industry. This, far more than any lack of specific engineering knowledge, is the key to their limited grip on manufacturing strategy. Their opponents in West German and Japanese firms are typically committed to making a success of manufacturing in a particular industry or specific industry grouping.

During periods of intense merger activity industrial concentration provides a strategy in itself and, from the firm's point of view, an effective substitute for industrial investment. The success of firms is increasingly measured by their capacity to exploit stock market conditions and expand by taking over other firms. From the standpoint of the acquiring firm, another firm is an investment in additional productive capacity: it is like buying a second-hand machine. Expansion by acquisition is often cheaper and less risky than expansion by internal investment in new capacity. Firms can increase their market share in a given industry by merger or acquisition, and they can diversify by buying into profitable industries or non-manufacturing sectors. Even the largest firms tend to adopt defensive and risk-averse strategies in these conditions. They need to maintain their stock market price and that means declaring satisfactory profits and paying reasonable dividends. Large and long-run investments in new products or in major new production processes are thus risky. Indeed, taking a long-term view at all is risky. Far better to concentrate on impeding the domestic competition, the one kind of competition you can control, by means of takeovers.

British senior managers today give a very low priority to introducing new products to improve their competitiveness in existing markets or to enter new ones.[10] This is in marked contrast with the priorities American, European or Japanese managers give in response to similar surveys. British industry gives a low priority to research and development, to the introduction of new products and to seeking innovations in production processes and production organization. Indeed, some commentators[11] have placed the major blame for British manufacturing failure on poor R&D effort. The particular characteristics of British industrial concentration have thus helped to institutionalize the management priorities and practices that lead to competitive failure in manufacturing. The managers actively engaged in product development or production organization are far removed from the top of the managerial tree in Britain. They are subaltern personnel, without the financial decision-making autonomy to pursue their own strategies. They are often at risk from the remote top management of a group that has recently 'acquired' them.

If firms have been driven toward increasingly financial considerations and to a response to competition in terms of concentration, they have responded to problems of production largely in terms of a mentality that emphasizes hierarchical control and the rigid specification of the tasks of labour. Britain has been and remains virtually unique in its excessively rigid division between shopfloor and management, emphasizing that they are separate social classes. At the same time management has been severely hierarchical. The managers directly involved in production are often badly trained and confined to narrow spheres of responsibility and specialized roles. 'High flyers' are plucked out of management careers in manufacturing and join a top management that thinks in purely financial terms. British manual workers are the worst educated and trained in the advanced industrial world. In this respect the situation has worsened and the 1980s mark a new low. Management has consistently attempted to specify workers' tasks in detail and to deny them autonomy. This is rationalized as a response to traditional union obstructiveness and as part of the logic of getting higher productivity out of a reluctant labour force. There is little evidence that such rigid work organization does promote higher productivity. On the contrary, more flexible patterns of authority, allowing workers more autonomy, are the best way of ensuring continuity in production. It is continuity far more than intensity of effort that is crucial. Simply working hard is not the basis of high productivity. Working effectively by actively preventing bottlenecks and stoppages is the way to get high productivity; that demands the active and constant co-operation of workers and production organizers. Treating labour as the 'enemy' to be excluded from any responsibility simply cuts off such cooperation at root.

Finally, Britain still suffers from its nineteenth-century legacy of conceptions of the role of the firm. British policy makers, managers and economists have perceived the firm as a self-sufficient entity, standing in purely competitive relations to other firms. However interventionist at the macro level, however ener-getic in promoting rationalizations or mergers, governments have not seen it as their role to help build collaborative and cooperative networks between firms. Labour in 1964 never intended the National Economic Development Office (NEDO) as a means of bringing firms together in order to cooperate in the day-to-day work of their industries; it was meant to coordinate economic information for macroeconomic planners and to make the invest-ment decisions of firms coincide. It remained part of a predomi-nantly Keynesian macroeconomic strategy, which tried to operate on firms through common policy measures and adopted a 'hands off' approach to the actual microeconomic decisions of manage-ment.

Still failing – 1979–88

The Conservatives' strategy since 1979 is officially an anti-Keynesian one. Its approach to economic revitalization is based on removing the impediments to the free working of markets. It views the consequent development of intense and unrestricted competition between firms as a pure gain for economic efficiency. But who is most effective at international competition? By no means those who encourage cut-throat competition between national firms at home.

Current Conservative policy envisages only two possible econ-omic entities: wholly independent firms and efficient, because unregulated, markets. But it by no means follows that the isolation of firms in purely competitive relationships really does stimulate the efficiency of these firms. Jonathan Zeitlin and I have used the phrase the 'dis-economies of competition' to explain the phenomenon of firms isolated in purely competitive relationships being unable to acquire all the inputs they need from exclusively market relationships with other firms. Many firms simply cannot bear the full costs of research and development, commercial information and market services, worker training, and so on. In Britain, even large firms often fail to provide these necessary inputs for themselves, training being a good example. The classic responses of firms to their training needs are to demand more of the state or to freeload off other firms, pinching skilled labour by a wage premium much less than the full cost of training a new worker.

What Britain has singularly lacked is patterns of cooperation between firms and between firms and public agencies to provide essential common services and to develop industry. We may call this an 'industrial public sphere', a set of institutions through which firms can cooperate to mutual benefit as well as compete.[12] In other countries, industry associations and regional and local bodies often perform these functions. The public sector, whether it be the central government or the municipal council, will cooperate with and aid firms. This is done without such networks of cooperation and common industrial services becoming simply state agencies themselves. Especially for the smaller or medium-sized firm in manufacturing, such patterns of cooperation can provide valuable information about markets and services to enable entry to new markets, information about the latest industrial processes, and the collective upgrading of the skills of the labour force. Large firms may benefit from patterns of cooperation if they develop constructive and ongoing relationships with suppliers and subcontractors, often investing in them or sharing information with them.

These patterns of cooperation, especially the cooperative relationships between subcontractors and large firms, have been common in Britain's major competitors like Japan. This is not to say that foreign firms do not compete; they do, and they often struggle fiercely to best one another, but they also cooperate. Large British firms almost never adopt this attitude: they see suppliers in purely commercial terms and seldom trust them. Suppliers, in turn, take on more work than they can cope with. This is understandable as they are being perpetually let down by large firms who promise major orders, demand keen prices, and then cut back at will. In Britain, industrial concentration has taken the place of common services. Most manufacturing firms are subsidiaries, without the autonomy necessary to contribute to industry associations or local networks.

These reasons for the failure of management decision-making are institutional and qualitative. It will take more than a change of attitudes and an enhanced attention to management training to cure them. They are also not amenable to 'quick-fix' strategies at the level of the individual firm. Too often British firms have simply tried to copy foreign manufacturing methods and management techniques, frequently with poor results. One cannot grab aspects of another country's whole economy, and ignore the fact that those aspects depend for their success on a social and institutional context that we cannot easily copy.

In 1979 the Conservatives believed in a 'quick-fix' solution: weaken the power of organized labour; deregulate and derigidify markets; remove controls and constraints on management imposed by regulatory legislation. Management would then be free to manage; it could make the best and most rational decisions. The macroeconomic evidence suggests that that hasn't happened. Moreover, there is disturbing micro evidence that since 1979 British firms have continued to make the same mistakes and indulge in the same old bad practices. In fact, the continuities in British manufacturing practice and performance stand out more clearly than do radical changes, and this at a time when manufacturing strategies and methods have changed in Britain's major competitor nations like West Germany, Italy and Japan.

To begin with, the stimulation of domestic demand has given the UK firms that managed to survive the 'shake-out' of 1979–82 something like 1960s market conditions again. To be sure, foreign producers may have a large market share, but British firms can sell all they can make. Survey evidence shows that there has been no significant improvement between 1975 and 1985 in the performance of British firms at making delivery dates. A shocking 23 per cent of firms responding to an authoritative survey failed to meet the hardly demanding target of 50 per cent of orders delivered on time.[13] Firms have not extended capacity to overcome these blockages. They are happy to work close to capacity and are able to ensure that they do so by taking on more orders than they can possibly meet.

In the early 1980s British firms in hard-pressed sectors like textiles and clothing enjoyed a boost as retailers adopted new and more flexible strategies, involving rapid feedback from sales and rapid responses to orders for repeating successful lines by manufacturing suppliers. This favoured local sourcing in the UK, and in the mid-1980s British firms regained market share and import penetration was halted. Foreign suppliers, particularly in the Far East, have responded by cutting their own reaction times and offering dramatic improvements in quality, so imports in these areas are once again on the increase.

Britain's failure to exploit the latest production technology continues. There is strong evidence that British firms have failed to make efficient and flexible use of bought-in new, and generally foreign, capital goods. A case study shows that British firms that have invested in flexible manufacturing systems (FMS) – highly automated equipment, capable of manufacturing a variety of products and greatly enhancing the versatility of appropriately skilled labour – have used them as if they were specialized single-purpose machinery.[14] It appears that firms have made such purchases looking for short-term cost savings and to control labour by the rigid use of automation. Foreign firms utilize such technology to increase the flexibility of their output. Survey evidence also shows that British firms have not made proper use of the latest (and generally imported) technology. A very high proportion of firms reported that they had either negative or fairly low results from processes like computer-aided design/computer-aided manufacture (CAD/CAM), FMS and robotics.[15] This is a very disturbing finding: if British firms are failing to exploit these technologies, Britain's future as a competitive manufacturing nation is bleak. The reason British managers cannot utilize these technologies is not because they are stupid but because of the old vice of short-termism. They are expecting direct and immediate benefits in terms of manufacturing costs. Foreign managements are willing to look toward longer-term gains, in terms of productive flexibility, and are willing to change their whole manufacturing organization to get them.

The secrets of our competitors' success

The 1973 dramatic rise in oil prices signalled the end of the long post-war boom for our competitors as well as for the UK. The international economy faltered into depression. Oil prices quadrupled for countries like Japan in 1973. Japan faced serious inflationary pressures and the need to adapt its industries to the challenge of higher energy costs and more volatile international markets. Sweden faced serious problems of structural adjustment with the rundown of major and previously successful industries like ship-building and steel. The more dependent a country on the export of manufactured goods, the greater the threat from the growing competitiveness and the fragmentation of international markets. Countries that had based their economic strategies on export-led industrial growth had to adapt quickly or face prolonged recession. The UK had not followed such a strategy; although a major exporter, its growth and its industrial output were oriented toward domestic demand.

How did the most successful countries adapt? By carrying out programmes of macroeconomic adjustment, by trying to cut down energy inputs and therefore oil imports, and by trying to improve the productive efficiency of their manufacturing sector. It is often assumed by economic commentators that the success of countries like Japan in competing with Britain and the USA, in areas like motor cars and consumer electronics, is due to the fact that they have simply become more efficient at the basic processes of mass production. They have learned the secret of high productivity and economies of scale. But we all know as shoppers that Japanese goods actually compete in terms of product quality, reliability and above all variety, to suit differing tastes and pockets. These reasons for Japanese success are actually antithetical to competition in terms of cheaper prices based on sheer volume of production. Often Japanese goods command a price premium; we say they are good value but often they are not cheap. Japanese goods in a particular industry, like motor cars, sell world-wide, to differing national markets and to differing segments within markets. This demands that Japanese motor manufacturers offer a wide variety of models and variants. These are tailored to specific market conditions, and the output of the models can be varied depending on their relative success.

It should be obvious that traditional processes of the mass production of standard goods for undifferentiated mass markets – the classic American system of mass production – simply cannot cope with such demands. Mass production relies on long runs of standard goods, and it uses special-purpose machinery and unskilled or at best semi-skilled labour to make them. However, without such mass markets the strategy is undermined: production of varied goods no longer offers the 'economies of scale' that will justify highly specialized manufacturing machinery. The Japanese are the leading exponents of a quite different manufacturing strategy, geared to changing and differentiating markets, called 'flexible specialization'.[16] Flexible specialization is the use of general-purpose machinery and broadly skilled, adaptable labour to produce a wide and changing range of semi-customized goods. Such a system can switch quickly to producing more of the most successful variant or model of a good, as it can also cope with changing and uncertain demand by producing more than one type of good by means of the same process or plant.

This strategy can be followed by a wide range of types and sizes of firm – by big multinationals and tiny factories no bigger than workshops. In the case of the larger multinational, multi-product firm, the way of adapting to the need for flexibility is to decentralize its constituent operating divisions into a loose federation of sub-units. Each division specializes in some area of activity and coalesces and cooperates with other divisions within the firm when necessary. Operating units thus enjoy high autonomy and the capacity to conduct their own R&D. Multinational corporations like Fiat, Xerox and Bosch are following this strategy. In the mass production era, multinational firms tended to centralize their operations, giving each of their subsidiary units a place in their international division of labour and often moving parts across the globe from one specialist mass production unit to assembly plants. Ford is the classic example of such a strategy and persists with it. We are talking of tendencies here, clearly, not all mass production plants and firms will cease. Who wants a customized lightbulb?

In the case of a major nationally based producer within a single main industry, like motor manufacture, flexible specialization involves developing flexible internal manufacturing and work practices that can switch between models and variants and that can also ensure quality: multi-purpose equipment, a loose division of labour, and rigorous processes of inspection. It also involves such a firm building up ongoing relationships with suppliers and subcontractors, such that both the supply and the quality of components can be assured. A flexible firm aiming at high-quality products must be able to rely on its suppliers being as flexible and as good at quality control as itself. It may therefore have to invest in them, to share information with them and to help them out in periods of trading difficulty if it wants to get such performance. A great strength of Japanese industry is its commitment to such ongoing relationships, and the acceptance of obligations on both sides that are not purely commercial or contractual.[17] The Japanese motor industry and Toyota in particular exemplify this approach to manufacturing.

Another example of the institutional foundation for a flexible specialization strategy is the industrial district, that is, a network of small and medium-sized firms that not merely coexist and compete in the same area, but also share ongoing subcontracting relationships and contribute to common services.[18] Such districts are like multi-cellular animals, with a lively population of active firms specializing in some particular range of industrial activities. Typically the firms will use general-purpose equipment and a core of skilled labour, but flexibility is found not merely within the firm, but in the fact that firms can contract out work to one another and thus acquire specialized services, equipment and skills none of them could possess alone. The institutional framework of such districts is diverse. But the thriving industrial district will typically have developed means of combining and balancing competition and cooperation between firms. In such districts, market relationships, personal contacts, industry associations and public bodies all have a place. Firms thus compete one with another, but they also share work and information. They participate in public forums and benefit from collectively provided services, like market information, common promotion or common design facilities.

Such districts exist in Japan, but also in all the more successful export-oriented industrial economies – in West Germany and in Italy. Baden-Württemberg in West Germany, Emilia-Romagna in Italy and Sakaki in Japan are among the best studied and frequently cited of such districts. Such districts have many different specialisms, ranging from traditional goods like textiles or furniture, to more complex goods like medical equipment or high-tech auto parts. What makes them different is that they can vary their output quickly to cope with changing patterns of demand or new forms of competition. Even if they produce traditional goods they generally use advanced equipment and production goods to do it. Sakaki in Japan offers a good example.[19] It is a mountain township which has developed from an old-style peasant and artisan economy into a go-ahead network of some 300 small production units. The artisans and small businesses of Sakaki use advanced numerically controlled machine tools to produce a wide range of products varying from medical testing equipment to typewriter keyboards.

Such districts used to exist in Britain too.[20] For example, Birmingham was one vast district for the metal-working trades in the nineteenth century. But they have been broken up by mergers, by takeovers by major national firms and by the disappearance of firms with de-industrialization. Britain's manufacturing industry is highly concentrated, and small and medium-sized firms have a less important and less independent role in it than in many other more successful manufacturing countries. Small and medium-sized firms are frequently no more than very dependent subcontractors for major firms and are treated purely commercially, not in terms of ongoing and mutually beneficial relationships as in Japan. No wonder major British firms suffer from poor-quality components and parts, leading to lower productivity and more unreliable products. No wonder British firms fail to meet delivery dates because they too have been let down by suppliers. British management is very impressed by Japanese 'just-in-time' systems for minimizing holdings of stocks of parts by ensuring that subcontractors deliver them in exactly the quantities needed for current production. But so far they seem to have been less than willing to enter into the new and partly non-commercial relationships with suppliers this implies. They seem to think they can secure a better performance out of suppliers by relying on market and contractual terms alone.

Britain is ill-placed to adopt a flexible specialization approach to manufacturing. It demands the sophisticated use of general-purpose machine tools and specialist equipment. But the British capital goods industry, and the machine tool industry in particular, is weak. British firms thus tend to buy foreign machines 'off the shelf' and to misuse them. With weak domestic producers, managements purchasing capital goods lack access to firms with the local skills and advice needed to build customized or semi-customized equipment for particular plants demanding a certain kind of flexibility. Flexible manufacturing requires skilled labour and puts a premium on training. Britain is currently facing shortages of labour. A widespread shift toward flexible specialization would produce an acute crisis in labour supply.

The lesson offered by Japan is that small and medium-sized firms are a vital part of the main industrial dynamic based on flexible specialization. Such firms are the key to exploiting the numerous specialized market niches in an advanced industrial economy. Japan shows, as does Italy, that such firms succeed best in an environment somewhere in between the intense competition of isolated firms in the market and the state interventionist direction of industry.[21] They need either a cooperative local environment, like an industrial district, or an ongoing and partly non-commercial relationship with a larger firm. Pure Thatcherism can see virtues only in free markets and in competition. Other countries, and not least their industrial managers, have seen the need to temper competition with cooperation. In a way, Britain's nineteenth-century free market legacy has continued to hamper it. It was replaced by imperatives to state intervention and industrial concentration which have destroyed the autonomy of many firms through mergers into larger ones, and which have left British industry owned by a relatively small number of large and inflexible firms, whose managers are remote from manufacturing.

Flexible specialization thus poses a major threat to British industry if it is the dominant new manufacturing strategy and the key to competitive success. The reason is that it doesn't rest on some particular management technique one can copy or some new technology one can buy in, it rests essentially on social institutions. It rests on industrial districts, on cooperation and trust between subcontractors and major firms, on cooperation and trust between management and skilled workers who take an active interest in what is made and how, on a strong population of small and medium-sized firms that are autonomous and controlled by managers with an active commitment to manufacturing, and on a sophisticated interaction between public bodies and private firms, an interaction closer to dialogue than state 'intervention'. It is just such institutions, and the public culture needed to build them up, that are lacking in Britain. The leading political parties have little experience of such a collaborative 'public–private' culture. The Conservatives stress the free market, competition and the freedom to manage. The Labour Party is slowly retreating from a long history of seeing state intervention as the sole solution to all economic problems. Changing our *political* attitudes about the economy may be one of the preconditions for economic success.

British top management have been fêted by the Conservative government. They have been confirmed in every prejudice, allowed to richly reward themselves, and allowed to run an unprecedented new wave of merger mania. The message of flexible specialization will be unpopular in boardrooms too, because it involves dialogue and cooperation. Top management do not want to give recently acquired production units in firms they have just taken over great autonomy, nor do sophisticated managers want to be on pally terms with subcontractors, thinking of them as just one step up from a prole. Snobbery is so institutionalized in Britain we call it 'class'. The pampering and over-rewarding of top management in the Thatcher years has done nothing to promote dialogue with the shopfloor or with the smaller firms who act as suppliers.

There are, of course, examples of better practice. Everyone cites Marks and Spencer. Yes, they have tried to develop ongoing relationships with suppliers, and to give preference to British firms, but, not to put too fine a point on it, they are a diamond on a dunghill. They also firmly remain in the distribution sector. British firms in this sector continue to be strong and successful. They have, moreover, adopted flexible marketing strategies, minimizing stocks and rapidly assessing sales patterns so that they can switch orders to the most successful lines. British manufacturers in areas like food and clothing have had to fit into flexible retailing, but the evidence that they have switched to flexible manufacturing methods is not strong.

Flexible distributors will purchase abroad if British firms fail to meet their requirements. With a few exceptions, they feel they owe British industry nothing and will switch suppliers if foreign manufacturers are more efficient and if home sourcing in areas like food and clothing becomes less necessary. This could result in the de-industrialization of the food-processing sector too – a very large employer – and further rundown of areas like textiles and clothing. There is little evidence that major British manufacturers are doing what the retailers are doing. There is a great deal of management babble about 'flexibility', but little apprehension of what flexible specialization means. The strong growth of retailing, other private marketed services, and financial services offers both profitable opportunities for investment and good management careers. The British remain good at selling and bad at manufacturing. Manufacturing is the cinderella sector of the British economy, and this is reflected in the drain of entrepreneurial and management talent away from manufacturing activities, even in industrial firms. Who wants to get caught up in 'metal bashing' anyway?

The secret of expansionary policy – 'electoral Keynesianism' 1982–8

This sort of attitude is a close reflection of the government's economic policies since 1983. If the Conservatives' diagnosis of Britain's problems was largely wrong in 1979, if their macroeconomic policies from 1979 into 1982 were disastrous in their impact on the manufacturing sector, how do we account for the growth and prosperity in 1983–8? The answer is to return to my analogy at the beginning of this book: the monetarist tradition of Toryism gradually lost out to the opportunist. Political defeat seemed a real possibility at the end of 1981. Mrs Thatcher, the conviction politician, dropped her monetarist convictions at a stroke, and set out to copy Harold Macmillan. Most of the problems of the British economy in late 1981 had been either caused or exacerbated by the government's own macroeconomic policies: an overvalued pound, high interest rates, a restrictive monetary policy and severe constraints on public spending (which nevertheless remained high because of unemployment).

Since 1982 Mrs Thatcher has followed an explicitly expansionary policy. Only half ironically I shall dub it 'electoral Keynesianism'. It is a policy geared to ensuring electoral success and political survival. It benefits those Mrs Thatcher has most need to please, the shock troops of her victories at the ballot box – private sector employees in what are both the most prosperous and the most Tory parts of the country. Electoral Keynesianism concentrates expansionary policy on those parts of the country and the economy that need stimulation least. It is an expansionary policy for those who have: tax cuts and easy credit can only help the unemployed or the depressed areas by supposed 'trickle down' effects.

Keynes' strategy was quite different. Keynes wanted to preserve capitalism. A sophisticated liberal, he loathed state socialism and administered collectivism. However, he saw that in the conditions of the 1930s one could only do so by actively trying by public policy to compensate for capitalism's worst features: unemployment and bleak poverty. Keynes' analysis of the causes of depression was in essence simple – a deficient level of consumption and too high savings. His strategy for dealing with unemployment was also in essence simple – to boost effective demand through public spending and deficit finance of that spending by the public sector. The state would spend in order to compensate for deficient private spending, and it would borrow or print money to do so. It was gambling on the successful stimulation of the economy to sort out the state's finances in the longer term, but Keynes was a good gambler. It was not a reckless policy in the 1930s when there was underutilized industrial capacity, when prices and interest rates were falling, and when the domestic economy was protected by tariffs on foreign goods. Keynes' proposals were not merely expansionary, but also redistributive: putting work in the hands of the poorest and unemployed boosted demand of those who most needed to consume. Keynes thought he had solved both the problem of the trade cycle and the problem of social justice with one policy stroke. Keynes was remarkable both for the sophistication with which he demonstrated the theoretical practicality of his ideas within the system of neoclassical economics and also for the extreme simplicity of his policy measures. They involved politicians abandoning obsolete economic dogmas, but no changes in the fundamental institutions of either state or society.

'Electoral Keynesianism' is something else again. It is an expansionary policy that takes place in a quite different situation and with quite different goals. It takes place in an open economy without protectionist measures, where interest rates and prices have a strong propensity to rise, and where there is little surplus industrial capacity, most of it having gone to the wall in 1979–82. Nigel Lawson's expansionary strategy has been to boost effective demand in the most affluent parts of the private sector, by holding down the growth of public expenditure and stimulating current consumption at the expense of investment. Lawson's predecessors were explicitly anti-Keynesian, because they opposed a demand-led expansionary policy and argued a strong dose of depression to check inflationary pressures. Nigel Lawson has until recently taken inflation to be beaten. He is anti-Keynesian, not because Keynes' policies were expansionary but because they were redistributive. Keynes' policies also aimed, indirectly, to stimulate investment. Nigel Lawson seems to have devised policies that, one supposes unintentionally, act as a disincentive to investment. After five years of such policies, prices, interest rates and imports are all rising above sustainable levels. The rich and the affluent employed have prospered; the poor and the unemployed have lost out. Keynes is probably turning in his grave, but at least he is mocked by an expansionary policy aimed at growth. The right-wing economic gurus Milton Friedman and Friedrich von Hayek are probably spinning in their chairs at Lawson's recklessness.

In many ways the later years of Nigel Lawson's chancellorship resemble the phenomenon of the Barber boom* in the early 1970s – dramatic overheating of domestic demand, strongly inflationary wage pressures, a run-away property boom, and an intense merger boom. The difference is that we don't have 1973 and OPEC to contend with, nor is the current Tory administration prepared to see public sector expenditure and employment rise in the way Mr Heath's did. Tory administrations

* Mr Anthony Barber, Heath's Chancellor, adopted a strategy of dramatically increasing Britain's rate of growth based on a strongly expansionary economic policy.

are closer in some ways than the advocates of a new Conservatism and a break with the past would like.

How did the Conservative government manage to turn a particularly serious depression, albeit substantially of its own making, into five years of expansion? First, Mrs Thatcher's administration received a big present from the USA. The pound fell against the dollar largely as an unintended consequence of American monetary policy in the period up to 1985. This restored the competitiveness of British exports. This situation has now changed. Because of the government's own exchange rate policies and also because Lawson has chosen to use high interest rates to sweat inflation out of the economy, the pound is likely to remain strong.

Secondly, the growth of UK public spending has been controlled, although public expenditure has not been thrown dramatically into reverse as radical Tories hoped in 1979. The household sector has thus benefited from cuts in the rate of direct taxes. Despite continuing high unemployment (about 2 million by the government's figures in early 1989, probably at least 0.3 million more if revisions in the methods of counting are excluded), this control of public expenditure growth has been possible because of public revenues from oil, because of the large-scale sales of public sector assets in the privatization programme, and because of the higher than expected growth in revenues from indirect taxes like VAT as a result of booming customer spending. The government has thus been able to achieve a surplus of revenue over expenditure and borrowing without savagely cutting public expenditure, and has thus sustained the purchasing power of these regions heavily dependent on state employment and state benefits. Without sounding like a Tory apologist, the public expenditure policies of 1983–8 have been much less deflationary than an orthodox free-marketeer or monetarist would deem healthy.

Thirdly, since 1983 consumer credit has been allowed to grow unchecked. Without doubt this is in line with the government's policies for liberalizing the financial sector, but is directly contrary to monetarist imperatives to restrain the rate of growth of money supply. To control the creation of credit-money is the first objective for the monetarist if inflation is to be controlled. The

abolition of exchange controls in 1979 and the continuing programme of financial deregulation, culminating in Big Bang in
1985, have meant that credit controls are a thing of the past.
Many foreign lenders have entered the economy and the previous
close control over financial institutions and bank lending by
public agencies has ended. This leaves the government with only
interest rates to control the level of borrowing.

Fourthly, the government has done nothing to control private
sector wages. In 1979 Mrs Thatcher swore to have nothing
whatever to do with corporatism or incomes policies. Workers
were to be free to bargain, within the steadily increasing restrictions of industrial relations legislation, and managements to pay
what they could afford. Private sector wages have increased more
rapidly than either inflation or productivity growth for several
years.

The result is a consumer boom of the good old-fashioned
1960s type, stimulated by easy credit, tax cuts and inflationary
wage rises. The household sector has gone on a spending spree.
Rising inflation, balance of payments problems, an overheating
consumer boom, wage rises above productivity – we could be
back in the 1960s. Indeed we could, if we shut our eyes to the 2
million unemployed, to Britain's status as a major oil producer,
and to the fact that the government has simply given up worrying.
Rising inflation and growing balance of payments problems are
just a 'blip' and Mr Lawson is eager to assure the markets that a
dose of high interest rates will calm the domestic consumer
boom down just enough to have a 'soft landing' and not a new
depression. In early 1989 it looks like the stock market and foreign
purchasers of sterling believe him.

Having grossly overheated the most affluent parts of the economy, the Chancellor is now pleading for restraint. In the 1960s
a Conservative chancellor faced with the familiar phenomenon
of a consumer boom overheating and facing an economy with a
balance of payments crisis had a whole economic toolkit available
for macroeconomic management: foreign exchange controls,
credit controls, taxation policy, interest rates, devaluation, and
incomes policies. Incomes policies are now anathema (even the
Labour Party shuns them), exchange controls and credit controls
have been dismantled beyond repair, raising taxes has been

forsworn – the result is to leave Mr Lawson with one all-purpose tool of macroeconomic management, interest rates.

Interest rates have simultaneously to cope with inflation and domestic demand – the higher costs of borrowing squeezing household incomes and the growth of credit, and the resulting rise in the cost of living hopefully falling away as the economy stabilizes. One must wait and see. Mrs Thatcher's luck may last: she may be able to go to the country in 1991 without a new stock market crash, without a depressed property market, without a balance of payments crisis, and with inflation under control. This is pushing luck too far perhaps. But the opposition will not win in 1991 simply because the economy is in a mess. Even in that case, it will only win if it looks like a credible candidate for tackling the mess. Sneering at prosperity and wishing the economy into depression will not help, as Labour's leadership knows. Gloating at Lawson's difficulties alone will not help; offering constructive criticism based on viable alternative policies might.

One ought to be glad that there are strong points of comparison with the 1960s today. Better the problem of an overheating boom than some other scenarios. Yes, one can challenge the Thatcher government for failing to use the bonus of North Sea oil for industrial recovery and industrial investment. To be fair, however, no credible or viable policy was proposed – merely a good deal of ill-considered rhetoric. But we should be glad that we haven't had a regime daft enough to follow monetarist economic dogmas to the letter, like Pinochet's Chile. One should therefore be glad the Conservatives were inconsistent and had abandoned a monetarist-inspired strategy by 1982. There may have been strong elements of political opportunism in this, but, given the Labour Party's drive to make itself unelectable and the SDP split in this period, a monetarist Mrs Thatcher might even then have won the 1983 election and had another four years to carry on nailing the economy to the monetarist cross. Mrs Thatcher's conversion to a kind of economic pragmatism should, therefore, be welcomed and not just ridiculed – although her constant references to her consistency and her convictions make it very difficult to resist showing her up for the opportunist she is. The fact that the economy has grown rapidly for five years should be welcomed too, both in the sense that Britain would be much worse off had it not pulled out of the trough of the depression, and because no post-war government managed to sustain uninterrupted growth for that long. If growth based on consumer spending were to continue for long enough, then British manufacturers might feel confident enough to invest in new capacity, and there were signs that this was happening at the very moment Mr Lawson has raised interest rates to 13 per cent.

Japanese and German growth were hardly presided over by attractive politicians. If Mr Lawson did manage a British *Wirtschaftswunder* one would have to confess that, whatever its economic and social limitations, it would be a welcome and necessary process of economic recovery. Too many on the left and in what the Tories sneeringly call the 'chattering classes' can only carp at Conservative economic policy. They are fundamentally uninterested in the creation of wealth and the extension of the scope for enterprise. Personally I would sooner live in a successful, enterprising and changing society than in a stagnant one whose members are prey to *ressentiment* and who seek to solve all problems by the redistribution of existing wealth. Too many people on the left – and in the centre too – really enjoy gloating at stories of Yuppies losing their jobs and their Porsches. They would be horrified if the same relish were expressed at the redundancy of a well-paid manual worker. Views like these are rather comparable to the crazed revolutionary socialist in Belgium in the late nineteenth century who complained that the workers were becoming rich and soft – far from being starving as in the good old days, they could afford bicycles!

Too many people in Britain indulge in the politics of envy. They also miss the simple facts that a genuinely successful reversal of industrial decline will not merely create wealth, it will create wealthy people. Too many people in the Church of England, higher education and the political left simply cannot stomach what economic success *has* to mean – some people getting richer than others, fast. The Labour Party leadership has avoided that distaste for wealth and, in a striking reversal of attitudes, sees the necessity of pragmatism in respect of individualism and wealth creation. If anything, it is too sold on the reality of current 'prosperity' and overestimates the extent of the switch to individualism in core social values. There is a real difficulty here. Reversing industrial decline means shifting the balance of national income from consumption to investment, and from sectors like services and housing toward manufacturing. It means trying to keep the economy on a long-term course of steady growth, which means finding ways of making the growth in incomes correspond to that in productivity. The problem is that meeting the challenge of the 1990s involves things being rather tougher for the average employed worker than they had been in the mid-1980s. This is not because of some socialist austerity drive, but simply because we have been living above our means. It means that if we want a higher standard of living we have to invest to get it.

An active policy of meeting the problems of the 1990s (by creating an economy based on manufacturing industry and with high per capita incomes) is no less directed toward wealth creation and no less requiring of enterprise than the one that the Conservatives have claimed to follow. It is as well to remember that, and not to join the smug, and generally well-to-do, modern anti-industrials. Staging a British *Wirtschaftswunder* is what *all* serious British politicians have aimed at since the days of Macmillan and Wilson. Prosperity and economic success remain popular and broadly shared goals, not least because Britain is one of the poorest of the advanced industrial countries. A policy that seemed to offer a serious possibility of reversing industrial decline would command cross-party and cross-regional support were it advanced by a credible political force. Is that possible?

The invasion of compulsory suburban morality

Britain is fast becoming two nations and an unbridgeable gulf is growing between them. I refer not to North and South, rich and poor, but to those who follow the new *mores* of suburban respectability and those who don't. I am not a snob; I don't want friendly bombs to fall on Slough; I also don't want others to dictate how I should live. Suburban *mores* are tyrannical because they demand that the world be made safe and cosy; no shocks, no rough and tumble, no bad language. The new world of private estates, each house detached, no matter how tiny or close to the next, built in a variant of the new English vernacular – with or without half-timbering – and linked by the private car with the key sites of shopping malls and garden centres, is one for which I have little liking. It is, however, one many aspirant and upwardly mobile people like, and that is their own business. I am no cultural legislator, but equally I don't want to be regimented into any new suburban utopia.

That is now a serious threat. The right to shop without hindrance or upset is today fundamental in certain areas. And the government seriously contemplates banning the drinking of alcohol in public. Many cities and councils are introducing restrictive bye-laws, but the action of Basingstoke town council must take the biscuit. It has allowed an insurance company to own and run a substantial part of the town's shopping centre. The company has decided to make things 'safe' for shoppers by having its security guards exclude undesirables. I don't particularly like loud-mouthed and drunken kids, but I don't want them run out of town because they don't look 'nice' and don't hurry round quietly spending their money. Shopping centres turn what were public spaces – the streets of towns – into the interiors of buildings or private spaces. It is frightening that people set so little value on their own freedom of conduct. They don't recognize that they or their children might change and live differently; instead they are willing to put up with restrictions on dress, language and deportment enforced by security guards. One would like, as an experiment in social engineering, to give a shopping centre into the hands of the Hell's Angels and let them enforce their view of the world on the respectable. Bad language and mass public drunkenness are not particularly admirable, but we used to tolerate them. When we had a big navy (and we still did into the 1950s) our dockyard towns were full of drunken and half-riotous sailors. I can remember Union Street in Devonport as a long road of pubs, none too savoury on a Saturday night, even with the shore patrol. Respectable people knew they lived off the fleet and its sailors: they bit their lips, shut up and took the money. If our shopping centres catered for a semi-drunken and half-riotous mass their owners would do the same, but the drinkers, the punks and the yobs are a marginal minority who can be shut up without threat to business. Just to be safe, any teenage kid who doesn't conform can be silenced along with them.

CHAPTER 5

Economic Recovery: the Failed Contenders

IT WOULD BE NICE to be able to launch straight into my view of the alternative to Nigel Lawson's policies. But we have to clear our way through a thicket of competing 'alternatives' first. Even if all major social interests and political parties share the common goal of economic recovery, it is also the case that this consensus dissolves into squabbling factions the minute one turns to consider the means to that end. Several competing economic diagnoses and strategies have to be shown to be unsatisfactory before we can turn to the exposition of the one I think viable.

Who needs manufacturing in a 'post-industrial' future?

It will be obvious that I regard the manufacturing sector as the key to meeting the challenges of the 1990s. But this is to make a major assumption and one that is hotly disputed. It is not necessarily the case that a strong manufacturing sector is the core of a successful advanced economy. Many people, ranging from academic futurologists to commercial forecasters, believe that the era of manufacturing is, quite simply, over in the advanced world. Manufacturing is a strategy that suits newly industrializing countries (NICs) like South Korea or Singapore. Britain and the USA are the most mature advanced economies, but far from being in decline they are the leaders in the wave of the future. Gloomy prognoses stem entirely from looking at such countries with old ideas based on manufacturing. Countries like West Germany are not ahead on this view; they are locked into backward specializations like 'metal bashing'. The future international division of labour will be between the information-rich advanced societies, with information processing and service-based industries, and the less developed mainly ex-Third World countries that concentrate on manufacturing and assembly. The advanced world firms control forecasting and marketing through large data banks, they control product development and research, and they specialize in science-based industries like genetic engineering. Information banks, consultancy firms and science parks are the key units of this new post-industrial economy, not assembly lines and industrial plants. Control of advanced scientific knowledge and commercial data will generate high profits and high incomes for workers. The post-industrial economies will therefore maintain their dominance of financial markets and financial services. In a post-industrial economy with very high disposable incomes, sophisticated services and cultural products will take the place of physical goods as the prime objects of expenditure. Advanced leisure and culture industries will attract consumers throughout the world and contribute to positive balances of payments. 'Invisibles' are the core earners of the future, and physical trade will become supplementary to them and not the other way round as at present. The advanced economies will continue to control the international communications media and the dissemination of cultural images; they will therefore be able to manipulate and control the demand for advanced commodities.[1]

This is the strongly 'post-industrial' and futurological version of the argument against the saliency of manufacturing. But there are more pragmatic versions. Thus it is often argued that financial services, tourism, distribution, etc., will take the place of manufacturing in the British economy. We can offset the balance of trade in physical goods with strong earnings on invisibles. This argument simply accepts the rundown of UK industry and claims that we can compensate for it by strength elsewhere. In economists' jargon it means Britain has a comparative advantage in financial services and other marketed services, but not in manufacturing.

Usually this pragmatic version of the argument is less optimistic about uniformly high standards of living and high per capita incomes. It is recognized that services are labour intensive and that they often demand little skill; wages will therefore tend to be low. There will be a 'high-tech/no-tech' mix of advanced service-based industries and financial services, and a large service sector with mainly low-wage and low-skilled jobs. The highly qualified Yuppie banker buying a hamburger from a part-time, low-paid and ill-educated teenager working in a fast-food chain sums up the two extreme social types in this economy. The labour force will be more and more differentiated between a well-qualified and well-paid core of executives, professionals and skilled specialists with career jobs, and the unqualified and un-skilled mass, many of whom are part-time or only intermittently employed.

In such a society, egalitarian social policies make no sense. Quite different policies are required for those on either side of this fundamental divide – different forms and levels of provision in education, housing, health care, etc.: for the professionals and the skilled, a market-based, high-quality system; for the rest, a minimum-quality system provided primarily from public funds, in which resources are scarce and rationed and which aims to provide no more than a safety net. This view is quite close to current Conservative attitudes on social policy. It should be clear that it flows from an economic analysis as much as from anti-egalitarian prejudice. It assumes an economy dominated by labour-intensive, low-pay and low-productivity services. It assumes that such a radical division of labour between skilled/career and unskilled/casual workers is inevitable in a service-based economy. Social policy will reinforce this tendency to low pay by offering the majority of people a poor system of underfunded health, education and welfare, with badly paid health workers, teachers, etc. It is almost inevitable that, if one thinks in this way, one abandons the goal of a near full-employment economy with high per capita incomes and based on high skill and productivity in both manufacturing and services. This is the achievement and not just the goal of successful advanced economies like Sweden.

There are a series of issues here and the best thing is to separate them out into a series of distinct questions:

(1) *Is* there a decline in the saliency of manufacturing in the most advanced economies and in patterns of world trade?

(2) Can financial and other services meet the shortfall in the

balance of payments caused by the competitive failure of manufacturing in a country like Britain?

(3) Is there a meaningful distinction to be drawn between the manufacturing and the services sectors? On the one hand, are not many services aimed at manufacturing industry, and, on the other hand, are not a quite different but very large range of services aimed at the purchasers of manufactured consumer goods?

(4) Is not a great deal of the 'post-industrial' argument dependent on a restrictive view of what 'manufacturing' is? For example, genetic engineering can be regarded as manufacturing just as much as cotton mills. However, such new manufacturing relies on R&D and applied science, in both of which Britain is weak compared to its industrial competitors.

To begin with the first question. The idea that Britain and the USA are the leading economies because they are shifting toward services is a curious one. This shift is partly due to 'de-industrialization' following from competitive failure in manufacturing. Britain and the USA have a lower GDP per capita than the most successful major industrial economies like West Germany and Japan. Britain and the USA have large balance of payments deficits compared with large surpluses in West Germany and Japan. Moreover, world trade in manufactured goods continues to grow more rapidly than that in services. On all the important current indicators the successful manufacturing states seem to have made the correct choice.

For all its 'post-industrial' trendiness, the view that tries to separate information and execution, R&D and production, depends on an old-fashioned view of manufacturing. It conceives manufacturing as the physical execution of given tasks, and the model for this is the assembly line. We have seen, however, that a revolution has taken place in manufacturing that closely links conception and execution, integrates R&D and production skills, and in which highly skilled labour is central. It is less easy in a manufacturing system in which flexible specialization strategies dominate to envisage the division of labour between the information-processing First World and the assembly-line Third World. Information-based applications in manufacturing bring computers into the heart of production itself, as with CAD/CAM.

Most advanced applications of information technology imply the close interaction of computers and advanced engineering, as in robotics, advanced passenger aircraft, etc. Countries with strong traditions of high-quality engineering but that are not major computer producers, like Switzerland and Sweden, are adopting strategies that emphasize their expertise in contributing to producing integrated computer/mechanical systems. Japan, which combines strongly competitive computer and engineering industries, is thus favourably placed to maintain its lead as the most successful manufacturing nation. Those newly industrializing countries that have moved close to First World standards, like South Korea and Singapore, see the need to move into more advanced manufacturing sectors, and realize that to do so they must have a well-educated, computer-literate population. The idea that they will accept a division of labour in which they remain subservient to First World data processors is absurd. A country like the UK may have real problems competing to world standards in manufacturing, but we should not fool ourselves that manufacturing is ceasing to be the key sector of the advanced economies.

To turn to the second question. Britain is an economy highly dependent on the import of foodstuffs, raw materials, components and capital goods in an open international economy. In the past, Britain had a positive balance of trade in manufactured goods, and relied on 'invisible' earnings to provide a positive balance of payments – earnings from shipping and insurance, etc., helping to pay for goods like food and raw materials. The argument that 'services can take the place of manufacturing' is an ambiguous one, since it remains unclear how much of the manufacturing sector is going to remain in this argument. It should be obvious that the manufacturing sector remains important to Britain; we cannot be indifferent to its success or expect services to make up for any given level of de-industrialization.

What matters is manufacturing output and its value. Even if employment in manufacturing were to fall to, say, the same percentage of the labour force as that engaged in agriculture (3 per cent), that would not alter its salience to the UK economy. British agriculture has very high productivity by international standards, and it produces a large percentage of the food we consume. Thus the key issue is that industrial *output* continue to rise and the balance of trade in manufactured goods be favourable. Falling employment in manufacturing says nothing about that sector's role in the structure of the economy. It can have various causes: rising productivity, a cyclical depression, or structural 'de-industrialization'. Thus employment in manufacturing in Japan fell from 27.5 per cent of the employed labour force in 1973 to 24.7 per cent in 1980, but GNP attributable to manufacturing rose from 32.2 per cent to 36.8 per cent.[2] Evidence of 'post-industrial' tendencies based on percentages of the labour force employed in manufacturing evade the central point.

If 'de-industrialization' is not to cause serious problems in a hitherto highly industrial and import-dependent economy like Britain's, then other sectors must make a correspondingly larger contribution to employment, to GDP and to balancing the trade coming into the country. Britain would therefore have to either export primary products or persuade foreigners to buy its financial services or other marketed services in sufficient quantities to balance industrial decline.

Is there any evidence this can happen? We can dismiss primary products. Even with North Sea oil at peak production, Britain has balance of payments deficits. In the case of financial services, Britain will have to compete hard to keep its present share of the major markets. It will be difficult to do so if the manufacturing and trading base of the economy is eroded. International competition in financial services like insurance, bond-dealing, etc., is intensifying no less than in manufacturing. Tourism also presents a problem. Areas like London are close to capacity. The declining transport system, the creaking air travel infrastructure, and the grubby public face of Britain must both set physical limits to tourism and deter people from returning. Britons are also tourists themselves, and there is no guarantee of a positive balance in this area if domestic living standards remain high (there was a net deficit in 1988 it appears).

As for other marketed services, there are two problems: the first, as we shall see, is that many services are tied to manufacturing and, if that sector declines, so will the services allied with it; the second is that many services simply are not internationally tradable. The reason world trade in manufactures has grown faster than in services is that goods are easier to move and less subject to cultural differences and national tastes. Services like hairdressing are obviously impossible to trade, while many forms of consultancy or financial advice involve local knowledge and knowledge of the relevant national legislation in particular. Exporting services is subject to serious constraints of tradability and it really cannot be assumed we have any long-term competitive advantage in those marketed services that are tradable. To put it bluntly, a technologically backward and ill-educated country is ill placed to compete in the kind of up-market services that foreigners are likely to want to buy. The creation of an integrated European market in 1992 will make it easier for EC-based providers of those financial and other services that are internationally tradable to compete with domestic firms. German insurance companies, French accountancy firms, European-wide management consultancy firms, etc., will become eager bidders for a share of the British market. Britons' poor facility with languages and their provincialism will hinder their doing the same in Brussels or Frankfurt.

The third question has been the subject of some interesting arguments.[3] Manufacturers are obviously consumers of services, from quite ordinary things like contracting out the supply of washroom towels through to specialized advice, like computer consultancy. A large manufacturing sector in decline threatens domestic providers of services to industry. To give an example, Britain's major ports, although not manufacturing industry, were the centre of a complex web of manufacturing and services – of repair yards, ships' chandlers, brokerage firms, hostels for sailors, and so on. The decline of the major ports decimated their thriving hinterlands, leading to large losses of business and employment outside the docks as the cargo-handling facilities declined. Liverpool is the classic example: a thriving city was reduced to a wasteland. Similar effects can be seen on a lesser scale from the decline of the motor industry in the West Midlands.

Much of the successful service sector – the new warehouses and smart offices in the brand new developments off the motorway network in places like Swindon or Milton Keynes – consists of the distribution and maintenance investments of foreign manufacturing firms servicing the British market. A strong service sector is not only compatible with de-industrialization, it may be a direct reflection of it. As such foreign firms become major employers and traders they create an obstacle to policies which favour British industry. Restricting the import of German or Japanese cars, for example, even if it were possible, would raise howls of rage from Toyota or BMW dealers and their employees. We can see that a lot of the service sector is directly tied to supporting household purchasers of manufactured goods: TV repair shops, service centres for washing machines, prefabricated kitchen installation firms, etc. These services may provide domestic employment and opportunities for British business, but they are closely tied to the success of manufacturing. If the manufacturing sector is substantially foreign, that does not make Britain a 'post-industrial' economy in any sense other than that the core of manufacturing is not located here.

Fourthly, my final question. If high-tech areas like genetic engineering, computer-based manufacture and design, fibre optics, robotics, etc., are not 'post-industrial' but simply the latest wave of industrialism, even though they don't take place in old-style smoky factories, then Britain has no cause for complacency. We simply are not doing very well in such industries or investing enough to develop them properly. We have seen that British firms seem to have made poor use of such technologies and to have derived few benefits from them. We might also note that Britain has a huge balance of trade deficit in information technology. Far from being information rich and good at R&D, we are really below par for both. If there is a switch to new science-based industries, then our weak effort in civilian high-tech R&D and our abysmal record at producing scientifically trained and numerate manpower will cripple us. Far from being ahead of countries like South Korea and Singapore, we are behind them in advanced education; we have the lowest proportion of our youth in higher education of any advanced country in Europe. The future, whether advanced industrial or post-industrial, if it depends on knowledge and information, is likely to leave Britain behind.

I have dealt with this issue at length because it is the subject of so many illusions and so much clutching at straws in British debates on our economic future. We have no option but to try and compete in manufacturing, and across the widest range of industries, from high-tech ones to old-fashioned ones like clothing and furniture. We probably have to accept that, until our systems of education and industrial training, our R&D effort and our business strategies improve dramatically, then the less sophisticated and low-tech end of manufacturing will offer more scope for significant improvements in competitive performance. This is a very negative conclusion perhaps, but one better justified by the evidence available to us than is the myth of our moving into an era of 'post-industrialism' as one of the leading economies.

Why economic liberalism should not be given a second chance

The last chapter strongly criticized Conversative economic policy, and a central plank in that case was that economic liberalism is a non-starter as a strategy for economic recovery and industrial renewal. But some more argument is needed here. Economic liberalism is a tenacious economic doctrine and some of its most ardent advocates feel it has been misapplied or insufficiently applied by the Conservatives. Economic liberals trace their ancestry from the great Scottish eighteenth-century economist Adam Smith. In its modern version, championed by thinkers like Friedrich von Hayek, it captured the minds of many of the world's leading economists, central bank officials and leading politicians, in close combination with monetarism, in the later 1970s. It is not merely a 'right-wing' theory, although it is the official economic doctrine of the current Conservative government. Labour parties like those in Australia and New Zealand have adopted economic liberal ideas and policies.

Put in its simplest form, the guiding idea of economic liberalism is that it is individual economic actors – entrepreneurs and consumers – who make the best economic decisions if they are given the freedom to do so. Free markets are the best information system for an advanced and open economy with many independent economic decision-makers. When markets work freely, they provide neutral and impersonal economic information. If prices can rise and fall according to the economic laws of the market, then consumers can see comparative prices and decide to buy the cheapest goods (encouraging the most competitive producers) and entrepreneurs can see and decide what is the most profitable line of business and choose to enter it or stay in it. Free markets punish inefficiency and encourage enterprise. Governments and large corporations undermine this uniquely efficient information system when they use their power to interrupt the free workings of the market in the service of special interests. They protect privileges and existing ways of doing things. The more they interfere with markets, the less effective such mechanisms become, and the resulting 'imperfections' of markets force governments and big businesses to intervene more and more to compensate for blockages in their working. Administrative discretion and politically biased allocative choices come to be substitutes for the workings of the laws of supply and demand and the process of competition. Such administrative and interest-based decision-making actually favours the strong vested interests in society, not the ordinary consumer.

Like all successful social theories there is a big grain of truth in this. Adam Smith was a radical; he wanted to benefit the hard-working businessman, the ordinary worker and consumer, not rich aristocrats or officials who derived unfair benefits from state-sponsored monopolies. Mrs Thatcher likewise believes she is offering real power to the people, the power of economic choice. A centrally planned economy like the Soviet Union tries to replace the workings of the market and price system with a system of administratively set prices and resource allocations that reflect plan targets, that is, the priorities of those in power. We can see its inefficiency and unpopularity, its failure to deliver consumer goods and standards of living comparable to those in the West. The partial conversion of Soviet and Chinese reformers to economic liberalism seems to reinforce the rightness of Western economic liberal ideas. But we must be careful; 'liberalizing' a command economy is a long way from creating a free market.

The great problem with economic liberalism is the reverse side of one of its great virtues, theoretical simplicity. It is a highly schematic model of an economy, one that assumes that economic decision-makers are equally able to have access to information and resources and that the information that markets give to decision-makers is a sufficient guide for their actions. This happens to be less than adequate for complicated Western national economies, let alone Soviet-style systems. In Western economies there are three great obstacles to the workings of such a free market system.

The first is that economic decision-makers are not roughly equal. Big corporations have access to privileged resources and information, they can block entry to markets and they can set prices and terms of competition in their own favour. A model of an economy appropriate for small firms and individual consumers, none of whom is strong enough to influence the workings of the market, will not do for modern, highly concentrated corporate economies. What economic liberalism does in practice is to legitimate the actions of powerful economic agents, like corporations, by pretending that markets are free and open.

The existence of big corporations gives rise to economies in which a large part of economic decision-making is based not on markets but on the internal planning and administrative procedures of corporate officials. Because corporations are so large they need special actions of government to help and protect them, on the one hand, and government regulations are necessary to protect the public against the actions of corporations, on the other. The rise of collectivism and 'big government' has been in part to help and in part to control the corporate economy. The 'mixed economy' is an uneasy partnership between big corporations and big government. For good or ill, and both outcomes occur, the mixed economy is a fact of modern economic life. It is no more than rhetoric and sophistry to pretend that the corporate economy and the public management of that economy can be undone by piecemeal measures of liberalization. Mrs Thatcher's government has got no closer to a 'free' market than will Mr Gorbachev's reform programme, *perestroika*.

The second great obstacle to an efficient free market is that market information provides only a fraction of the information necessary for many important economic decisions. Market information is current and quantitative; it gives prices, current profits, and so on. But narrowly financial information as currently available cannot guide a decision about a major R&D initiative or an investment project in a new industry where perhaps there is as yet no market for the good envisaged and where the production of that good is some years away. Such decisions are a mixture of planning and gambling. They require forecasts of demand, likely markets, prevailing costs of production, and so on, in the future. An economy that, although not a perfectly free market, has extensive profitable opportunities to trade on current markets in which the immediately available financial information provides sufficient basis for decisions will tend to make long-run industrial investments less attractive and more risky. If markets in securities, national currencies, primary commodities and property offer profitable returns based on immediate information (for example, share prices), then those economic actors who want short-term profits and easily calculable risks will tend to give preference to them. That is what happens in the USA and Britain. In neither country is there a system of long-term industrial finance geared to the development of manufacturing like that offered by the close collaboration of big industrial firms, investment banks and state agencies in West Germany and Japan. In both Anglo-Saxon countries, leading managers tend to give priority to short-term financial information, but many of the factors in industrial investment cannot be summed up in the conventional forms of accounting and financial reporting. Far from being current and quantitative, the required information is often long term and qualitative.

A 'free' market in industrial finance, linked to a strong non-industrial financial sector, makes long-run industrial investment more risky and less profitable than short-term purely commercial and financial activities. This may not matter when industrial firms are very successful and are able to grow by internal financing and retained profits. When industrial firms start to fail or when some wholly new technology requiring massive investments beyond the existing earnings of firms occurs, then the problems begin. It is quite clear, for example, that ordinary financial markets would not underwrite a project like the Channel Tunnel or the Japanese information technology industry's Fifth Generation computer development programme without state support and guarantees, or in the latter case without the willingness of the major industrial banks to help if need be.

The third great obstacle to the creation of a free market is that competition is neither local nor national but international. It is quite correct that inefficient producers in an open international economy with relatively few barriers to free trade will suffer from foreign competition, however much national governments may subsidize them. The economic liberals have been correct to challenge government policies that underwrite competitive failure rather than try to get national firms to meet international competitive standards. It does not follow, however, that the way to do this is simply to open national firms to international competition, on the assumption that successful foreign firms have succeeded because of free markets at home. On the contrary, such a policy is suicidal where competitors do not operate free markets in industrial finance or *laissez-faire* regimes in areas like product development and the provision of services to industry. Competitors aided by their governments, by industry associations, by banks closely linked to the big manufacturing firms and by successful patterns of cooperation between industry, labour and the state have a real and not unfair advantage; that is how one competes in world markets.

Economic liberalism is thus a risky policy for a country with a weak domestic industrial base and a strong financial system that does not give either priority or privileged terms to its own manufacturing firms. Economic liberalism is a non-starter for policies of industrial revitalization because it exposes domestic firms to strong international competition without actively helping them to compete on the same terms as successful foreign manufacturers.[4]

Most critics of economic liberalism concentrate on three failings: first, the distributional effects of free markets, which lead to inequalities in income; second, the unfortunate welfare effects of the free market system, when the business cycle and long-run competitive failure of firms lead to unemployment; and third, the imperfections and failures of the market system in supplying certain goods or producing certain outcomes, failures that lead market actors to impose costs on everyone, like pollution, or failures that concentrate costs on the weakest who lack the resources to pay for a good, like health care. These market failures and imperfections may all be true, but to the convinced economic liberal they are tolerable blemishes if the free market delivers the crucial goods of economic efficiency and technological dynamism, economic growth and the investment to sustain it. The economic liberal can then argue, if this is true, that in the long run the wealth will be created to compensate for and to pay for these deficiencies of provision or those unfortunate side-effects, and that, if the market is granted sovereignty in all but special cases, then the exceptions like 'public goods' (clean air or defence) or specific cases of market failure (a bare minimum social security safety net for the destitute) can be tolerated and government action permitted to remedy them.

It is just this case that we must deny to the economic liberal. If we do not, then every form of public provision and public intervention has to be justified on economic liberal terms, as a necessary evil. However, if economic liberalism does *not* deliver the goods, if it does not make possible sufficient industrial investment to ensure economic efficiency, technological dynamism and economic growth, then the case for such free market policies fails. The ultimate standard of efficiency in our advanced industrial economy is not the free working of markets, it is the success and continued growth of the manufacturing sector. That sector has been the engine of modern industrial growth; it has not generally succeeded because of free market policies in industrial investment, and its success cannot be sacrificed to the dogmas of economic liberalism. In the end, dogmatic economic liberalism has no other standard of economic efficiency than the degree to which markets approximate to perfection. It is a 'formal' economic theory; that is, it judges economic performance by the extent to which a particular allocative mechanism – the price system in a perfectly competitive market – works without interruption. But almost all the economic goals we actually have are 'substantive': we want more wealth, better products, more leisure time, full employment, etc. We can never be satisfied with simply accepting whatever it is that efficiently operating markets, which happen to meet the economists' formal criteria, happen to deliver. An economic Dr Pangloss may be happy with economic liberalism. He may say that whatever the market happens to give is the best that can be had in the best of all possible worlds. Most of us measure economic performance differently and are willing to sacrifice economic theory to our substantive economic goals, to look at how successful economies actually succeed, and to try to find the means to such success ourselves.

When we look at how other countries succeed we must be careful, moreover, to distinguish between official rhetoric and reality, and between policies in one sphere and those in another. It is often pointed out that neither Germany nor Japan adopted 'Keynesian' doctrines of macroeconomic management after the Second World War. Both countries followed the sort of orthodox lines on fiscal and monetary policy advocated by monetarists and economic liberals today. However, neither set out to create or to follow free market policies in the normal economic liberal sense. Their governments were in fact highly interventionist and their corporations did not subscribe to free market ideas about the virtues of competition. Some commentators have tried to explain Japan's success in free market terms, but the evidence against such a view seems formidable.

In 1945, West Germany and Japan were shattered societies and economies. They rapidly rebuilt their institutions, but, far from creating free markets or promoting ceaseless change in economic institutions in the way a policy of open competition would imply, they tried to rebuild durable social relationships as part of the world of work and not merely rely on market, contractual or competitive relationships. In fact there is good evidence that this choice was correct, for not only did Japan and West Germany prosper in the boom years, but they adapted well to the turbulent international economy after 1973. Successful adaptation to international competition proves to be best accomplished where the strong continuity of efficient firms and effective institutions of economic cooperation has precedence over the free market. Technical change and productive flexibility within the firm are more likely to be accepted by those subject to change where those processes can be contained within stable institutions and thus not disorder the individual's whole context of social relationships. Thus societies, like Japan, whose managers and workers accept rapid economic and technical change do so on the basis of strongly conservative economic institutions and patterns of behaviour in the wider society. In 1945 the Japanese had the choice between re-inventing the old and adapting it to new conditions, and wholesale Westernization, adopting not merely American technology but American management practices and free market values. They clearly chose the former course. Enthusiasts for modern Japan will tell you that its central social institutions are the family and the firm. The family provides stability and support, which cushions members against the disturbing effects of change and makes them more adaptable at work. In the firm, the system of guaranteed employment and single-status membership for the core employees of large firms, and the perception of both management and workers of the firm as an ongoing social unit in which all workers have a stake, provide the certainty about the future and the active cooperation that make possible flexibility in terms of tasks undertaken and working methods. Management and workers are linked by common bonds of commitment and trust.

In West Germany things are obviously rather different. Nevertheless, the system of 'co-determination', which offered workers some say in German industry, the close and not purely commercial relationships between the industrial banks and major firms (with bank officials sitting on company boards), and the re-creation of strong regional governments, all provide parallels with the Japanese case. Clearly, the Japanese take manufacturing so seriously that they do not regard it as merely a 'business', just one way to make profits rather than another. The outlook, derived from economic liberalism, that a firm's business is making money is central in modern British management. The long legacy of economic liberalism, and not merely its modern 'Thatcherite' forms, has crippled management thinking, even into the era of big corporate capital. Economic liberalism is a non-starter not merely because of arguments about the efficiency of markets but because of its corrosive effects on the outlook of management and workers alike.

In a way Britain does need a change in economic values, not toward those of economic liberalism, of which it has had if anything too much, but toward an attitude that is better able to balance competition and cooperation, making money and making things. I shall soon argue that without new social institutions and new attitudes an active industrial policy will fail. The reason is that what we need to do most is to recognize that economic relationships are embedded in social relationships, a proposition which the idea of an automatically working market based on purely contractual relationships seeks to deny. We are junkies for the idea that the economy is subject to 'laws', that there are inescapable logics of economic and technical efficiency which impose the same choices on all those who want to survive the process of competition. If that were true, if 'laws' worked, then people would get punished for disobeying them. But the Japanese have ignored economic 'laws' and won. If the Japanese had believed the prevailing ideas about the 'law of comparative economic advantage', they would still be colourful peasants weaving silk. In fact there are economic constraints, but they fall far short of 'laws'. They leave a large area of choice about how to organize the economy – choices that can best be called 'political'. These choices involve not just market conditions or approved methods of financial calculation, since both treat the economy as a flexible realm of socially neutral technique, but also the complex ensemble of institutional relationships, ways of thinking and social contexts that allows some economic actors in some countries to do things that others elsewhere regard as impossible, or too risky, or simply don't think of at all. Unfortunately, all the business schools in the world can teach this lesson, but then managers in firms are actually stuck with the choices that are possible in their own society. They cannot invent a new social context by 'working smarter' in the firm. They may have to link up with other firms, with their workers and with public bodies to do that. The lessons that the economy is embedded in society and that the forms of economic organization adopted are as much political choices conditioned by society as they are the results of 'economic laws' have to be re-learnt once again.

Why Keynesianism and socialist planning cannot reverse industrial decline today

The reason that this process of re-learning has to start from scratch in Britain is that the two main forms of challenge to the sovereignty of the free market – Keynesianism and socialist planning – neither understand these lessons nor will suffice as the basis of an active policy of industrial recovery in the present context of British manufacturing failure. Keynesianism and socialism also believe in economic laws and inescapable logics of economic necessity. Keynesianism considered that market-based laws had important exceptions, and that there were techniques for modifying the action of these economic laws.

Keynes was a liberal. He wanted the market to remain as sovereign as possible – when it worked. When it did not, and to prevent the evil of a state socialist solution, it was permissible to interfere with the market using the powers of government. Keynes saw his measures for restoring effective demand, through deficit financing of public expenditure, as neutral techniques to be used by state officials; they did not involve radical changes in the wider society. Keynesian measures involved no active administrative discrimination between one firm and another or between one person and another. Managers remained free to manage, consumers to consume, and all the state had done was to alter the state of the market, by increasing demand, thus leading economic actors to make their own self-interested choices in this new state of affairs. Keynes was an economic liberal who saw the need for exceptions to orthodox 'sound' fiscal and monetary policies if the market system were to survive.

Keynesianism offered simultaneously a way of stopping socialism, while changing neither ownership nor the existing relationships of political power, and a solution to the pressing problems of capitalism. As a 'neutral' bundle of techniques of economic management it relied on one thing above all, that the managements of private firms would remain efficient enough to deliver the goods. The current crisis in the British economy is due not to a deficiency of effective demand, but to the failure of firms in the manufacturing sector. An economic policy that depends on adjusting macroeconomic aggregates and then relies on an effective manufacturing sector where managements make the appropriate investment and production decisions is less than useful when it is precisely those decisions that are the root of the problem. Keynesianism, in its traditional policy guise as demand management, has little to offer in an open economy in which domestic demand is growing too rapidly and in which an expansionary macroeconomic policy may simply suck in imported foreign manufactures. Keynesian 'hands-off' techniques are no substitute for an active, interventionist industrial policy.

Socialist planning might seem a better option in that case. If Keynesianism has failed, why not try the solution Keynes fought so hard to prevent? Let us ignore the political unpopularity of socialist centralized planning, and let us also ignore the watered-down versions of planning promoted by the Labour left called the 'Alternative Economic Strategy', which have got nowhere since when they were first proposed in 1973. We can say with some confidence that planning works best when setting overall goals and for a stable and predictable environment. It presupposes efficient managements that get on with the detailed job of putting plan targets into effect and it tries to make their job easy by making the surrounding economic environment certain.

Translate this to Britain in 1989. We face world market conditions characterized by unpredictability and uncertainty. We face managements who may well not make the right decisions. Planning cannot easily be superimposed on a very open and rather ailing capitalist economy. Too many of the major economic variables are not under control. Planners tend to try to protect and subsidize producers so that they don't have to face the full rigours of international competition. This may be possible in conditions of semi-autarky. It is a disaster in an open economy. One ends up in the same state as Poland is today, desperately uncompetitive by international standards and yet forced to trade in international markets to buy oil, raw materials and capital goods.

Centralized planning or some lesser substitute for it need not detain us further.

The arguments advanced against Keynesianism and socialist planning here are not meant to disparage either of these techniques of economic management as such. Keynesianism would have been beneficial in Britain in the 1930s, if it had been tried. Some state socialist countries have been efficient at building up strong industrial economies; East Germany is a case in point, if a very exceptional one. The point is that these techniques of economic management are answers to particular problems in particular circumstances. They are not magic solutions to all and every economic problem as some of their more naïve and enthusiastic advocates believe. They will not solve the problems of manufacturing failure in an economy open to intense international competition. Economic theorists – whether orthodox economic liberal, Keynesian or socialist – tend to argue as if there is only one right way of analysing any modern economy and just one set of policy solutions to economic problems. The analysis of the economy as embedded in the wider society, as dependent on its institutional context, and as subject to a range of political choices necessarily leads to a more complex country-specific and situation-specific account and to policies which are a mixture of techniques of economic management, institutional changes, and political changes.

A British MITI?

The case so far indicates the need for an active interventionist industrial policy and one sophisticated enough to give directions to individual firms. Some critics of British manufacturing, such as Keith Smith in *The British Economic Crisis*, argue that what we need is an equivalent of the Japanese Ministry of International Trade and Industry (MITI). MITI is often seen as the engine of Japanese manufacturing success, directing firms into new successful industries and aiding the rundown of sectors that are seen to be low value or threatened with decline. Japan's key ministry is thus supposed to 'pick winners'.[5] There are numerous reasons to dispute this, and David Friedman argues strongly against overrating MITI in his excellent book on Japanese industrial success *The Misunderstood Miracle*. Japanese success is not, he argues, to be ascribed exclusively to the state direction of industry or the efforts of the major industrial groups. The local regulatory role of local governments and economic associations, the thriving industrial districts, and the adoption of flexible specialization strategies on the part of the large and active population of small and medium-sized firms have played a very important role in sustaining Japanese success since the mid-1970s. MITI is not all-wise and all-seeing. Some of its policies have been at best ill-considered, some amounted to picking lame ducks, and some have been resolutely refused by Japanese firms. For example, MITI has advocated building up virtually from scratch a civilian aircraft industry to compete with the USA, or inappropriate and strongly resisted mergers and rationalization of capacity in the motor vehicle and machine tool industries.

Enthusiasts for MITI are, therefore, asking us to copy what is at best a fallible institution. But even if it were infallible, it is by no means evident that it can be removed from its social context and imported into a country like Britain. MITI depends on an intimate, informal and often highly corrupt culture of close contacts between the leaders of the major firms, senior government officials and politicians. It can give directives to individual firms because these are not seen as orders but emerge from informal and often unspoken agreements between elites. It can favour one firm rather than another. Culturally, that is simply anathema to Western publics; public servants are supposed to be neutral and to treat everyone equally fairly.

Even if the British public were willing to tolerate civil servants having the degree of administrative discretion that an active industrial policy on MITI lines in the British context would imply, could these officials make good use of it? British industry-level planning by central government has been plagued by a series of bad decisions. In the nationalized and quasi-public industries, a series of disastrous decisions have been made – for example, planning the expansion of basic steel-producing capacity on the assumption of optimistic forecasts for economic growth in the early 1970s, or the successive rationalizations of British Leyland/Austin Rover. A civil service that can completely mismanage predicting the demand for school teachers or that cannot get its road traffic forecasts right is hardly equipped to staff a British MITI. Far from 'picking winners', British industrial policy, in so far as it has existed heretofore, could be better called 'making losers'.

There is no reason to suspect that public officials will have better information or superior ideas about products, production processes or business strategies than the managements of firms. Even if the state has a large part in creating an environment favourable to investment and to industrial renewal, it is not evident that the state should have an equally active part in directing and determining the investments that are made. I shall turn in the next chapter to just what an industrial policy would look like that is not based on the direct state control of investment but that is strongly interventionist. Before I do, it is important to knock on the head one final major contender for an alternative industrial policy, protectionism.

A new protectionism?

Protectionist advocacy is currently very strong in the United States. Powerful industry lobbies, including sections of the computer industry, and some political advocates of industrial policy favour protectionist measures as a way of beating what they see as unfair competition. For many years Professor Wynn Godley and his team at Cambridge were strong advocates of protectionist measures in the UK.[6] A large-scale protectionist policy for Britain faces three major problems: first, it involves breaking with GATT and the Treaty of Rome if tariff barriers are to be high enough to work; secondly, given the extent of de-industrialization, it makes very optimistic assumptions about the speed with which British firms could extend capacity; and, thirdly, it tends to ignore how dependent Britain is on importing essential inputs for the domestic manufacturing sector. Britain simply lacks the economic strength to force favourable terms of trade on its own out of a country like Japan. Such protectionist measures also imply a triumph of Little Englander values and a retreat from European economic integration; something to be avoided on *political* grounds, even if it were to be economically possible.

There are few influential advocates of generalized protective tariffs in Britain today. But there are intelligent advocates of sectorally limited protectionist strategies, such as Professor John Williams and his collaborators.[7] They base their case on a persuasive analysis of manufacturing failure that reaches the very pessimistic conclusion that British industry cannot meet international competition without help. They are well aware that generalized protectionism is politically impossible, and that a 'siege economy' behind tariff walls is likely to be inefficient, simply putting off competitive failure for a time whilst imposing heavy costs on consumers. What they propose is that Britain's negative balance of trade could be virtually eliminated if the British market could be protected in just two industries – motor cars and consumer electronics. They propose that this would be done not by tariffs but by local content regulations, requiring, for example, that a car sold on the British market should incorporate 80 per cent of locally manufactured components. They also argue that this regulation would encourage efficient producers to

178

establish British subsidiaries, like the Nissan plant in the North East, which would quickly meet the need to extend capacity and maintain strong competition in the British market. While clever, the proposed policy has two main drawbacks: it would break EC rules, if it were applied to Germany, and so European cars could still be imported, and it presumes Britain can hold import penetration to these two most-affected industries. But import penetration is extending across a wide industrial range, and giving favoured terms to these two industries would both fail to stem industrial failure elsewhere and provoke cries for similar protection from other sectors. It is thus less a general strategy for industrial renewal than a stopgap for containing decline.

Each of these failed 'alternatives' represents a straightforward way of resolving Britain's economic problems. The post-industrialist thesis does so by saying they don't exist. The others do so by using established economic theories – economic liberalism, Keynesianism and socialism – and readily available policy instruments based on governmental action. Each has ultimately a simple recipe for recovery involving a single main policy. Economic liberalism expects the government to unblock institutional rigidities to the free working of markets. Keynesianism uses government fiscal and monetary policy to regulate effective demand. State socialism substitutes centrally planned priorities for those of the market through a system of planned targets for productive enterprises and administrative prices corresponding to those targets. MITI 'picks winners' and protectionism reduces foreign competition by means of tariff walls. The alternative I shall propose is much more complicated, but consistent with my view of the economy as embedded in social institutions. It is also one in which the state no longer plays the primary role; nor is it a neutral and technical 'delivery service' for economic policies. The state's role is secondary to that of the leading political parties and organized social interests, whose role is that of coordination and orchestration of cooperation. The alternative view I shall propose is, therefore, less an economic 'policy' in the traditional sense than a doctrine for the 'governance' of the economy.

The 'Future of socialism'

It has become almost obligatory in the Labour Party to debate the 'future of socialism'. Even practical politicians like Neil Kinnock and Roy Hattersley feel the compulsion, although cynics might say that the only future socialism has is to keep intellectuals out of harm's way debating its future. As a member of the Labour Party and having written extensively on socialism, I should explain why I have practised a self-denying ordinance here. This book is addressed to people inside and outside the Labour Party, to socialists and non-socialists. Most people couldn't care less about the future of socialism, but almost everyone cares about the future of Britain. This book tries to offer solutions to Britain's ills, solutions that start from the problems before us. When addressing the electorate a political party seeking office in a democracy like Britain is bound by two necessities. First, to speak to, and to try to act for, as many of the people as possible, not just certain interest groups closely allied with the party. It has to speak to people who may never vote for it, about difficulties that they feel, and offer solutions in a language they understand. Secondly, whatever its political doctrine, it must provide solutions to certain pressing and inescapable dilemmas, such as the decline in British oil production in the 1990s and the weakness of our manufacturing base.

Socialism has met neither of these necessities in the 1980s. Socialist language has become threadbare and exclusive. Socialist 'solutions' have become improbable. Socialism in Britain has become identified with nationalization and collectivism, and elsewhere with single-party states and command economies. Socialism has lost its hold on the language of liberty and the hope of a better future that gave it such persuasive power when it began to be a mass movement in the 1880s. Socialism will only renew its appeal and relevance if the party at least nominally committed to it can share in governing and be seen to be effective in doing so. I have tried to indicate how Labour can seek a road back to office and how it can address the major economic problems that face Britain. Providing a socialist 'pedigree' for such ideas is largely irrelevant; it is an inward-looking act, a seeking to propitiate the old party gods. Socialism will matter when it can speak to people other than socialists. It will be relevant when it finds ways to go forward within practical politics, starting with the issues that dominate the mainstream political agenda. A socialism that cannot start with the politics imposed by circumstances not of its making, that must hope to re-order the world in order to be relevant in it, is not worth speaking of.

Socialism has become identified with certain institutions proposed by competing dogmas; centralized planning, nationalization, and collectivist welfarism. Yet it began with certain principles about how society should be organized and how people should be treated, principles that contradict the ethos of competition and individualism preached by economic liberalism. Those principles still make sense, even if some of the institutions proposed to put them into effect do not. Competition is an aspect of social life, inescapable and even healthy, but it cannot become society's guiding principle without undermining the cooperation and solidarity that are necessary to any collective enterprise. Individuation ought to be the goal of any worthwhile social doctrine: only a truly independent individual can exploit and enjoy liberty. Yet it is difficult either to become an individual or to enjoy liberty without associating with others.

If socialists return to those principles, they will discover two things: one is that they are an effective criticism of the current Conservative philosophy; the other is that taking cooperation and solidarity seriously obliges socialists to work with others with whom they share certain objectives in common, to recognize themselves as members of a society and not masters over it. This latter recognition is essential, and the ability of socialists to speak to others who do not identify with them stems from it. That ability is the precondition for political success in a democracy. Socialism becomes an exclusive idea when it claims a monopoly of political virtue and political power. British socialism has never gone that far, but it has sought to 'run' things and order people for their own good. People do not want to be 'run' nor told what is good for them, whether by Sidney Webb's old-style Fabianism or by Roy Hattersley's modernized paternalist collectivism. A socialism that grows out of new strategies for social cooperation, that is enriched by collaboration with non-socialists in common political and economic enterprises, has some prospect of not being feared and rejected, and some prospect of finding a language that can speak without awkwardness to most members of society. The social pact at the core of the argument in this book is the starting point for such a socialism.

CHAPTER 6

A Strategy for Industrial Renewal

THE CHALLENGE FACING BRITAIN in the 1990s is daunting. A pessimistic analysis of industrial failure since the early 1970s and an assessment of the increasing economic difficulties that will result from the decline of oil production and intensified European competition after 1992 seem sufficient to encourage gloom. But is it worthwhile remembering that other countries have faced very severe economic challenges and acute economic crises and have been able to adapt. Japan, as we have seen, responded rapidly and effectively to the severe oil price shock in 1973. Sweden was very hard-hit by the Great Depression. It faced a particularly sharp depression in 1931–3, with about 25 per cent of the members of trade union benefit funds unemployed. The Swedish Social Democrats came to power in 1932, on the basis of an agreement with the Agrarian Party, and engineered a very successful reflationary programme which cemented the Socialists' long period of uninterrupted rule. It should not be imagined that this process of recovery was easy or stemmed from a pre-ordained consensus of the social interests in Sweden. Workers' and farmers' interests were not identical, and there was strong resistance from business interests and advocates of orthodox economic policies. Sweden was as bitterly divided on class lines as many other countries.[1]

Another pertinent example is the rise of the 'Third Italy', in such regions as Emilia-Romagna and Tuscany, during the 1980s. While the old industrial areas of the North stagnated, the new regions grew rapidly, based on new manufacturing sectors and small- to medium-sized firms. The new industrial growth of these districts is largely responsible for the spectacular performance of the Italian economy in the 1980s when Italy's growth rates out-performed the average for the EC. Rapid industrial recovery and spectacular industrial growth of new regions are thus as much in evidence in recent economic history as severe depression and regional stagnation. Countries like Italy show that dramatic changes are possible in regions and industrial sectors hitherto regarded as backward or marginal: the province of Modena, for example, jumped from nineteenth in the league table of income per capita in Italy in 1970 to second place in 1979.[2]

This does not mean that such changes will happen in Britain in the 1990s, merely that they are possible and that we *could* succeed if we tried hard enough. I shall argue that it is changes in the institutional context of the economy and in the political institutions sustaining economic cooperation that are essential to such a recovery. A successful industrial policy is above all predicated on changes in political attitudes and in social institutions. This is difficult and faces very strong obstacles in Britain, but it is not impossible. Above all it requires a new style of political leadership. This is required not just for economic reasons. It is also the precondition for the political success and electoral victory of an alternative government to replace that of Mrs Thatcher and the Conservatives. It implies the cooperation of the opposition political parties and also some of the major social interests.

One strong ground for optimism is that the terms of manufacturing success and industrial competition seem to have changed. Fragmented markets and flexible specialization strategies in manufacturing give a key place to small and medium-sized innovative firms, bound neither by rigid managerial structures nor by traditional divisions of labour. This offers the prospect of outflanking the highly concentrated, rigid and risk-averse major firms in British manufacturing industry. A new industrial policy does not have to rely exclusively on the sclerotic giant firms wedded to given markets and mass production methods. It is less bound by the union traditionalism which is still strong in big firms even after ten years of Mrs Thatcher. It involves new investment, large in aggregate but spread over a wide range of industries and smaller firms, and no longer concentrated in a few major 'make or break' projects. It therefore involves the central state less in 'picking winners' and can be accomplished with the support of a decentralized range of alternative investment funds and public agencies. It thus allows effort to be diversified without being dissipated and minimizes the risk of the inevitable failures that a large programme of new investment carries with it. It also allows a centre–left government to build bridges to the smaller business sector, making the smaller business firm the ally rather than the sworn enemy of the non-Conservative political parties.

Lest this latter point seem silly and pie-in-the-sky, look again at Italy. The communist regional government in Emilia and the municipal government in Bologna have worked actively with thrusting entrepreneurial firms, and won their respect.[3] The Catholic entrepreneurs of the Veneto have worked well with non-communist but still radical trade unions. Coalitions of social interests are *not* fixed and they can be changed by the right political attitudes and policies. Small manufacturing industry need not be wedded to Mrs Thatcher. Robert Chesshyre's *The Return of the Native Reporter* provides excellent anecdotal evidence of the dissatisfaction of small manufacturers with many of the present government's policies. It shows that smaller entrepreneurs feel resentful that little is done for them, that industrial finance is difficult and that the present economic system is stacked in favour of big business and the City. Obviously, they will not support an anti-business Labour Party, wedded to the big unions and to the public sector. But Labour Party policy is changing, as I shall show when I consider the Policy Review document 'A Productive and Competitive Economy'. Labour is no longer dominated by an anti-business and anti-competition mentality. If it can go beyond its recent commitments to a new economic outlook and also come to see the need for a new overall *political* outlook to complement it, then the prospects for the Party are no longer as bleak as the opinion polls would seem to indicate. As I shall argue, however, that is a big 'if', for it involves the Party in a new strategy of social leadership, making itself the pivotal force in a new coalition for recovery. Such a strategy involves dialogue with the other opposition parties and with social interests that are not traditionally part of Labour's 'camp'.

That sort of political change can, however, be accomplished. The Swedish Social Democrats triumphed over adversarial and class politics to build such a coalition in the 1930s. Improbable constellations of political forces and interests have provided the political foundations for industrial success in the newly successful Italian regions. The dissatisfaction with adversarial politics, the desire for more consensual economic and political relationships, and the retreat from political class identifications are all strong in contemporary Britain. What that mood needs is a new institutional and political focus.

Economic and political power has concentrated in modern Britain to a degree that is unacceptable to a large section of its population. A strategy that aimed to break that concentration would command widespread support. Big government and big business have cemented their grip during the Thatcher era. Privatization has generated a large sector of unaccountable private government. Industrial concentration has proceeded apace, as has the financial concentration of the City. A new political and economic strategy aimed at the decentralization of power and the parallel growth of cooperative networks of consultation and bargaining to lay down major agreements about public policy offer a way out of this tyranny of large, hierarchically managed and essentially unaccountable units. As I argued in the discussion of the constitution in chapter 2, political change in and of itself is unlikely to be the basis for a new policy of challenge to concentrated authority and the unaccountable rule of the manager and the official. Political change linked to economic revitalization, the building of new forums for economic cooperation and the generation of consensual policies is much more likely to succeed and to command assent for radical measures.

Radicalism is clearly needed if the institutional context of the economy is not to atrophy in a way that locks us into economic decline, and that allows a favoured few and some favoured regions to prosper as others stagnate and decline. It has to be a new style of radicalism: one that cuts across traditional party lines, one that is neither dogmatically free market, nor dogmatically collectivist. Such a radicalism cannot be painless, nor can a 'consensus' about policy simply reduce agreement to the lowest common denominator of 'moderation'. Moderate polices will not revitalize the British economy, if by 'moderation' we mean a policy of minimum change. Radical policies imply conflict, but not traditional class conflict. Many of those most favoured by the

Thatcher years will find them deeply disturbing and unacceptable and they are to be found on both labour's and capital's side of the fence.

That is why we need a broad coalition of interests and parties with a stake in change to make those radical changes possible. New policies that promote accountability, economic flexibility and social dynamism will be resisted by the elites that stand to lose. A management culture whose idea of accountability is 'blame the bosun' will be shaken by such change. A governmental culture based on secrecy and strategic leaks whose watchword is 'blame it on a junior official if you are found out' will be shaken to the core. Those in the Labour Party who see coalition and consensus as middle-of-the-road have little idea of the genuine radicalism involved in the new political style. They still dream of using central state authority as an engine of social reform and laws passed at Westminster as the source of social change. Far from being radical, that is a conservative strategy that fits together the oldest illusions of Labourism and the most ossified traditions of the British state. Such traditional Labour ideas are more in need of radical demolition than they are radical.

The strategy for reversing industrial decline thus requires radical political changes, because there is no new technical economic 'fix', no new smart economic theory and no new instruments for managing the economy by the neutral action of state officials. Political changes are necessary both because traditional economic policies have reached an impasse and because Britain's economic failure stems from a culture that has stressed the competition of firms and has neglected the coordinative and cooperative relationships necessary to sustain industrial investment and innovation.

The strategy outlined

A viable strategy can be summed up in two propositions:

(1) it is necessary to increase the proportion of national income devoted to investment in manufacturing and in the infrastructure of an advanced industrial economy;

(2) that investment must be in firms, products and production processes that meet the prevailing conditions of international competition.

Easy to enunciate, but difficult to accomplish.

Only central government macroeconomic policies can begin the process of redirecting national income from consumption to investment. Keynesianism, in the general sense of active macro-economic management rather than the restrictive sense of de-mand management, is not dead. Japan, as we know, invests some 30 per cent of GDP, Britain less than 18 per cent (1985 figures). Unlike Japan, Britain has a much bigger slice of national income taken up by state expenditure and a much lower rate of saving by the household sector. Japanese GDP is larger than Britain's and its manufacturing base stronger. Because of the different structure of the two economies, it may be difficult to aim directly to meet Japanese levels of investment. All the more important then both to try to increase the overall rate of investment by as much as is feasible and to ensure that the *composition* of that investment is shifted as far as possible toward manufacturing and to the infrastructure that supports it.

How can this be done? A good deal can be done by such traditional macroeconomic instruments as fiscal policy, if it is geared to new objectives. Most parties approach tax reform primarily with regard to the household sector: the arguments are largely about the fairness of tax burdens between different classes of taxpayer or about the overall burden of tax on households. The argument here is that a good deal can be accomplished by adjusting the government's fiscal policy to provide an appropriate structure of incentives to companies and households. The aim should be a system of tax allowances to companies that strongly favours manufacturing investment and, in particular, gives the greatest incentive to those firms that are adding to capacity. If business tax relief were concentrated on investment in the manufacturing sector, a gradient would be set up favouring it over other forms of investment. Even existing large British firms would have an incentive to favour the manufacturing aspect of their operations. In order to have premium allowances for new industrial buildings, machinery and R&D projects, many existing allowances that apply to all firms irrespective of sector and type of investment would have to be reduced and certain obnoxious allowable expenses like company cars or business entertainment would be simply scrapped. This policy would be quite orthodox and neutral between firms: it would apply to big conglomerates, major foreign firms and small workshops. Large manufacturing industry would have no cause to complain, nor would incoming or existing foreign firms.

To encourage the household sector both to save more of its income and to invest it in manufacturing, more radical innovations in tax policy and in financial institutions are needed. The current government has tried to widen share ownership and create a 'people's capitalism'. This has largely taken the form of selling shares in privatizations of what then become big 'blue chip' companies like British Telecom or British Gas, and hardly represents much help for the small or medium-sized manufacturing firm seeking new funds. Wider share ownership is not the way to promote the household sector's investment in new manufacturing industry. Shares have high transaction costs, smaller firms may not be quoted on the stock market or involve risks to small investors, and above all the stock market is a risky and expensive source of finance for the firms themselves.

Moreover, another part of 'people's capitalism' – the active promotion of a 'property-owning democracy' – militates against household saving. British tax policy has encouraged the household sector to borrow in order to 'invest' in housing and has given the building societies a privileged position in order to attract the funds of savers. Mortgage interest relief should be finally phased out, as should relief on private occupational pensions. The building societies are mutual institutions which successive governments have supported; their main effect has been to divert a large portion of national income into private housing. Why not give a tax-privileged position to mutual institutions that act as industrial lenders and give households allowances if they save through these? The state could thus encourage and underwrite a new range of industrial lenders: specialist industrial banks, industrial credit unions, cooperative finance agencies, etc. A combination of tax reliefs and government guarantees would enable such institutions to lend to the manufacturing sector at below the prevailing rates of interest.

The aim of fiscal policy would be to encourage all decision-makers in manufacturing to invest more. Two quite different policies are implied. One is a structure of simple tax allowances that would provide incentives to existing big companies. The other is a combination of tax allowances to households and policies to encourage a new type of investment institution. The latter policy would make industrial finance simpler for the small and medium-sized manufacturing firms. If a firm's assets were below a certain net value, it then could borrow from such institutions at privileged terms. It would thus be able to avoid the risks and costs of going public on the stock exchange, or the caution and high interest rates of the commercial banks. Small manufacturers frequently complain about the restrictive effects of their inadequate access to investment finance and the constraints of the existing institutional sources. If finance is a major brake on the small to medium-sized firms, such a system of tax-based incentives and new government-sponsored lending institutions could make a real difference to the growth of this sector and, if the experience of Italy and Japan is anything to go by, the whole economy. Other types of ownership of firms could also be encouraged by the creation of such new mutual financial institutions – for example, cooperatives or management/worker buyouts from big firms. Such tax policies would help to counteract the concentration of ownership, at the same time as they gave incentives to big firms to invest too. A tax policy of this kind would thus encourage all types of industrial growth, not penalizing the big firms willing to exploit tax advantages whilst providing privileged lending to small ones.

Such a policy to promote investment through tax incentives could only work if the macroeconomic climate remained propitious to investment. Deflationary policies or volatile changes in levels of domestic demand would undercut any system of incentives to increase domestic manufacturing capacity. This implies that the government should pursue an expansionary policy directed toward sustainable growth. It also implies that macroeconomic policy be pursued consistently over a period of at least ten years and that macroeconomic regulation be dominated by the needs of the manufacturing sector. The aim is to shift toward investment-led growth and a reversal of import penetration in manufactures. This is so important that all other objectives should be directly subordinated to it. A policy of this kind will inevitably prove difficult, since governments can control neither world trade nor, beyond a limited point, exchange rates, particularly if a major policy aim is to reduce interest rates and keep them low. Therefore, any policy designed to smooth out fluctuations in exports or domestic demand has to give priority to protecting investment.

An expansionary policy that aims to switch national income from current consumption to investment can work only if the household sector's income is not permitted to grow faster than the rate of growth in productivity and if that sector can be encouraged to save more. Without some form of control of household incomes, an expansionary policy will see current consumption rising as workers in the expanding industries push for higher wages, and it will be difficult to keep inflation low – something that is essential if the aim is a high level of investment at relatively low interest rates. For the moment, the precise form of control of incomes can be left on one side. The point is that it is a macroeconomic necessity. It is this key constraint on sustainable growth that makes a broad and enduring consensus on economic policy necessary. That consensus must be big enough to discourage consumers' revolts from turning into the marginal electoral swings that topple governments.

Controlling the household sector's income from employment is *the* crucial component of stabilizing the economy for an expansionary and investment-oriented long-term strategy. It is the one major economic variable that *can* still be controlled within the national economy. Its control, as we know, has been virtually impossible in Britain. Previous expansionary policies have stimulated current consumption and the economy has overheated due to excessive household demand, inflationary wage rises and accelerating levels of borrowing to finance current spending. This has always cut short periods of rapid growth in Britain. A long-run strategy based on growth in investment is no less threatened by inflationary wage rises, but, as it has to last far longer, it needs a stronger institutional framework for the control of incomes than a short-term 'wages freeze'.

In the 1990s public expenditure will remain under severe constraint and, in particular, oil revenues will probably fall. It will be difficult to keep direct personal taxation to the current low levels. A government adopting a new investment-based expansionary policy will have to counter thirteen or more years of under-investment in infrastructure and in basic public services. Pressures to spend more will be inexorable, and there will be strong pent-up demand for wage rises in the public sector, from such groups as teachers, health workers, local authority workers, etc. Whatever its preferences, a new government will have to have a clear set of priorities for public spending and it will have to have an explicit strategy for directing and controlling rising public expenditure. One cannot unlose more than a decade of restrictive public expenditure policies at a stroke. The argument here is that priority be given to manufacturing and infrastructure investment over current public sector spending on wages, transfer payments, consumables, etc.

Two factors may help to ease this constraint, but it is as well to be explicit from the start that priorities should be toward economic recovery in the long run rather than meeting pent-up demand for health, education and welfare spending. This will be very difficult for the Labour Party since so much of its propaganda has been directed toward criticizing underfunding in the health, education and welfare sector. Labour appears too often not to have thought out the priorities implied in the expansionary policy contained in 'A Productive and Competitive Economy' as against its wider plans to attack poverty and build up the welfare state stated in other Policy Review documents.

The first factor easing the constraint on public spending is that an expansionary policy will help to reduce unemployment, although it cannot abolish it at a stroke – particularly as the employment effects of an investment-based strategy may be less dramatic in the short run than a classic Keynesian policy directed toward stimulating the household sector's current consumption. However, if unemployment does continue to fall, tax revenues will grow as the unemployed enter the active economy and public expenditure on unemployment benefits and welfare will fall too.

There is thus a modified place for Keynesian arguments for an employment-boosting strategy; that is, it will reduce purely unproductive public spending and release resources for diversion to other sectors. Investment in infrastructure will help in this respect, since construction remains a relatively labour-intensive industry. Infrastructure investment is necessary as a complement to a manufacturing-based strategy; fortunately it has old-style 'public works' effects of a Keynesian type too. If aspects of policy that can be considered 'Keynesian' are introduced into a policy that aims at a 'supply-side' recovery based on manufacturing investment, then such macroeconomic policies do have a place, but they are ancillary to a strategy that is no longer an orthodox 'demand management' manipulation of the household sector's spending.

The second factor is that, if taxes have to rise to meet increasing demands for revenue and public expenditure, this may have positive effects if this distribution of the tax burden is shifted toward higher income earners. This is not a traditional socialist 'soak the rich' argument; it merely registers that higher income earners have benefited differentially from current tax cuts and continue to enjoy the benefits of a wide range of allowances available only to the relatively wealthy. Cutting allowances and making moderate increases in higher rates of tax would help to cut back the current consumption of the well-to-do. It is they who have the greatest propensity to buy foreign consumer durables and to spend abroad on such things as frequent foreign holidays. Cutting the disposable incomes and the tax-subsidized consumption of the well-to-do makes good macroeconomic sense. Most BMWs or Porsches are company cars. Taxes would act as a kind of substitute for protectionism. Cutting back on the over-stimulated demand of the wealthiest 10 per cent of households would reduce the demand for the sort of luxury goods that are differentially imported. If British industry became more efficient and its products more attractive this would not even impose severe 'hardships' or lead wealthy consumers to devote a higher proportion of their falling disposable incomes to foreign goods. Trying to keep the value of the pound relatively low would also both help British exporters and put a price premium on foreign goods. The aim, therefore, should be to withdraw the many tax allowances which primarily benefit the better-off and to raise the higher rates of tax up to the European average. Britain is no longer a high-tax country and there is plenty of room to increase the tax take from the better-off without worsening 'incentives' relative to our European rivals. It is also clear from opinion poll data that a large majority of the population would be willing to see higher taxes in order to have better public services. If such a tax reform were part of an explicit strategy to revitalize the economy, such a move is likely to be not unpopular.

One final point that may simplify the problem of simultaneously increasing public investment and countering the underfunding of spending on current consumption in the public sector is that the Conservatives' expenditure cuts have in many cases been so cheeseparing that relatively minor increases in spending will have quite dramatic effects. A health authority or a local authority may be faced with radical cuts in services to find quite minor sums; to save sums of often no more than £2–3 million, wards have to be shut and roads left unrepaired. Modest increases in current budgets may, therefore, have quite dramatic effects in the short run.

Another area in addition to taxation policy where quite orthodox central government policies may have dramatic effects is in public sector spending. Despite Mrs Thatcher's avowed ideology, the public sector remains large. The state remains responsible for a wide range of goods and services, and a planned programme of infrastructure spending can therefore have substantial expansionary effects. The planning and administration for infrastructure spending will be a relatively straightforward matter since both central and local government retain the capacity to initiate and administer such projects. Big government has not been turned into little government, despite Tory claims. Local governments in particular have the personnel and the project management capacities to put higher levels of infrastructure investment into effect. In fact many local authority planning and architect's departments are currently distinctly underemployed. The share of investment in government expenditure in goods and services fell from a high of 21.6 per cent in 1973 to a low of 6.7 per cent in 1982. In 1985 it stood at just 8.8 per cent.[4] As in the household sector, government spending has been heavily skewed toward current consumption. The Conservatives have controlled the inexorable rise in public expenditure that characterized the 1970s, but largely by drying up spending on capital projects.

Infrastructure investment in Britain as a share of GNP is now much lower than in other advanced industrial economies. It is not my purpose here to set priorities for infrastructure investment – that requires public debate and serious assessment of priorities by central and local government agencies. The point is that such investment will tend to be in construction. Investment in buildings and general construction has substantial effects on employment because it is relatively labour intensive and it relies on manufactured inputs that are still largely sourced from British suppliers. The construction industry is no longer as depressed as it was in the early 1980s, but it may suffer if the current property boom and office and retail building boom peters out and if the economy slows down under the impact of high interest rates. Infrastructure investment will both help to fill the gap and to keep up and increase employment and output in what remains a largely domestic industry. To expand infrastructure investment needs two urgent measures, however. One is to increase the supply of trained building labour by an urgent crash programme: there are currently severe skill shortages in the construction industry. An expansionary policy without such training measures will merely exacerbate such shortages and lead to rising construction costs as firms chase a diminishing supply of labour. The other is to encourage the development of capacity in the building-materials industry and to enhance its ability to source the more high-tech inputs to construction. If this does not happen, a British infrastructure boom will suck in imports to a greater degree in this industry too.

So far I have remained at the level of macroeconomic policy. It is clear that a policy that favours manufacturing and infrastructure investment requires the right sustained macro policy environment and that this means a stable and durable government with quite different policies from the present one. An industrial policy of itself cannot work in such an unpropitious climate as the present one. An industrial policy implies *continuity* in macroeconomic policy, ensuring that public agencies and companies are able to follow through initiatives until the completion of the investment cycle and that expansionary investment becomes cumulative and self-reinforcing. A successful strategy implies the difficult task of coordinated programmes of regulation of the economy both at the macro level and at the micro level of the firm. An investment policy is no good unless firms are able and encouraged to make the 'right' investment decisions. Boosting business confidence and investment is no good if the resulting expansions to capacity are not viable. We have seen that firms cannot be left to do this on their own; they need a regulatory framework that helps them to expand and in the right ways. A major increase in investment cannot be limited to known 'winners' and low-risk projects. If big business is left to pursue its own risk-averse strategies it will make at best the minimum extensions to capacity even in an expansionary climate. It will work profitably at high or over-capacity utilization, and leave the remaining demand to foreign producers.

An active industrial policy must thus complement an expansionary and investment-oriented macroeconomic policy. Industrial decision-making has to be a public policy concern, and economic management cannot concern itself merely with aggregate levels of consumer demand or industrial investment. That is why Keynesianism, like patriotism, is not enough. It does not follow, however, that an active industrial policy must take the form of the direct state control of investment decision-making. In a period of rapidly changing technologies, fragmented markets and changing patterns of international competition a *dirigiste* policy will simply lack the sophistication and flexibility required to respond in the many different ways that will be needed at firm and industry level.

The state needs to be the orchestrator but not the executor of industrial decision-making about investment. It needs to facilitate investment rather than to make it itself. Too often an active industrial policy is envisaged as a concentrated and centralized policy run by public officials and a few key quasi-governmental institutions. That is how the radicals in the 1974–9 Labour administration saw industrial policy. The state cannot simply create a few central institutions like the old National Enterprise Board or the proposed National Investment Bank and hope that they can provide the assessment of investment needs and projects necessary to a strategy of recovery in manufacturing. Such strategies will inevitably tend to favour industrial concentration and big firms, since they are easiest for a centralized body to deal with. Thus Labour's 1973 'Alternative Economic Strategy' envisaged coordinating the investment plans of the 100 largest companies and forcing them to increase investment by state fiat. We have seen, on the contrary, that the larger British firms are both cautious (rationally, given a long history of failure) and largely directed by short-term financial strategies. They are an unlikely engine to pull the whole economy onto a path of investment-led growth.

Local economic strategies

The industrial policy to be followed should therefore decentralize investment decision-making as much as possible, should give a significant place to small and medium-sized manufacturing firms and should be fairly catholic about the type of industries in which investment is encouraged. This is a new strategy for Britain, one that aims for a model of industrial policy closer to that in the Third Italy than that taken from socialist planning strategies or popular perceptions of MITI.

As a first step the government should try to encourage two new types of institution to promote investment and local economic cooperation. First, it should work actively to encourage a range of new investment institutions on the model outlined in my discussion of taxation policy above. Pluralism in provision here has an obvious advantage. A range of alternative funding institutions offers more choice to those seeking investment funds, it encourages competition between alternative lenders, and it allows learning about diverse markets and industries. The more successful lenders will, therefore, tend to become models for the whole sector, in the way that the more successful building societies have stimulated the development of the whole mutual sector in housing finance. A range of central government, local government, quasi-public and private mutual agencies (such as industrial credit unions) would provide a wide mix of lenders, central governmental agencies acting as lenders for major strategic initiatives and to plug gaps in provision. Some direct government participation in alternative lending is desirable, just as exclusive state control is undesirable, not least because it provides direct experience through central agencies of the complexities, problems and needs of such a sector.

Secondly, government needs to act as a 'matchmaker' in creating public/private networks of consultation and cooperation between firms. Bodies like industry associations, local collaborative agencies combining local authority representatives and firms, etc., need to be encouraged and set actively to work to provide advice, information and common services for their industries and localities. As we shall see, the more enterprising local authorities have already tried to do this in a very hostile climate and with minimal central government support. A sympathetic central government would find a great deal of enthusiasm and expertise waiting to be tapped, both in the local authorities and in business firms. The principle here is to build up a 'public sphere' for the industries and localities concerned, encouraging cooperation between public agencies and firms, and creating hybrid public–private institutions. Collaboration and dialogue are of the essence here; *dirigisme* and anti-business sentiments are actually long since past in the more go-ahead Labour local authorities. Only if new investment institutions can plug into such networks will it be possible to acquire the kind of robust and informed base of knowledge on the part of both firms and investment agencies required for local coordinative planning.

Britain retains a wide range of industrial sectors and, as we have seen, big firms and high-tech projects are only one route to industrial recovery, and a very risky one at that. Concentration on such firms and projects has a tendency to become a self-fulfilling strategy. Central state agencies inevitably tend to work best with the major firms and to support the rationalization of industries in their favour. One should reject theses about industrial development based on hunches derived from the 1950s and 1960s claiming the inherent advantages of big firms and economies of scale. This obsolete common sense of industrial economics leads inevitably toward concentrating investment on a few major 'national champions' in what are perceived to be 'key' industries. It restricts public investment funds and intervention to this large-scale sector. The economic rationale for picking a small core of 'target' industries has declined. Trends in industrial organization and manufacturing strategy are now more pluralistic, and they favour a strategy of going for a wider range of options and more plural choice. The old hunches of indicative and sector planners are less relevant now and were often inappropriate even in the 1960s, when state-sponsored rationalization created fewer options and fewer firms. This is true not only in Britain, but, for example, in the rationalization of the textile industry in the Lyons region in France – which created fewer and less adaptable firms, offering a less flexible and less varied range of specialist products.

A policy that seeks to encourage investment and promote competitiveness at international standards across as many types of firms and sectors as possible has definite advantages. It reduces import penetration across a broad range of industries if successful and it minimizes the risk of failure in any given sector or locality. Traditional industries like textiles and clothing, and furniture can be turned round and made success stories in advanced industrial economies.[5] In Italy, for example, both sectors are very successful and major export earners. They are not inevitably doomed to fall prey to competition from the NICs, since labour costs are not the crucial factor, nor is price competition the dominant issue – except at the bottom end of the market. Both industries, and many others like them, desperately need both public assistance in investment and the collective provision of those industrial services individual firms cannot afford to create. However, both industries are organizationally diffuse and characterized by many small firms – and the same is true in many similar sectors, like light engineering. Investment choices here depend on the detailed knowledge of the potential of firms, new processes and products, and the state of markets. Only given such knowledge can one avoid a rigid conception of the nature of these industries, and superficial assessments that write them off as inevitably part of Britain's industrial 'sunset belt'.

To know which sectors, localities and firms have potential in such diffuse sectors is a task beyond the scope of central government. Central government can only find out what is and is not possible in such areas if the right networks of information, assessment and policy formulation are created at sector and local level and are then able to feed back measured conclusions to central government agencies as a guide to policy. The knowledge required cannot be derived from aggregate statistics or conventional forms of financial reporting alone. To assess the potential of medium and small-sized firms, which are good investment risks and which bad, requires informed and qualitative knowledge about their potential. This involves knowing not only markets and industrial processes, but very often the character of key personnel. It is the sort of knowledge local public agency officials, industrial association staff, and alternative lending agency officials acquire gradually by long immersion in the trade or region. It is a knowledge that cannot just be found on a balance sheet or presented through the conventional forms of financial reporting. It requires both trust and judgement. The great economist Alfred Marshall termed it 'intimate' knowledge for just this reason. Such knowledge is only rarely found among central government officials or the analysts in national banks and the City. It is therefore essential to create decentralized networks of information gathering and lending if one is to pursue a catholic policy of broad-based investment for industrial recovery.

Firms will not participate in such networks if they are mere talking shops. Access to alternative finance provides an incentive, as does the prospect of public assistance to build up common services. If firms see the advantages of such common services as forecasting, exhibition centres, promotion and public relations for the industry or industrial area, common facilities for sharing expensive capital equipment (like CAD bureaux) and hire services for other equipment, then they will begin to contribute actively to the 'public sphere' of their industry or area. Local authorities can contribute to this by specialist advice, like research by the economic strategy unit on the local economy, and by training business people in how to build up patterns of cooperation, based on best practice elsewhere.

The main aim of industrial policy at the local level should be to help rebuild industrial districts in areas that have suffered industrial decline and to promote cooperation to sustain further growth in the successful manufacturing areas such as those in the South East. Industrial districts cannot be legislated for; in the end only the active and successful cooperation of public bodies, firms and local labour can do that. The creation of a local and industrial 'public' sphere, and the building-up of a district by active local collaboration, means that, if successful, that district will tend to survive. Owners and managers enter into a different relationship with their locality. Local councillors and officials will come to realize the centrality of the area's manufacturing base and its needs. Firms are more likely to stay and to fight to survive if they are assured loyalty and support from other firms and the local authority. An organized industrial district becomes tenacious and resilient; it derives its strength not just from cheap finance or common services, but from 'political' attributes, like cooperation, common concern and the existence of forums in which to debate problems and devise solutions. Industrial districts without these 'political' attributes have often suffered decline precisely because there was no economic organization or information above the level of the firm.

Such a policy as that proposed here inevitably rewards local success and local activism, since alternative investment funds will inevitably flow toward the successful, the organized and the articulate. Any policy that relies on local initiative and building from the base up will tend to do this, and it would be a bogus egalitarianism that would gainsay it. Contrast this policy of building up industrial districts with the regional development policies pursued in Britain in the 1950s and 1960s. Such policies relied entirely on cheap infrastructure and investment allowances and other financial incentives to encourage inward investment to depressed areas. Firms were attracted solely by bribes, had little connection with the area, and either closed or left as soon as conditions became difficult. The policy advocated here encourages firms with strong local loyalties and the will to fight along with local government to preserve output and employment.

Such ideas sound strange in Britain, because we don't expect firms to behave 'politically'. The contesting ideologies of the free market and statism have squashed all such thinking to the margins. For the free market dogmatist the firm is sovereign, both free and isolated. Labour left dogma still finds the idea of active support for and collaboration with 'private' business abhorrent. Such old left ideas of local intervention involve 'rescuing' failed firms for the sake of labour as the sole legitimate objective. That this often means buying out failure on relatively generous terms, rather than investing in success, has, however, gradually sunk home with all but the most inflexible in the ranks of Labour's local economic strategists. Much better, in particular, to give money to groups of enterprising workers who want to start producers' coops than to try to convert into a 'coop' the labour force of a unionized firm that showed complete indifference to the cooperative idea before it failed and who were previously content to be waged workers. Local economic strategies based on 'enterprise boards' that practise mini-versions of the 1974–9 Labour government's nationalization of failing firms are both economically and politically counter-productive. Ultimately they impress and appease only that section of unionized labour that wants undemanding secure waged employment. Labour has that support already. Labour will never win the support and respect of local manufacturers, getting them to stick with a district through thick and thin, and at risk to themselves, if they pursue such strategies.

However, Labour local strategies and local economic policies are now very different and are changing out of all recognition. No one could accuse Glasgow of being hostile to private business. Even the GLC's Greater London Enterprise Board, after some unfortunate experiences with local 'nationalizations' and some flirtation with 'popular planning', came to see the need for careful investment assessment and to adopt different strategies than simply to take ailing firms into public ownership. Many other Labour local authorities see the need for new strategic thinking on local economics and are aided by able economic development workers. Nottingham City Council and the West Midlands Enterprise Board are good cases in point. Labour local authorities have tried to set up industry-wide networks like Local Action for Textiles and Clothing and the Motor Industry Local Authority Network.[6]

At the local level, Labour councils, concerned about the erosion of their industrial base, are willing to be pragmatic. But Conservative policy toward local government has stifled any attempts to compensate for national policies by alternative local economic strategies. Central government policy has both restricted the finance and the autonomy of the existing local authorities, and abolished an entire tier of local authorities such as the GLC and the West Midlands County Council. Active strategies are thus enfeebled. The Conservatives see this as stopping the waste of ratepayers' money by unaccountable local socialist councils. But many councils learned the error of their ways, and what Conservative action has cut off is the freedom to learn and experiment. Labour councils are to be reduced to centrally policed local welfare delivery agencies, burdened with duties they cannot fulfil and cannot afford. The result of cutting off active experiment is to weaken such local authorities' most intelligent and upbeat side. Labour is struggling to put a credible face on local government – to counter such disasters as the Militant and ultra-left control of Liverpool, the mindless and unjust persecution of Maureen McGoldrick* by Brent Council, and so on.

In Italy, regional and municipal government remains strong and distinctive. All the major parties have their local bases and their distinct versions of local economic strategy. The municipality of Bologna has served as a shop window for Italian communism. Successful public regulation of the economy in Italy has rested with those local and regional authorities able to take the initiative. Local government in Britain, however, has become little more than the executor of central government policy. Strong political centralization in the hands of Whitehall and strong industrial concentration in the hands of the largest firms have between them managed to wreck both local political and economic autonomy. The effects of this centralization are clearly damaging to British manufacturing industry. If Labour mounts a campaign for local government on the need to restore local autonomy to permit local economic regulation to assist manufacturing, then it will provide a new and clear rationale for this much-maligned level of authority – one, moreover, that indicates that Labour local government is interested in not merely spending local wealth but making it. Labour's local government image is

---

* Mrs Maureen McGoldrick was a successful and respected junior school headmistress whom Brent Council tried to dismiss on grounds of 'racism'. The only evidence for this charge was remarks she was alleged to have made on the telephone to a junior council official. That anyone could be dismissed on the basis of such evidence is shocking: it allies the Labour Party with rank injustice.

so tarnished that conducting such a campaign becomes central in terms not only of the requirements of economic policy but of Party propaganda.

Labour has been stressed here because it remains the key challenger to the Conservatives in the centres of industrial decline. However, policies for alternative investment institutions and an industrial 'public sphere' with networks of collaboration and common services between firms are important for *Conservative* authorities in certain regions of the South East too. They desperately need to unlearn as much free market dogma as Labour authorities do collectivist dogma. If they do not, then their manufacturing sectors will be priced out of the market by the very effects of rapid and uncontrolled growth in the South East that the Conservative Party at Westminster is so eager to praise. Manufacturing in the South East is threatened by shortages of development land, acute shortages of skilled labour, and strong pressure on wage costs stemming from the high cost of housing and competition from other sectors for workers, and the labour shortage is compounded by the barriers to the entry of new workers to the region constituted by high housing costs. The case for a *Conservative* local economic strategy for manufacturing is clear enough but, even if local councillors were in favour, such activist policies would be condemned and countered from Number 10.

Labour's economic policies

In early 1988 the Labour Party published the results of the first phase of its review of its major policies. The document, 'A Productive and Competitive Economy', emphatically rejects the traditional collectivist shibboleths that have helped to make Labour unelectable. The contrast with the bankrupt and *dirigiste* statism of the Labour left's old 'Alternative Economic Strategy' is striking. Clearly, much of this is due to the energy and intelligence of Labour's trade and industry spokesman Bryan Gould. It recognizes that the object of economic policy is to promote an internationally competitive private sector that is capable of producing growing levels of wealth for Britain. It also recognizes the crisis that is likely to face the British economy in the later 1990s when oil production declines and the effects of the current under-investment and under-provision of training bite home. Labour policy will have to meet this crisis by working to enable firms to meet foreign competition by being more enterprising, efficient and innovative. We cannot, however, rely on free markets to improve competitiveness. Unregulated markets do not of themselves ensure satisfactory levels of industrial investment, product innovation or the supply of appropriately skilled workers. The state must both create a favourable macroeconomic climate for increased rates of investment and encourage the microeconomic developments which ensure that investments lead to satisfactory products. The aim is a medium-term industrial strategy that both sets targets and stabilizes the economy so that these targets can be pursued through market fluctuations.

The document envisages a mixed economy and explicitly rejects any attempt to counter Conservative privatization with renationalization. It raises the questions, however, of how privatized public utilities are to be regulated and the future of forms of 'social ownership'. It makes clear that there are forms of control over such utilities other than nationalization, and that the Morrisonian public corporation is not the only type of public ownership. Thus the report envisages that a new type of highly regulated, but not state-owned, company may have to be created in law to apply to these privatized utilities – 'the public interest company'. Similarly, it recognizes that public ownership and state ownership are not the same thing, and that there are a variety of forms of social ownership, including cooperatives. It is through a combination of public regulation and the promotion of social ownership that the 'mix' is to be restored to the mixed economy and private sector managements rendered publicly accountable.

What is wrong with this outline framework for a new industrial strategy is that it fails to face up to two key problems. One is the *political* obstacles to a successful policy of economic recovery and the political measures needed to overcome them. The other is the failure to see the extent of the problems represented by privatization. We should confront this last point first.

By the early 1990s a vast shift in ownership and economic power will have taken place as the major public utility and publicly owned manufacturing companies are privatized. The only real equivalent to such a large-scale and rapid change in ownership engineered by the state in British history was the dissolution of the monasteries by Henry VIII in the sixteenth century. As Hilaire Belloc, an acute critic of collectivism, was at pains to point out in his book *The Servile State*, the sale and transfer of the monasteries' lands created a new class of wealthy landowners who were both virtually unaccountable within their domains and had great influence on the policy of the state. The ferret-faced, shifty-looking Tudor bagmen who stare down from the walls of many a stately home are the 'ancestors' of many of the grandest noble families of today. Privatization today also threatens to place such unaccountable private power and excessive public influence in the hands of a new stratum of managers. It is difficult to see how British society can be called 'democratic' when so much highly concentrated, hierarchical and unaccountable decision-making power is put in the hands of the senior managers of major privatized companies like British Telecom or British Aerospace and in the hands of the heads of the large conglomerate firms created by the merger booms of this century, especially that of the 1980s.

It is as inadequate to respond to this by arguing for a 'stiffer regulatory framework' as it is to propose wholesale renationalization. The latter, even if it were politically possible and economically feasible, would simply re-create big *public* bureaucracies, nominally answerable to ministers, who in turn are 'answerable' only to the backbenchers of their own party. The issue here is large-scale hierarchical and unaccountable government – whether it be nominally 'public' or private is a secondary matter. It is about time that Labour and radicals in the opposition generally took the problem of the power of the big corporations seriously. Labour in the past has been all too sympathetic to big companies and it has made very little of the Conservatives' failure to open up markets to competition by an active anti-concentration policy, reducing the control of major sectors by a few giant firms. The Tories are actually slavishly pro corporate capital; Labour could be more anti without appearing to be converted to economic liberalism. The answer to this over-concentrated private government of the economy is not to preach the 'free market' but to offer a new doctrine of the public government of the corporation. That means not merely 'regulation' but active intervention to change the way that companies are organized and run *from within*. The aim is not merely to revitalize the 'mixed economy' by checking its dominance by big private corporations, but also to try to restore the accountability of management for its actions to members of the company.

Let us begin putting some flesh on the bones of Labour's proposed public interest company (PIC). Suppose that a special section of a new Companies Act creates such a new legal status, what should the legislation contain? First, it should explicitly describe the company as charged with fulfilling a *public* function, that of providing a service. The fiction that the PIC is a 'private' company, whose management is 'free to manage' and answerable only to its shareholders should be denied. Most PICs will enjoy a monopoly or quasi-monopoly position in relation to most consumers. That they are privately *owned* does not mean they should not be publicly accountable and liable for the very last detail of providing an efficient and economical service to the consumer – that is, publicly *controlled*. Private 'ownership' is a paradoxical notion, since the corporate property rights in question are a creation of public policy.

Each PIC should, therefore, be directly accountable to an independent inspectorate for each industry area, like gas or telephones. Each PIC should have a two-tier board: a Supervisory Board, composed of one-third shareholder representatives, one-third employee representatives directly elected by secret ballot (and not nominated by the unions) and one-third community and consumer representatives, nominated by the industry-specific consumer council but also perhaps by members of, say, the Association of Metropolitan Authorities, would have the duty of appointing and overseeing a Management Board responsible for operations but subject to an overall strategic framework set by the Supervisory Board. The PIC would have an explicit legal requirement to have due regard for the interests not only of shareholders but also of employees and consumers. The PIC Supervisory Board would be obliged to create boards for any area agencies or specialist operating divisions within the company, creating a federation of self-governing sub-companies.

All PICs would be given a series of public duties as a condition of enjoying a quasi-monopoly position, and a quasi-public status through their right of access to local authority land and public roads, etc. (i.e. publicly granted legal privileges). If a firm qualifies for PIC status it is certainly a 'blue chip' company, a safe investment for shareholders and, if run with reasonable efficiency, able to make profits from a virtually captive market. While it must be prevented from milking the consumer, this means that the existing management and shareholders should be willing to concede a good deal to enjoy this privileged position. Legislation should, therefore, specify the following conditions:

• that the company create a comprehensive system of co-determination, with workers' representation and consultation in joint councils at all relevant levels, from the shop to the area division;

• that the company establish a single employee status with the same holidays, pension rights, terms of service and social facilities – on the model of the most progressive Japanese companies;

• that the company give a Japanese-style lifetime employment contract to all permanent full-time employees and that it employ no more than 30 per cent part-time and casual workers – this would force the company to find efficient alternative work for the employees affected if it wants to 'rationalize';

• that the highest salary paid to an employee have a differential of no more than six times that of the lowest and that this apply to members of the Management Board;

• that, whenever the company declares a dividend, 10 per cent of the total is given in new shares to be divided evenly between the employees and consumers and held in trust by the employee and consumer representatives on the Supervisory Board, the future income from such shares being used either to increase the joint holdings of the two groups or for employees' and consumers' welfare;

• other new share issues to require a 60 per cent majority of the Supervisory Board;

• that the Supervisory Board conduct and oversee an active policy of 'internal privatization', that is, to contract out all possible services and activities either to cooperatives of former employees, the Board making loans based on its share of dividend where necessary, or to firms with full public mutual company status (see below) – in this way PICs would deconcentrate slowly to the minimum core necessary to perform the central service.

In other words, the best response to privatization is to require firms to behave as socially responsible self-governing associations. A government has a very strong lever precisely because such firms require legal privileges and public policy support. Changes in company law are necessary not only to convert privatized firms into bodies that are more democratic and more accountable than the nationalized industries from which they sprang, but to deal with the growing crisis of accountability of business corporations generally. Modern big companies are relatively recent, and they are creations of company law. The Companies Act of 1862 made it easy to form modern limited liability companies, and after the 1880s British business began slowly but increasingly to take this form. The limitation of shareholders' liability to the value of the amount of share capital subscribed and the grant of corporate status (giving certain legal immunities to managers as agents of the corporation) were considerable privileges granted by the law and, therefore, by the public. Most managers and shareholders think of them as just a natural part of 'property', but managers would feel very uneasy if they could not hide behind the facade of corporate personality, as would shareholders if they were liable to the extent of their assets for any failure or fault of the company. Corporate property is 'privileged' property and should be seen as such. Before 1862 being a shareholder was a risky business and before the 1850s the formation of a private company was a relatively difficult affair.

When corporate status and limited liability were granted in 1862, an elaborate series of measures were adopted to ensure the accountability of companies to their shareholders and for the protection of the public. Companies had to keep a register of shareholders and to file public annual accounts. More importantly, the company was to be seen as a democratic republic of shareholders. The shareholders were to elect the board of directors, who were to be accountable to the shareholders at an annual meeting. This structure of company government and accountability, adequate in the 1860s when the primary interest to be safeguarded was that of the investor, has, quite simply, broken down. The 'republic' of shareholders is no longer credible: boards of directors are virtually self-perpetuating oligarchies, supported by major institutional shareholders. Answerability to the shareholders is, therefore, hardly any check on a company's policy. What the oligarchy fears most is a hostile takeover bid, and they anxiously watch their stock market rating and dividend levels.[7]

If we want to make companies internally accountable we must change who they are accountable to and for what. In addition to the PIC above, a new Companies Act would create a new legal status – the public mutual company (PMC) – to add to those of the existing limited company and public limited company for all firms with more than 1000 employees or a capital of £100 million (these figures to be the aggregates of any group). All PMCs would have to show they had complied with the conditions set out for such status within five years or lose the privilege of limited liability. The object of a PMC would be to convert the company into an effectively democratic self-governing association (the intention of the 1862 Act) and to give recognition to the mutual interdependence of the major interests in modern economic life.

A PMC would be required to democratize its governance and widen its ownership. Like the PIC, it would have a two-tier board, in which the Supervisory Board appoints and oversees the Management Board. In this case the Supervisory Board would again be composed of one-third each of shareholders, employees and community and consumers' representatives, with the difference that the first two groups would each nominate half of the third in the first instance (subject to independent arbitration by a new regulatory body, the Companies Inspectorate, if either side thought the other was 'packing' their community share of the Board). The employees' representatives would be elected directly and by secret ballot. Again the company would be under a direct and explicit obligation to consider and give proper regard to the interests of employees, consumers and the community in formulating policy – and, of course, to be subject to legal penalties if it could be shown to have acted detrimentally to any of these interests. The Companies Inspectorate would be empowered to give special legal aid to any employee or member of the public who could establish *prima facie* a serious grievance.

The company, like the PIC, would be expected to give 10 per cent of the value of any dividend in the form of share issues to be held in trust by the employee and community representatives in equal parts; as with the PIC, these shares would have normal voting rights to be used by those representatives. Again, new share issues would require a 60 per cent majority approval by the Supervisory Board. All share options should be equally available to all employees and of equal value to all.

Like the PIC, the new company would be expected to create a single status for all employees, although it would be subject to less stringent conditions on lifetime employment and the reduction in differentials (granting such status to all employees who had a record of five years' continuous employment with the firm – a policy of contracts or sackings to defeat this would be illegal – and allowing for differentials of eight times the lowest full-time wage). Again the PMC would be required to introduce a comprehensive package of co-determination procedures below board level. In the case of groups of companies, each subsidiary company would be required to have its own two-tier board. The employee and community representatives on the main group Supervisory Board would be nominated by the corresponding members of the supervisory boards of the subsidiary companies. As far as employee and community representation is concerned, the group would become a federation whose highest forum is elected from below, in contrast to the top-down authority of the present relations based on ownership.

In and of themselves such new legal requirements would not convert the big firm into something other than a profit-seeker dependent on its performance in the market. What it would do is to open the firm up to wider internal scrutiny and to force it to take notice of a wider range of interests. If it be objected that lifetime employment would threaten management's right to hire and fire, the answer is that it would. It might also increase senior employees' commitment and sense of belonging. It has had little adverse effect on the performance of those Japanese firms that practise it. The same can be said of co-determination and workers' election of representatives to supervisory boards. British management and unions will alike scorn 'industrial democracy'. That is why it should be entrusted not to the unions but to a free and secret vote.

Britain will have to have some measure of industrial democracy to comply with the directives for harmonization of EC company law. One can say emphatically that those countries that have adopted comprehensive co-determination measures, like West Germany, can hardly be called economic or industrial failures. The idea, widely scouted, that British citizens will not give time as consumer or community representatives on supervisory boards seems to be answered by the relative success of most representative governing bodies of such institutions as schools or colleges and by the apparent willingness of many Britons to undertake voluntary public service and to run the voluntary sector. In any case, those arguments are virtually all specious. They are cloaks for management's 'right to manage' and for the unions' right to have a monopoly of the representation of labour. Neither right is defensible in and of itself. Management was originally intended simply to fulfil the express directions of the shareholders, not to make company policy on its own and virtually without consultation. If the unions refuse to take an active part in co-determination, they have no right to sabotage it.

The above measures would render companies more accountable. Two other measures would act against the excessive concentration of company ownership and the very active programme of mergers and takeovers which enhances that concentration. First, *all* mergers and takeovers, mutually agreed or hostile, should be referred to a reformed and strengthened Monopolies and Mergers Commission. The Commission would consider each case in the light of a general directive that the presumption be 'no', unless a positive case of advantages to the *public* be proven to the Commission's satisfaction. The dealing in the shares involved would be suspended until the Commission had reported. Secondly, the reverse of the old Industrial Reorganization Corporation, the Industrial Decentralization Commission (IDC), should be established. This body would have two major tasks: to help finance and assist management/workers' cooperative buyouts from large companies, on the one hand, and to advise on and to assist large firms to devolve to become a federation of semi-autonomous sub-units, on the other. The IDC would encourage and advocate the deconcentration of large firms, pointing to the advantages of substituting ongoing relations of cooperation for hierarchy and showing how market relations between semi-autonomous sub-units could convert centralized firms into active federations of the kind that favour flexible specialization strategies.

If these changes in company law seem draconian, the answer must be that the very strong and active intervention of the public power is necessary to check and to compensate for the growth of private and undemocratic economic power. Mere 'regulation' will not do. The Conservatives have wielded public power in a draconian fashion to force unwanted, unnecessary and often economically irrational privatizations. At the same time they have regarded private corporate concentration with indulgence, and adopted a complete 'hands off' policy. That the 'shareholders know best' and should decide, and that 'managers must have the right to manage', are the only answers offered by Conservative ministers to all public policy issues in this area. But shareholders and managers are only one interest in the complex issues surrounding the governance of firms. The big firm is a social product, its property rights are created by the public power, and 'its' actions are of legitimate interest to employees, consumers and local communities. There is no reason why the profits of shareholders should come before the rights of employees or the effects on local communities (when, for example, big firms choose to close successful privatized manufacturing firms they have acquired solely in order to benefit from lucrative property deals). Such misuse of the authority that stems from ownership of property is a weakening of social obligations. Public power is therefore justified in being used to redress the balance.

Pussyfooting changes will not tackle the political issue of the governance of corporate private property; only a strong commitment to make firms behave in a socially responsible way can alter the balance of power in the direction of greater economic democracy. The measures advocated here involve the strong intervention of government through legislation, but they emphatically do not involve the direct state control of industry. On the contrary, they place powers in the hands of citizens, who are then expected to take active steps to ensure the responsible governance of companies. They are, moreover, powers of super-vision and of the legal defence of certain interests; they require supervisory boards not to 'run' the company, but merely to oversee its administration. Managers are still required to manage and to devise appropriate strategies. The power to manage re-mains and, indeed, the duty to manage well is enshrined in law. The difference is that managers are to be accountable for how they exercise that power and discharge that duty. The proposals advocated here are certainly radical, but they are far from being utopian. The opposition to them rests on the indefensible case that the incremental growth of unaccountable privilege should be converted into a 'right', that is, that 'company policy' become publicly unquestionable and that senior management need answer to nobody but those few owners big enough to make their voices heard.

The political conditions of industrial renewal

'A Productive and Competitive Economy' is written in a calm and even tone, like a paper for a university seminar. And that is the main thing wrong with it. A sense of urgency, of unease at the growing crisis of Britain's manufacturing sector, and of determination to rouse both the Party and the country to do something about it are simply missing. It could be written for Sweden, or some other relatively successful country, so relaxed is its tone as it discusses under-investment and the future decline of oil production. A party with an appropriate sense of urgency and a taste for good old-fashioned propaganda would have called it 'Britons Awake!'

But to call it that requires something more than a politician like Churchill or a writer like Chesterton, with a taste for the grandiose; it requires a willingness to make the changes in the settled routines of politics necessary to achieve such national mobilization. For that is the issue. A party government trying to make headway by legislative reforms and state macroeconomic action is simply inadequate to the task in hand. Labour has little chance of becoming a strong majority government, nor, if my analysis is correct, will conventional government action alone address the economic problems we face. The active cooperation of major social interests and economic actors at both national and local levels is a precondition for economic recovery, and this cooperation must be more than grudging and short term. A party government simply cannot command that depth of support for long enough. Labour can expect the support of no more than a fraction of the major social interests. Indeed, it has made little effort to ensure that the key organized social interest associated with it – the trade unions – is willing to adopt the new policies and practices that are necessary to a long-term programme of recovery. An incomes policy, for example, is still a taboo subject for the Labour leadership, which has proved unwilling to tackle the commitment of a number of the major unions to 'free collective bargaining'. Some of these unions, in the private sector in particular, still think they can benefit their employed members in private and successful firms far better by following the present free-for-all policies in industrial relations and wage bargaining. Tory policies are acceptable to too many unions, even if they would like some repeal of Conservative industrial relations legislation, for purely self-interested reasons.

Many of the major British firms likewise can see no need for such policies of active cooperation. They are doing well enough. They enjoy the support of the existing government, with its outright commitment to managements' unquestioned and un-challengeable power to manage in the private interests of their own shareholders. If they are strong enough, present policies allow them to take over the competition and rationalize domestic markets to defend their own market share. If they decide to relocate within Britain or invest abroad they will face no challenge from the state and they are accountable to nobody else. That is the law of the market, and so be it.

Labour's economic policy document implies a strategy of *social* mobilization if its economic objectives are to be attained. Labour will be unable to get such a mobilization started, let alone see it through, if it cannot present itself as a dynamic and modernizing force capable of calling forth the energies of the whole nation. Labour is still not a one-nation party. It is a regional party, with a social base in certain substantial but declining social interests – welfare claimants, public sector workers and the trade unions. To become the political core of a strategy of social mobilization for national economic goals centred on the revitalization of manufacturing, the Labour Party itself will have to change and to modernize.

Labour must be seen as a party capable of orchestrating a credible industrial strategy, a party capable of both working with and leading the private sector firms and the unions to change manufacturing techniques, management strategies and working practices. Without a broad base of sustained effort stretching from senior ministers to local councillors, such a strategy cannot have the depth and energy necessary to take effect. Without a genuine willingness to collaborate with, to bargain with and to compromise with other parties, with business and with other social groups, Labour cannot lead. It cannot expect others simply to follow a *Labour* programme, to be bound by the Party Conference, and to accept that they must take orders.

In advancing its new economic policy, Labour must accept the political logic of that policy – that it makes demands not only of the main actors in the British economy, not only of its own governmental skills, but of its own capacity to act as leader of society. Its failure to do so is because to pose the problem involves seeing that the Party is currently unfit for such a task. It needs first to be convinced of the need to undertake it before it can call forth the energies to renew *itself* in order to do so. It will take a colossal effort to convince the Party that it must regain the dynamism and the flexibility to lead the nation. It lacks the confidence to call credibly for national renewal. Mrs Thatcher, in her own dogmatic way and in the service of her own narrow and divisive solutions, has that confidence, which gives her a genuine advantage over every other party and every other Conservative leader. The advocacy of an industrial policy is not just one piece of the policy jigsaw, just one of seven equal 'policy reviews'. It is the core component in a strategy which proposes the economic renewal of Britain and presupposes the political renewal of Labour.

I stress leadership and conviction not in order to steal Mrs Thatcher's clothes. It is not a leadership like Mrs Thatcher's – which is authoritarian and dogmatic, which merely says 'no', which cuts and closes, which permits the indulgence of private self-interest – that we require. The task is infinitely more difficult than merely using government power to force others to behave as one's own prejudices dictate. Government leadership has to call forth cooperation and commitment from the wider society, giving direction by making dialogue possible, helping to orchestrate bargains and overseeing them so that they stick, showing alternatives by argument, and so on. Switching the balance of national income from consumption to investment depends on political commitments to that objective well outside the governing party, and in particular a willingness to accept some current sacrifices in the interests of longer-term goals, to forgo immediate personal benefits for the public good. It runs counter to the Thatcherite ethos. Such a switch involves workers being willing to accept wage rises limited to no more than the rate of growth of GDP overall or the rate of growth in productivity in their firm if it is higher. It involves the management of firms being prepared to risk making new investments and being confident enough of public support to do so. Even if firms are offered incentives to invest and privileged rates of interest, 'economic' inducements alone will not make them behave in this way. A public policy of priority to manufacturing growth and widespread public support for it, institutions and forums where management can influence that policy and be heard – in a word, political inducements – will have much more effect. This will prove difficult with the risk-averse managements dominated by a stock market mentality we have today in most major corporations. Only if they see a massive consensus in favour of such a policy, a consensus cemented by institutions of dialogue and bargaining, and a consensus set to last, will they change their attitudes.

Labour will not get back to power because it ditches the old policies that made it unelectable. It will not get back because it convinces the electorate that the economy is in trouble. It will not get back because it convinces the electorate of the poverty and misery created by Mrs Thatcher's 'reforms' of the welfare state. The electorate can believe the economy is in bad shape and sympathize with the victims but still doubt Labour's capability to govern. Labour will probably not get back at all if it sees its role as a party government with a majority sufficient to ensure that only its own ideas prevail. It can get back only as a party of social and national leadership, credible because it looks outside itself and seeks to work with and listen to others. That means above all being willing to work with the other opposition parties and with those organized social interests outside its own camp.

Simple pragmatism dictates that Labour recognize two facts. First, even if Labour were, through some disaster shattering the Conservatives, to form a majority government on about 42 per cent of the vote, it would be a weak government. It would be weak because the tasks facing it are beyond the scope of orthodox governmental power and because it would command no more than a fraction of the social interests whose active cooperation is necessary if a strategy of economic recovery is to work. As a purely party government it would be buffeted by international pressures and bedevilled by a 'wait and see' policy on the part of firms and unions as they withheld commitments on the assumption that Labour would spend only a short term in office. Secondly, if Labour faces the need to cooperate with the opposition parties even if it were to win a majority, as the above point implies, it ought to take them seriously and start talking to them about policy now. The issue is not merely one of the need for electoral pacts, it is one of the need for a new style of government when elections are won. Accepting the logic of Labour's economic policy commitments means accepting ongoing dialogue with the other opposition parties and also a need to reach out to their supporters, showing that Labour intends to govern in a new style even if it were to have a majority. Doing this might help to make the Party electable; it would certainly reduce the fear in voters' minds about 'letting Labour in' if they vote for one of the other opposition parties.

What is proposed here as a political precondition for an industrial policy is that:

(1) national macroeconomic policies be established on the basis of a bargained consensus between the governing party/parties and the major social interests, that these policies be subject to

review by dialogue and negotiation, and that the parties to the bargain actively cooperate to make sure that the commitments they have made are honoured by their members – central to this agreement would be an ongoing incomes policy to set the norms governing wage settlements;

(2) that a range of local and sectoral institutions be established, paralleling the national collaborative forums, to build a 'public sphere' for industry, involving the active collaboration of firms one with another and the support of local and regional government – these local/sector forums would work to provide common services, to stimulate industrial development, and to oversee the alternative public/private hybrid investment funding institutions.

These national forums and local networks would make policy by dialogue and bargaining. Central and local government would play a pivotal role in organizing these forums, overseeing bargaining and orchestrating consensus, but they would not dictate policy. Central and local government would have to accept that policy would emerge from complex processes of consultation and bargaining, and that government's role was that of leadership not the imposition through state authority of party policy endorsed by a 'democratic mandate'. Far from weakening government, such processes of policy formation would strengthen it.

In essence this involves adopting analogues of the processes of national economic policy making found in, for example, Sweden, and of the processes of local economic regulation found in, for example, the Third Italy. This does not mean slavishly copying Swedish or Italian institutions. One lesson of starting such processes of national collaboration and local cooperation is that distinctive institutional styles emerge gradually as the leading politicians and the social interests learn to work together. If such processes *worked* in Britain, the results would be unlikely to resemble Sweden or Bologna.

The objection to such political conditions for an industrial policy is well known. It is 'corporatism'. Conservatives will claim that corporatism led to an era of weak consensus politics that nearly ruined the British economy. Trade unionists will object, like the Tories, that incomes policies cannot work. You cannot buck the 'laws' of the labour market, so free collective bargaining is best. The left will object that this smacks of class collaboration and is really just SDP ideology in new clothes. More careful academic voices will hint that the reason corporatism failed in Britain is because of the peculiar character of British trade unions and because Britain is just too big a country for such corporatist networks to function.

The truth is that Britain has never tried corporatism seriously.[8] We cannot draw lessons from the 'failure' of an experiment we never made. British politicians *talked* about collaboration between the major interests, they set up forums like the NEDO where industry, labour and the state could *talk* to one another, but they did not have collaboration high enough on the political agenda to do more than talk. One reason for this, as we have seen, is that it would have involved both Conservative and Labour politicians abandoning the 'Westminster model' and all the prejudices and privileges of party government that go with it. To decry incomes policies because they failed is curious, as if there were one type of incomes policy and one set of goals that it can follow, such that if you've seen one you've seen 'em all. Incomes policies in Britain under Macmillan, Heath and Labour were all short-term expedients designed to cope with a particular crisis of macroeconomic management, such as wage inflation. The unions saw them as temporary crisis expedients and were willing to accept them as such on the condition that normal collective bargaining was resumed as quickly as possible. No politician seriously tried to implement a long-run incomes policy as a tool of ensuring sustained growth, as a *permanent* device of macroeconomic stabilization.

In truth, the real objection to such 'corporatist' policies is not that they are old and tired, but that they are new and threatening in the British context. Despite Mrs Thatcher's claims, such processes of collaboration and bargaining have never been a strong part of the British political culture. The UK is a very centralized state and its traditions of government have never favoured corporatist consultation, let alone collective policy making. Mrs Thatcher has broken up whatever half-hearted institutions still existed. For her, centralized state authority (accountable to the voters every five years) and the management of the private firm (accountable to the annual shareholders' meeting) are the only two centres of effective decision-making in society. Their will must be unimpeded – everything else is weakness and produces only inefficiency, evasion and fudge.

Mrs Thatcher's claims seem credible to many, especially those who remember the 1960s and 1970s, but the real fact is they were years of weak centralist government rather than of corporatism. Wilson and Heath threatened industrial relations reform but lacked the authoritarian purpose necessary to realize it. The Labour governments of 1964–70 and 1974–9 entered into incomes policies reluctantly and of necessity, but lacked either the political will or the means to make sure that the bargains struck were followed through. They allowed the unions to make loose promises that they could not enforce on their members and the unions cooperated with government through immediate economic necessity rather than active commitment to a new regime of wage determination. If governments of the 1960s and 1970s were weak, it was because they stayed within the centralism of the Westminster model and yet lacked political drive. Mrs Thatcher has the latter and she has used the highly centralized power of British government to her own purposes. But curiously, for all her authoritarian *Sturm und Drang*, she finds herself back with the phenomena of the Heath and Wilson years – inflation over 7 per cent and private sector wages out of control. Yet she still insists that incomes policies are useless and has tried to render them unthinkable. She has succeeded remarkably well, since Labour is currently too scared even to think of them.

The reason Britain has failed to adopt corporatist bargaining is neither because it is too big nor because of its peculiar union structure. Britain is too big because it is too centralized and has ignored the possibilities of regional and local decentralization of government and economic regulation. Britain's unions lack discipline not because there are too many of them or because of their preference for local bargaining, but because national governments have not felt strong enough to insist that bargains stick – and the reason for that is that they have remained party governments prey to voters' revolts. The main reason corporatism has failed to take in Britain is because of our peculiar state structure and political culture. Both the major political parties have unquestioningly accepted the Westminster model. They have been committed to the idea of authoritative party government. A majority in Parliament gives a party both legislative sovereignty and sole control of the executive. In theory, therefore, the party should be able to carry out any reforms or policies it desires. Policy is a party matter, provided the voters elect the party. The changes determined by the party leadership are imposed as the lawful will of the sovereign, administered by a centralized and highly obedient civil service.

Who needs consultation? Why bargain? If changes are needed, wait for a general election and then return to office if lucky. The absence of regional governments, the limited autonomy of local government, the isolation of firms in purely competitive and market relationships, the sullen commitment of the unions to their own affairs, all enable party governments to ignore the need to consult or bargain. Mrs Thatcher has enjoyed the stroke of luck to be favoured with a weak and divided opposition. In 1979 she won by the classic means of voters rejecting a government, as with the old adage 'oppositions don't win elections, governments lose them'. In 1983 and 1987 the adage was reversed: Mrs Thatcher won by default, triumphing over a divided opposition and, in 1983, an unelectable Labour Party. The result is that she has enjoyed the electoral security that is the real condition of authoritarian party government. She has been able to dispense with consultation and bargaining completely and get away with it. Her opponents will never enjoy such advantages in government and, to the extent that they have a narrow majority and are electorally vulnerable, they will be weak.

Yet one can see what an addictive drug party government is and what illusions it creates in the minds of opposition politicians. The Labour left has lived in hope of 'another 1945', and decisive reform through legislation and government action. Roy Hattersley denies the need for PR because it would prevent majority governments able to use governmental power to implement exclusively party policies. Dr David Owen, for all his talk of inter-party collaboration, constantly postures as a 'Minister of the Crown'. The politicians and the political system they inhabit are the main obstacle to a coherent 'corporatist' policy, and therefore to industrial renewal.

If Labour does not manage to adopt a new role as the leader

of a social pact, which its commitment to an industrial strategy implies, if the opposition parties cannot collaborate, if they cannot so organize their campaigns that they can defeat the Conservatives in 1991, then all this advocacy will appear futile. Britain may then have to wait until the latter 1990s, when it may face an acute economic crisis, for the need for a social pact to become so pressing that the politicians finally see the point of it.

Advocacy of 'corporatism' may seem strange, both because it is an apparently 'failed' idea and because it seems 'un-English'. Yet we are about to become 'un-English'. Britain cannot halt the economic and political integration of Europe: 1992 is not merely about the removal of barriers to the free movement of labour and trade, it is also about the creation of a 'social' Europe through policies to counteract the concentration of wealth and industry in the most favoured regions. Europe will need to create new institutions of regulation and new corporatist forums through which the commitment of social interests to the new policies can be won. Mrs Thatcher shrilly condemns this agenda, openly rebutting M. Delors, but she can neither prevent the new Europe nor leave it. The future, we might say, belongs to corporatism. If the leadership of the Labour Party is too provincial and too cowed by the Tories' derision of corporatism that it cannot exploit both the growing crisis of manufacturing and the new agenda in Europe, then it is missing the greatest political opportunity it has had since 1979. Let us hope this is not so, and that 'A Productive and Competitive Economy' finds a politics appropriate to it.

A tale of two cultures

I used to think C. P. Snow a bore, and his idea of two cultures silly, but now I'm not so sure. The fracas over the reorganization of the Victoria and Albert Museum has provided a perfect example of it. Let us leave the rights and wrongs of the V&A controversy to one side, and savour this incident. Sir John Pope-Hennessy, a former director of the museum, lashed out in *The New York Review of Books* against the philistinism of the museum's new policy and by implication that of the government. He recalled conducting Mrs Thatcher on a visit to the V&A when she was Minister of Education. Mrs Thatcher passed through the museum as if it were a sewerage works, ignoring works of art by leading Renaissance masters. She came to life in the restoration department, when she met women who were fixing textiles with glue. Mrs Thatcher knew the formula for the fixative and talked animatedly with the restorers about it. Pope-Hennessy was beside himself; what horrified him was her philistinism and inability to grasp what he thought important.

Actually, this anecdote indicates Mrs Thatcher is both an engaging and relatively decent person. She does have private virtues and they do sometimes show in public. One of her virtues is that (despite her upbringing) she is not a snob. Why should she defer to the religion of 'art'? It is not compulsory. Feigned deference, without real comprehension or enthusiasm, is worse than honest indifference; most politicians are sufficiently good actors to leave Pope-Hennessy's prejudices intact. Mrs Thatcher took an active interest in the 'backroom girls' and she showed she still knows a little about chemistry. In his article Pope-Hennessy reveals that he obviously paid no attention to these specialist staff, whom he took for granted, and he neither knew nor cared *how* such valuable work was done in his own museum.

Such attitudes as his neither dent nor damage Mrs Thatcher today, nor will they change or challenge government policy toward the arts. They reveal the very worst of the old elite. My complaint against her is not that she is a philistine: her fault is that she has let too many of the cosy, pampered privileged off the hook. Miners or dockers she will tackle, but all too many stuffy closed rooms of the Establishment mansion, she has left unopened. The Pope-Hennessys of this world would truly loathe a cultured *and* anti-Establishment prime minister even more than they do Mrs Thatcher. The best way to upset the art establishment here would be for a formidably cultured, democratic and forceful politician to take over the arts portfolio. Britain's political tribe scarcely includes such a person, clear evidence why we are so backward, provincial and inept in the modern world. A Helmut Schmidt is almost inconceivable in British politics. Our cultured politicians are either distinctly Establishment or passively middlebrow.

CHAPTER 7

A United Opposition?

THE CASE FOR COOPERATION among the opposition parties
has been made repeatedly and in various quarters since the
mid-1980s. In 1986, the argument turned on the likelihood of a
hung parliament, a false hope as it turned out. In 1987, TV87
(Tactical Voting '87) tried to organize an anti-Thatcher coalition
from below, seeking to persuade ordinary voters to switch to the
strongest opposition party in their constituency in order to unseat
the Tory. The call of the 'great and the good' in the middle
ground went unheeded by the voters, there being almost no
evidence of tactical voting in the June general election. Since the
Conservatives' third victory a whole series of calls for inter-party
cooperation has emerged once again. TV87's successor organization, Common Voice, is seeking to build up grassroots cooperation in the middle ground. Charter 88 is an explicitly
cross-party body pushing constitutional change as the core common plank of the opposition. *Samizdat*, a journal seeking to
build a new opposition consensus, called in its first editorial for
something less and more than a pact, 'a popular front of the
mind'.

All this advocacy in the well-meaning middle ground, indicat-
ing a broad commitment among the intelligentsia to a cross-party
coalition, has failed to bear fruit. The opposition is further from
effective cooperation now than it has been at any time in the last
five years. The objective case for an electoral pact seems weaker
now than it was in 1986–7. Alliance support peaked in May 1987.
The disastrous handling of the merger of the Liberals and the
SDP has seen Alliance support fall back from 23 per cent at the
last general election to low single figures for the SDP and single
figures for the Democrats. The Democrats have been unable to
create a coherent party identity. Voters seem genuinely confused

by the loss of the term 'Liberal', and in many cases not to know the difference between the Democrats and the SDP. The Richmond by-election showed the disastrous consequences of the breakdown of the Alliance. An unprecedented collapse in Tory support could not be exploited because the two non-Labour parties split the vote between them. It would be difficult enough to create a credible electoral pact between Labour and a united third force. Labour would have to surrender the hope of becoming a majority national party, conceding most of southern England, in order to do a deal that the other opposition parties would accept. But the Democrats are too weak for such a pact even to be credible. The experience of Richmond shows that such a pact would certainly cost Labour seats and yet may fail completely to unseat Mrs Thatcher. Labour has even less reason to consider such a pact, as its own opinion poll support has grown to virtual level-pegging with the Tories in February 1989. Labour can also see that the other two opposition parties cannot agree on an electoral pact between themselves, let alone the infinitely more complex and difficult problems of a three-way pact.

The prospect of the parties being able to give electoral teeth to the consensus of the middle ground is thus remote and yet, without such an electoral agreement, the chances of unseating Mrs Thatcher are slim. Labour is unlikely to win a general election in 1991 unless there is a massive direct switch of support from Tory voters to the Labour Party. This is unlikely to happen if previous experience is any guide. Labour has strengthened its position but not sufficiently to beat the Tories in their south-eastern heartlands. A Tory Party elected on the basis of a *minority* of support in the South, and excluded from much of the North, Scotland and Wales, would be even more unrepresentative and yet would still ruthlessly exploit the advantage of a failing electoral system. Labour can see no advantage in trying to be other than a national party seeking a majority under the present electoral system and yet, given that system, it is unlikely to win a majority. It can only lose if it gives up its present stance and yet it cannot win if it persists with it. The current problem turns on an unspringable electoral trap and a Conservative Party indifferent to the national interest, completely unruffled by the growing crisis of legitimacy.

Mrs Thatcher is an anti-consensus politician. But so are Neil Kinnock and Dr David Owen. The opposition parties are hopelessly divided. Yet their differences turn mainly on slogans and symbols. Labour and the other opposition parties are closer in policy terms than they have been at any time since the early 1980s. Labour is strenuously trying to modernize its policies and to ditch the concessions to the left that made it unelectable in 1983 and 1987. The problem is that slogans and symbols *matter*, they are the substance of party identity. Under the present electoral system, each of the opposition parties has to maintain a distinct party image, to aim for the greatest possible exclusive party support from the voters. To blur that image is to lose electoral definition, and, in the absence of an explicit pact, to lose support.

A three-party electoral contest by the opposition necessarily involves emphasizing the differences between the parties, campaigning against each other as much as against the Tories. The Democrats and the SDP need to oppose Labour and seek to attract disaffected Tory voters by emphasizing that a vote for them is not a vote for 'socialism'. The terms of electoral competition are such that they tend to drive parties that have more and more in common further and further apart. Dr Owen in particular is a master at such spoiling tactics. The SDP in a no-holds-barred election will do everything possible to emphasize Labour's weaknesses. Owen has already pressed the born-again multilateralist Kinnock on whether he would be prepared to *use* Trident in a crisis. The SDP will thus make anti-Labour propaganda with disaffected Tory voters – emphasizing the 'socialist' nature of Labour and seeking to prevent a direct switch from Conservatives to Labour. Labour will campaign in the South on the basis that it is the only genuine national alternative party and that a vote for the parties of the old Alliance will not unseat Mrs Thatcher. The result is not difficult to predict.

Unfortunately, party interest and the national interest cannot easily be brought together. Parties are competing one with another and must seek to gain whatever exclusively party advantage is possible or suffer in consequence. Parties can survive long periods in opposition and still retain their identity and coherence. It is no advantage to a party to risk losing a relative gain in electoral support and more MPs in order to unseat the majority party. Even if Labour does not win in 1991 it will remain the second largest party and will gain in support. The Democrats will not disappear and will continue to enjoy pockets of regional strength sufficient to give them a small number of MPs and a strong position in local government. The SDP can survive if Owen and a few others are re-elected and if they continue to attract funding – indeed, anti-Labour money may well flow to them if the Conservatives weaken. Each party can see a second-best outcome that gives it some advantages and allows it to remain in the electoral game in the long run. Parties can operate on long time-scales and survive as organizations despite being out of office. Their second-best choices come first in party terms, so much so that they are willing to deny the realization of the anti-Thatcher aspirations of a majority of voters.

It would be silly to blame politicians for a lack of public spirit. One cannot expect electoral politicians to cease to be what they are, vote-getters for their party. They can only compete and seek advantage on the terms that are available. Parties cannot choose the terms on which they must compete. How then can the deadlock be broken? No party can be asked to make a self-defeating sacrifice in the national interest. Since only Labour can break the deadlock of the opposition parties, the question is whether it needs to make a real sacrifice at all. Can it make an initiative that reduces the adversarial competition of the centre–left without losing advantages itself? The issue is whether it concedes real advantages or positions that lock it and the whole opposition into defeat.

It has been the main positive argument of this book that Britain's political, social and economic problems cannot be solved by a conventional party government. The key to addressing the problems Britain will face in the later 1990s is a new strategy of revitalization of manufacturing. Such a policy programme cannot be carried out by a single party, given the need to build a broad coalition for economic recovery. A coalition between the opposition parties and the major social interests is necessary to create the legitimacy, the continuity and the conditions for effective implementation. Labour will not be electorally strong enough nor does it have the direct support of enough of the organized social interests to build this coalition from within a purely party basis of support. I have advocated the need for Labour to act as the orchestrator of a broad *social* pact, not a narrowly electoral pact. To do this Labour will have to accept that policy is derived from a process of inter-party and interest group bargaining, not from party manifestos or conference decisions.

I have argued that the logic of the Labour Party's own policy review in the area of economic policy leads in this direction. Such a policy needs a new political style and new structures of policy formation and implementation, rather than new techniques of economic management. For Labour to do this it has to become a 'one nation' party, not a regional and labour interest party. But to act as a 'one nation' party does not imply seeking to become an exclusive national majority party government. On the contrary, it involves abandoning such exclusivity and appealing to other parties and interests to join it in an ongoing social pact, rather than a temporary coalition to seek electoral advantage. Even if Labour were to form a majority government in 1991, it could not implement a strategy of economic and social renewal without reaching out to other sources of political and social support. As a conventional government it would be too weak and too threatened by the logic of competition between the opposition parties for exclusive electoral advantage. Switching national income from consumption to investment, and controlling household sector income, are policies likely to be threatened by voters' revolts unless there is a very broad political coalition that undercuts the logic of seeking short-term advantage by voters, parties and major social interests alike.

Such a 'one nation' strategy cannot be cobbled together *after* an election victory, nor can it be made to emerge from the necessities of coalition government in the event of a hung parliament. Such a strategy needs to be campaigned for well before the three-week run-up to a general election, and the ground needs to be prepared in advance.

Coalition is necessary even if Labour were to win a general election, the very event that conventional Labour politicians see as making such cooperation unnecessary. If Labour cannot govern without consensus, the argument for offering a *policy* coalition to the other opposition parties remains strong, and is, indeed, reinforced, as Labour gains in support and credibility. Labour as the leading opposition party, far ahead of the others in support, can credibly pose as a social leader. If Labour were neck and neck with the other parties, as in May 1987, it could not aspire to lead but would have to bargain from weakness. It could not then either offer or orchestrate a social pact; it would be desperately seeking party advantage.

My argument requires a strong Labour Party, at the very least pushing the Tories close, not a weak one. It is not to be gainsaid, therefore, by growing Labour support. This is a paradox most commentators and party leaders fail to appreciate. If Labour can comprehend the need for coalition from a position of strength, many of the arguments against dialogue between the opposition parties fall to pieces. A strategy of social leadership requires a bold initiative. Far from weakening Neil Kinnock as a national leader, it would form the basis for a considerable enhancement of his authority, within the Party and among voters. The Labour leadership has no reason to fear that a 'one nation' pact would undermine its position.

Labour does have to swallow one major concession in order to make its leadership of a pact possible, and that is PR.[1] I have argued that Labour's resistance to PR is both unprincipled and incoherent. Labour would gain not lose from PR, if it saw it as part of building up a new political system to replace the wreckage of two-party politics. Labour would be conceding the possibility of conventional majority government if it adopted PR, but the argument advanced here is that this is no real concession, since Labour is unlikely to be able to form a strong single-party administration, and it will require ongoing coalitions with the non-Tory parties if it wants to lead a lasting and effective government of economic reform. Refusing PR is to cling to a political past, one in which Labour's traditional strengths have become liabilities.

In a strategy of ongoing coalition government, being the largest non-Tory party and not having an overall majority is no great problem. Labour would be the core of a new governing coalition. It would have a route back to political power on new terms. It would also be able to become a national party once again, rather than a regional party. PR would enable Labour to regain seats in the South and it would enable the parties of the coalition to campaign as distinct parties without seeking the narrow forms of advantage that force parties into antagonistic and adversarial stances. It would allow the coalition members to campaign separately and yet cooperate.

The Democrats and the SDP in particular desperately need PR in order to institutionalize their electoral support. Without it, they are faced with a perpetual crisis of representation and with the need to opportunistically seek to benefit at Labour's expense in the South. The gain of PR to the other two opposition parties is so great that they would be willing to concede a great deal to get it. Labour is the only party both capable and conceivably willing to give it to them, and so, given a Labour concession on PR, they would be in a position of weakness not strength if it were offered well in advance of a general election. If PR were forced out of Labour in the aftermath of a hung parliament, the positions would be reversed. Labour has most to gain from offering PR now in combination with a strategy of a 'one nation' economic pact. With PR as the bait, Labour could expect to bargain hard about the policy terms of such a pact and cement its leadership role.

Even if Labour were to offer such a social pact, an electoral pact might still prove difficult. If the parties campaigned in terms of a common strategy, however, cooperation could prove easier. Labour cannot see coalitions and seeking to be a credible party of national government as opposed strategies. A coalition requires that voters for all three opposition parties see Labour as a credible party of government, otherwise the whole strategy would unravel. Making itself electable and working for coalition are conjoint objectives for the Labour Party. Tory voters will not switch to the Democrats and the SDP if they fear that will 'let in' an otherwise unelectable Labour Party. A 'one nation' pact in which Labour does not have exclusive control will make Labour less threatening and make it easier for wavering voters who have previously voted Tory to switch to one of the other opposition parties.

Labour thus needs to begin a process of dialogue with the Democrats and the SDP as soon as possible. An electoral pact is premature, and, without a common policy for action in government, bogus. Voters will not tolerate a pact based on pure expediency that offers the prospect of either uncertainty in government or a purely Labour administration. An electoral pact can only follow (if it does at all) exploratory talks between the parties about a common minimum programme and a set of explicit and agreed concessional goals. Voters may change their perceptions if Labour changes its own stance on government and if the three opposition parties can be seen to be trying to talk to one another.

Tory support is crumbling but it is not broken. It is obvious that the Conservatives do not have a magic touch in the way the myth of 'Thatcherism' has encouraged us to believe. Their handling of the economy is coming to be seen to be inept, and in direct contrast to their own triumphant hype. The Tories' very crying of 'success' is telling against them and after ten years in office they have no one left to blame. Economic problems are mounting to the point where ordinary voters are beginning to feel the pinch in a way they did not in June 1987. The unpopular policies of Mrs Thatcher's third administration are long term and will not be out of the way by 1991. Many of these policies touch the mass of ordinary voters directly and immediately in the way past reforms did not. The poll tax, unnecessary and bitterly contested privatizations (notably of the water and electricity supply industries), NHS reorganization, and the steadily emerging consequences of long-term neglect of central government and local authority spending will all simultaneously come to buffet the government at once in its mid-term. The image of an over-centralized and inflexible government, at one and the same time ruthless and opportunistic in conceding to favoured campaigns, like that mounted by the well-heeled villages of Kent against the Channel Tunnel rail link, has now got beyond media management and Central Office apologetics.

Tory unpopularity alone will not lose them the election. The Conservatives have a minimum bedrock of support that can survive in the face of a split opposition. Squabbling between the Democrats and the SDP, a crisis in the Labour Party over its new policies that shows the leadership is not in control, can further weaken the divided support of the opposition, and allow the Tories to win by default once again. The opposition has to make itself electable and to do this it must overcome its own divisions. This is no easy task; every pressure of our electoral system, short-term party interest, and our political culture tells against it. But the stakes have mounted with each victory the opposition has conceded to the Conservatives. If 1983 and 1987 are capped by a Conservative victory in 1991, the Tories will not be less partial and authoritarian but more so. They will be permitted to govern in a period when time is running out for economic and social reform. They will be able to pass the higher costs of a failing economy on to the poor and the weak. They will use the governmental power to force through unwanted change in the teeth of bitter opposition.

A heavy responsibility rests on the opposition, and the Labour Party in particular. Its leaders can see and know well the consequences of yet another Tory victory. They are still temporizing in the face of what can only be described as a disaster. The pressures against cooperation are real and they are easy to understand, but they cannot be allowed to prevail. The very failure of the opposition gives rise to the narrowest forms of 'realism', which treat this failure to cooperate as the acme of political toughmindedness and common sense. 'Realism' of this kind is actually the worst kind of illusion and an excuse for what is nothing less than a betrayal of the people. It can only persist because the political class does not bear the costs of its own failure; MPs and journalists do not suffer, the people do. A situation that calls for dynamism and new thinking is answered with cynicism and a retreat into the search for narrow party advantage.

Labour is the key to unlocking this crisis of the opposition. It is faced with the greatest choice and also the greatest opportunity in its existence. Unfortunately, it will not be faced with ruin if it flunks the choice. It will still be the second largest party. Yet Labour has always tried to be more than a political machine and a platform for oppositional interest groups. It has claimed to be a party of principle and national leadership. If it wants to make good these claims then an effort to break out of run-of-the-mill politics is essential. Previous attempts by the left to give substance to Labour's principles have come close to making the Party unelectable. But electoral success will not come by playing at machine politics or by sticking to playing it safe while ignoring the other opposition parties. The old hard left is in full-scale retreat and there is a desperate sense of the need to win in the ranks of Labour Party activists. Dialogue with the other opposition parties is a radical new departure and it is one that can only come from the top. Labour's leaders are currently far from seeking that dialogue, reinforced as they are in their purely party 'realism' by recent opinion poll success.

The strongest case for dialogue comes from the Party's own efforts at policy renewal. If Labour is willing to ditch nationalization and old-style 'socialist' shibboleths in order to achieve economic modernization, then it needs to will the political changes necessary to achieve that end. The Labour Party has only got half way toward understanding the full political logic of its economic policies. It needs rapidly to go the whole way. If the leadership saw the need for coalition and dialogue stemming from its own policy logic, not forced upon it as an external compromise threatening that logic, then perhaps it could adapt in time. This book is an extended argument in favour of such a change. I have tried to show why both the current political crisis and the problems of the economy require a new style of leadership and a new political culture. Coalition is the outcome of a political and economic analysis, dissecting Britain's failings and looking at the reasons for our competitors' success.

Labour opponents of dialogue with the other opposition parties have learned Mrs Thatcher's own diagnosis of Britain's failure all too well. They see consensus and dialogue as nothing more than compromise and dilution, giving way to a moderate and ineffective 'middle ground'. They have simply not understood how partial and provincial this diagnosis is, how far it flies in the face of experience elsewhere. Consensus based on strong leadership need not be weak, nor need it result in middle-of-the-road policies. Party governments without sufficient support for radical policies are, on the contrary, the true source of weakness. Labour has twice been propelled into office on this basis, in 1964 and 1974. Labour's recent history in government is the best argument against the orthodox and party-centred case.

Labour can only be really strong if it can reach well outside the ranks of its own supporters and voters. It both needs to do this in order to get a chance to govern at all and needs such broad-based support to carry out its objectives in government. The case for a social pact and for Labour as the only party capable of leading and orchestrating such a pact is overwhelming. Given its strength it need not fear dialogue if it has the will and the flexibility to exploit it. Labour's greatest obstacle to being a successful party of government is its own obsolete ideas about government. There is just time enough to change those ideas before 1991 and it is in the hope of persuading Labour of the need for such change that this book has been written.

After Thatcher has not wasted time being anti-Thatcher. There is and has been since the early 1980s an anti-Thatcher consensus. What has not existed are the means to organize that body of sentiment and that mass of votes. The reason the opposition parties have remained divided is that they have failed to break through the political and economic terms in which the Conservatives have been allowed to set the debate. They have failed because they lacked doctrines of governance and economic management that permit full cooperation between the parties. Cooperation has remained trapped in the illusion that it arises from mere expediency and short-term electoral problems. On the contrary, cooperation requires as a precondition that expediency and electoral short-termism be set aside. Coalition and dialogue between the parties and the social interests offer the best long-term alternative for sustainable reforming government and economic revitalization. No longer can Mrs Thatcher claim 'there is no alternative'. There *is* an alternative and it offers the prospect that, after Thatcher, the centre–left could govern Britain for at least as long as the Conservatives, and without Mrs Thatcher's legacy of political authoritarianism, social division and economic failure.

Notes

Chapter 1

1. I am far from underestimating the seriousness of the electoral problem facing the opposition parties, but dwelling on psephological studies of the last two elections can only paralyse political thought and action. Unlike some commentators on the left I neither ignore nor despise psephology, but politics is a realm of contingency and change and electoral politics is no exception to this rule. The political balance of the parties can and does change radically, under the influence of political events and the actions of the parties themselves. What appear to be long-run trends and political certainties can be reversed. The late 1950s and early 1960s were a period of obsessive debate about the secular decline of the Labour Party, characterized by the question 'Must Labour lose?' The mid-1960s were characterized by illusions about Labour as the 'natural party of government'. What will happen in the 1990s will be decided soon, and is partly in the hands of the opposition parties and partly subject to chance.

2. The best two studies of the Thatcher years are Peter Jenkins, *Mrs Thatcher's Revolution* (Cape: London 1987) and Dennis Kavanagh, *The Politics of Thatcherism* (Oxford University Press: Oxford 1987). The former is strong on the weaknesses of Labour in 1974–9, but consistently overrates Mrs Thatcher's success in revolutionizing Britain.

3. An excellent study of the rise and fall of 'liberal collectivism' based on the economics of Keynes and the welfare policies of Beveridge is Tony Cutler, Karel Williams and John Williams, *Keynes, Beveridge and Beyond* (Routledge: London 1986).

4. The best short accounts of monetarist doctrine and Conservative economic practice are Keith Smith, *The British Economic Crisis* (Penguin Books: Harmondsworth 1984; especially chapter 6) and Jim Tomlinson, *Monetarism: Is There an Alternative?* (Basil Blackwell: Oxford 1986). See also David Smith, *The Rise and Fall of Monetarism* (Penguin Books: Harmondsworth 1987).

5. Roger Jowell, Sharon Witherspoon and Lindsay Brook, *British Social Attitudes, the Fifth Report* (Gower: Aldershot 1988), p. 96.

6. ibid, p. 113.

7. ibid., p. 115.

8. See Stuart Hall and Martin Jacques (eds), *The Politics of Thatcherism*

(Lawrence & Wishart: London 1983); Stuart Hall, *The Hard Road to Renewal* (Verso: London 1988); the October 1988 issue of *Marxism Today* entitled 'New Times'. Andrew Gamble, *The Free Economy and the Strong State* (Macmillan: London 1988) is the most penetrating and balanced left account of Thatcherism.

9. Reprinted as chapter 18 of Stuart Hall, *The Hard Road to Renewal*, op. cit. (n8).

10. Three volumes, *The Affluent Worker: 1. Industrial Attitudes and Behaviour* (1968), *2. Political Attitudes and Behaviour* (1968); and *3. The Affluent Worker in the Class Structure* (1969; Cambridge University Press: Cambridge). If there is one other study that merits attention on the issue of social groups and voting behaviour it is Anthony Heath, Roger Jowell and John Curtice, *How Britain Votes* (Pergamon Press: Oxford 1985).

Chapter 2

1. A large literature now exists documenting the failings of Britain's constitution and political system; among the most telling contributions are: Ian Harden and Norman Lewis, *The Noble Lie* (Hutchinson: London 1987); Richard Holme, *The People's Kingdom* (The Bodley Head: London 1987); Cosmo Graham and Tony Prosser (eds), *Waiving the Rules: the Constitution under Thatcherism* (Open University Press: Milton Keynes 1988); Clive Ponting, *Whitehall, Tragedy and Farce* (Sphere: London 1986); Tom Nairn, *The Enchanted Glass, Britain and its Monarchy* (Radius: London 1988).

2. A. V. Dicey, *An Introduction to the Study of the Law of the Constitution* (8th edn, Macmillan: London 1920) remains unrivalled as an account of the sovereignty of Parliament.

3. Tony Benn, of course, favoured the democratization of *society* and, in particular, workplace democracy. But he favoured concentrating legislative power in the House of Commons and reducing the obstacles to radical legislation.

4. See Dicey's *Introduction*, op. cit. (n2).

5. Ivor Crewe's 'The grim challenge of the ballot box', *Guardian*, 1 October 1988, remains the best short account of the electoral task facing Labour.

6. David Marquand's defence of the 'mixed economy' in *The Unprincipled Society* (1988) is masterly and unparalleled.

7. This scepticism about governmental power is to be found in many nineteenth-century liberal thinkers, most notably Jeremy Bentham and Benjamin Constant. It was the abiding concern of leading Liberal politicians like Gladstone.

8. See Robert Dahl's *A Preface to Democratic Theory* (Yale University Press:

New Haven, Conn. 1956) and *Dilemmas of Liberal Democracies* (Yale University Press: New Haven, Conn. 1982).

9. A major source of such thinking is Michael Walzer's *Spheres of Justice* (Basil Blackwell: Oxford 1983).

10. For useful discussions of 'corporatism', see Alan Cawson, *Corporatism and Political Theory* (Basil Blackwell: Oxford 1987) and Philippe Schmitter and Gerhard Lembruch, *Trends toward Corporatist Intermediation* (Sage: London 1979). I have benefited greatly in what follows from Philippe Schmitter's advocacy of the reform and institutionalization of corporatist bargaining.

11. For an account of this process of unequal private influence on US public policy, see Thomas Byrne Edsall, *The New Politics of Inequality* (W. W. Norton: New York 1984).

12. For an account of these thinkers, see David Nicholls, *The Pluralist State* (Macmillan: London 1975) and for selections of their work Paul Hirst (ed.), *The Pluralist Theory of the State* (Routledge: London 1989).

Chapter 3

1. See *The Military Balance* published annually by the International Institute for Strategic Studies, London.

2. See C. Freeman, 'Technical innovation and British trade performance' in F. Blackaby (ed.), *De-industrialization* (Heinemann: London 1978).

3. The fairest and most balanced treatment of the rationale for British nuclear strategy is Laurence Freedman, *Britain and Nuclear Weapons* (Macmillan: London 1980); see also G. Segal, E. Moreton, L. Freedman and J. Baylis, *Nuclear War and Nuclear Peace* (Macmillan: London 1983).

4. For a very intelligent argument within military strategy for a unilateralist case for Britain, see Ken Booth, 'Unilateralism: a Clausewitzian reform', in N. Blake and Kay Pole (eds), *Dangers of Deterrence* (Routledge: London 1983).

5. Field Marshall Lord Carver is the clearest military voice in opposition to British nuclear forces and nuclear doctrine, yet within an overall Atlantic Alliance strategy based on acceptance of the US deterrent. See his *A Policy for Peace* (Faber: London 1982) and 'Getting defence priorities right', in John Baylis (ed.), *Alternative Approaches to British Defence Policy* (Macmillan: London 1983).

6. Despite its blatant right-wing bias, Correlli Barnett's *The Collapse of British Power* (Allan Sutton: Gloucester 1984) is invaluable in dispelling myths about Britain's role in the period after World War I. Paul Kennedy's *The Rise and Fall of British Naval Mastery* (Macmillan: London 1983) is excellent on the collapse of the Pax Britannica.

7. Anthony Barnett's *Iron Britannia* (Verso: London 1983) remains the most telling *political* account of the Falklands War.

8. For the 'emerging technologies', see Frank Barnaby, *the Automated Battlefield* (Oxford University Press: Oxford 1987).

9. Dan Smith's *The Defence of the Realm in the 1980s* (Croom Helm: London 1980) is still the best left-wing account of current defence problems. For a wide range of views on how British defence should develop, see John Baylis (ed.), op. cit. (n5).

10. This is a controversial view – sailors in particular seem addicted to surface ships – but it has many advocates, among them the influential military historian John Keegan in *The Price of Admiralty* (Hutchinson: London 1988).

11. For just such a NATO position paper that gives a central role to emerging technologies see ESECS, *Strengthening Conventional Deterrence in Europe* (Macmillan: London 1983), Part IV. The failed Labour parliamentary candidate for Bermondsey, Peter Tatchell, is the most enthusiastic advocate of self-defensive militia armies.

12. For an account of such countries' policy see Adam Roberts, *Nations in Arms* (Chatto & Windus: London 1976).

Chapter 4

1. See Nick Crafts, *British Economic Growth before and after 1979: a Review of the Evidence* (CEPR Discussion Paper No. 292, 1988), Table 1, p. 2.

2. ibid., Tables 2–3, pp. 2–3.

3. A very thorough, if inconclusive, debate on the issue of Britain's productivity growth and how to measure it is to be found in a special issue of the *Oxford Review of Economic Policy*, 'Productivity and competitiveness in British manufacturing', vol. 2, no. 3, 1986.

4. See, for example, D. N. McCloskey, 'Did Victorian Britain fail?' *Economic History Review*, vol. 33, 1970.

5. Nick Crafts, 'The assessment: British economic growth over the long run', *Oxford Review of Economic Policy*, vol. 4, no. 1, 1988, p. viii.

6. For a clear outline of this strategy see the Boston Consulting Group Ltd, *Strategy Alternatives for the British Motorcycle Industry* (HMSO: London 1975).

7. ibid.

8. See K. Williams, J. Williams and C. Haslam, *The Breakdown of Austin Rover* (Berg: Leamington Spa 1987).

9. For an account of merger waves in Britain since the 1920s, see Leslie Hannah, *The Rise of the Corporate Economy*, 2nd edn (Methuen: London 1979).

10. See C. New and A. Meyers, *Managing Manufacturing Operations in the UK, 1975–85* (Institute of Manpower Studies: Brighton 1986), Table 4.1, p. 28.

11. See K. Smith, *The British Economic Crisis* (Penguin: Harmondsworth 1984).

12. For a discussion of this concept and the importance of cooperation between firms in advanced industrial economies, see P. Hirst and J. Zeitlin, 'Flexible specialization and the competitive failure of UK manufacturing', *Political Quarterly*, vol. 60, no. 2, April 1989.

13. New and Meyers, op. cit. (n10), Table 3.6, p. 22.

14. See B. Jones, 'Flexible automation and factory politics: the United Kingdom in comparative perspective', in P. Hirst and J. Zeitlin (eds), *Reversing Industrial Decline?* (Berg: Oxford 1988).

15. New and Meyers, op. cit. (n10), Table 4.3, p. 30.

16. 'Flexible specialization' is a concept developed by M. Piore and Charles Sabel in *The Second Industrial Divide* (Basic Books: New York 1984). See also the Introduction and the chapter by Sabel in Hirst and Zeitlin, op. cit. (n14) and C. Sabel and J. Zeitlin, 'Historical alternatives to mass production: politics, markets and technology in nineteenth century industrialization', *Past and Present*, no. 108, 1985.

17. For an account of such ongoing 'relational contracting' relationships in Japan, see Ronald Dore, *Flexible Rigidities: Industrial Policy and Structural Adjustment in the Japanese Economy 1970–80* (Athlone Press: London 1986).

18. For a comprehensive survey of the new industrial districts, see C. Sabel, 'Flexible specialization and the re-emergence of regional economies', in Hirst and Zeitlin, op. cit. (n14).

19. For Sakaki see David Friedman, *The Misunderstood Miracle: Industrial Development and Political Change in Japan* (Cornell University Press: Ithaca, NY 1988), Ch. 5.

20. For nineteenth-century industrial districts, see Sabel and Zeitlin, op. cit. (n16).

21. For the role of small and medium-sized firms in Japanese development, especially after 1973, see Friedman, op. cit. (n19) and for Italy see J. Zeitlin, 'Italian small business growth: the social foundations of industrial success', *QED*, summer 1989.

Chapter 5

1. By far the most reasoned and developed example of the 'post-industrial case' remains Daniel Bell's *The Coming of Post-Industrial Society* (Heinemann: London 1974).

2. Ronald Dore, *Flexible Rigidities: Industrial Policy and Structural Adjustment in the Japanese Economy 1970–80* (Athlone Press: London 1986), Tables 2.1 and 2.2, pp. 30–1.

3. See Jonathan Gershuny, *After Industrial Society?* (Macmillan: London 1978).

4. Economic liberalism and free trade policies encountered strong and articulate criticism from economists in developing industrial countries like Germany in the nineteenth century for just this reason, the most famous of whom was Friedrich List in *The National System of Political Economy*.

5. The classic statement of MITI's role in Japanese economic development is Chalmers Johnson, *MITI and the Japanese Miracle* (Stanford University Press: Stanford, Ca. 1982).

6. Godley and his associates have now abandoned protectionism. For a recent account of their views, see T. Butler and P. Dunne (eds), *The British Economy After Oil: Manufacturing or Services?* (Croom Helm: London 1988).

7. See Tony Cutler, Karel Williams and John Williams, *Keynes, Beveridge and Beyond* (Routledge: London 1986).

Chapter 6

1. For an interesting account of Swedish anti-depression strategy, see Margaret Weir and Theda Skocpol, 'State structures and the possibilities for "Keynesian" responses to the Great Depression in Sweden, Britain and the United States', in P. B. Evans, D. Rueschemeyer and T. Skocpol (eds), *Bringing the State Back In* (Cambridge University Press: Cambridge 1985). For Japanese responses to the 1973 crisis, see Ronald Dore, *Flexible Rigidities: Industrial Policy and Structural Adjustment in the Japanese Economy 1970–80* (Athlone Press: London 1986).

2. See J. Zeitlin, 'Italian small business growth: the social foundations of industrial success', *QED*, summer 1989.

3. See Sebastiano Brusco, 'The Emilian model: productive decentralization and social integration', *Cambridge Journal of Economics*, vol. 6, no. 2, 1982.

4. See Jim Tomlinson, 'Macro-economic management and industrial policy', in P. Hirst and J. Zeitlin (eds), *Reversing Industrial Decline?* (Berg: Oxford 1988).

5. See J. Zeitlin and P. Totterdill, 'Markets, technology and local intervention: the case of clothing', in Hirst and Zeitlin, op. cit. (n4) and M. Best, 'Sector strategies and industrial policy: the furniture industry and the Greater London Enterprise Board' in the same volume.

6. See the papers by Zeitlin and Totterdill, Best, Elliott, and Marshall in Hirst and Zeitlin, op. cit. (n4).

7. See Tom Hadden, *Company Law and Capitalism*, 2nd edn (Weidenfeld & Nicolson: London 1977).

8. For an argument as to the necessity of corporate and collaborative political institutions as the key to British development, see David Marquand, *The Unprincipled Society* (1988) and for intensive studies of the crucial role of corporatist institutions in the industrial success of states like Austria and Sweden, see P. J. Katzenstein, *Corporatism and Change: Austria, Switzerland and the Politics of Industry* (Cornell University Press: Ithaca, NY 1984) and *Small States in World Markets: Industrial Policy in Europe* (Cornell University Press: Ithaca, NY 1985).

Chapter 7

1. I have ignored the issue of the form of proportional representation to be adopted, since this is largely academic whilst Labour remains opposed to the principle. I have no illusion that there is an 'ideal' form of PR that will act evenly and neutrally on the political parties. The argument about the form of PR can all too easily turn into a squabble between the parties in which each proposes a system that gives it the greatest advantage. My own view is that PR is best looked at in the context of overall constitutional and political change. As I strongly favour the creation of a federal United Kingdom with regional autonomy for Scotland and Wales and strong English regional government, my own preference would be for a system based on regional party lists. This would certainly break the connection between representatives and single local constituencies. The fact is that few MPs have strong connections with individual constituents, that most constituents have an MP representing a party they did not vote for, and that there are alternative ways of ensuring advocacy for individuals which are far more effective than the chance of getting a sympathetic and active MP to take up one's case – notably improved forms of administrative law and a more developed system of ombudsmen with wider powers. Regional lists would have two major advantages: they allow parties to put forward candidates who are not conventional professional politicians, experts at kissing infants and media manipulation; and they give substance to the new regions as political entities. From a purely Labour point of view, large regional lists, with a relatively low qualifying percentage of the vote, would enable Labour to strengthen its representation in the South.

Selected Bibliography

Barnett, Correlli, *The Collapse of British Power* (Allan Sutton: Gloucester 1984).

Belloc, Hilaire, *The Servile State* (1913, reprinted by Liberty Classics: Indianapolis 1977).

Chesshyre, Robert, *The Return of the Native Reporter* (Penguin: London 1956).

Crosland, C. A. R., *The Future of Socialism* (Cape: London 1956).

Cutler, Antony, Williams, Karel and Williams, John, *Keynes, Beveridge and Beyond* (Routledge: London 1986).

Dahrendorf, Ralf, *On Britain* (BBC: London 1986).

Friedman, David, *The Misunderstood Miracle* (Cornell University Press: Ithaca 1985).

Gamble, Andrew, *The Free Economy and the Strong State* (Macmillan: London 1988).

Graham, Cosmo and Prosser, Tony (eds), *Waiving the Rules; the Constitution under Thatcherism* (Open University Press: Milton Keynes 1988).

Hall, Stuart, *A Hard Road to Renewal* (Verso: London 1988).

Hall, Stuart and Jacques, Martin (eds), *The Politics of Thatcherism* (Laurence & Wishart: London 1983).

Harden, Ian and Lewis, Norman, *The Noble Lie* (Hutchinson: London 1987).

Hirst, Paul and Zeitlin, Jonathan (eds), *Reversing Industrial Decline?* (Berg: Oxford 1988).

Holme, Richard, *The People's Kingdom* (The Bodley Head: London 1987).

Jenkins, Peter, *Mrs Thatcher's Revolution* (Cape: London 1987).

Kavanagh, Dennis, *Thatcherism and British Politics* (Oxford University Press: Oxford 1987).

Kennedy, Paul, *The Rise and Fall of the Great Powers* (Unwin Hyman: London 1988).

Marquand, David, *The Unprincipled Society* (Cape: London 1988).

Olson, Mancur, *The Rise and Decline of Nations* (Yale University Press: New Haven 1982).

Piore, Michael and Sabel, Charles, *The Second Industrial Divide* (Basic Books: New York 1984).

Ponting, Clive, *Whitehall: Tragedy and Farce* (Sphere: London 1986).

Prais, S. J., *The Evolution of the Giant Firm in Britain* (Cambridge University Press: Cambridge 1976).

Smith, Keith, *The British Economic Crisis* (Penguin: Harmondsworth 1984).

Weiner, Martin J., *English Culture and the Decline of the Industrial Spirit 1850–1980* (Penguin: Harmondsworth 1985).

Williams, Karel, Williams, John and Thomas, David, *Why are the British Bad at Manufacturing?* (Routledge: London 1983).

Index

Index

Index

Index

Index